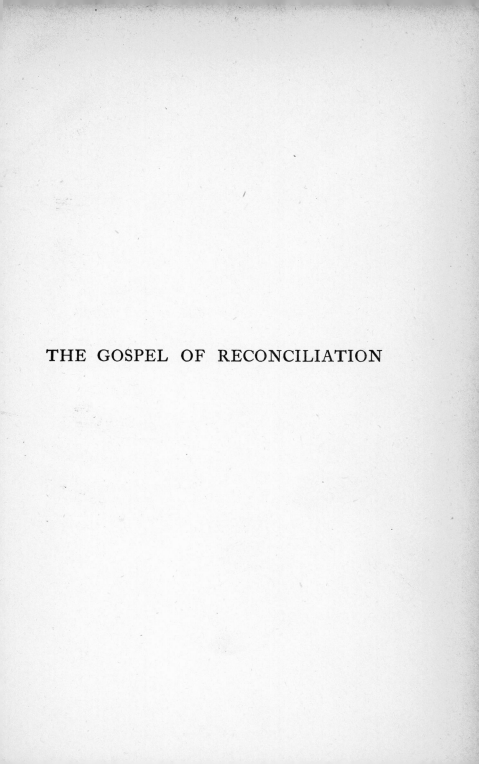

THE GOSPEL OF RECONCILIATION

THE GOSPEL OF RECONCILIATION

Or AT-ONE-MENT

BY THE

Rev. W. L. WALKER

AUTHOR OF
"THE SPIRIT AND THE INCARNATION" "THE CROSS AND THE KINGDOM"
"CHRISTIAN THEISM AND A SPIRITUAL MONISM"
ETC. ETC.

EDINBURGH: T. & T. CLARK, 38 GEORGE STREET

1909

Printed by
MORRISON & GIBB LIMITED
FOR
T. & T. CLARK, EDINBURGH.
LONDON : SIMPKIN, MARSHALL, HAMILTON, KENT, AND CO. LIMITED.
NEW YORK : CHARLES SCRIBNER'S SONS.

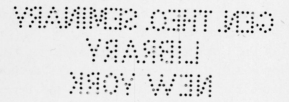

PREFACE

—◆—

ONE purpose of this Book is to set forth the Scriptural conception of the Cross of Christ as being, not an Atonement *to* God or Expiation of man's sin, but the means whereby God was effecting the At-one-ment, or Reconciliation, of the World with Himself. It is not written to support a one-sided "moral theory" of the Cross (although any true theory must be a moral one), but to state the Evangelical doctrine in its essential and abiding truth. An endeavour is made to show the real teaching of St. Paul and the truths underlying it, tested by the actual history and teaching of Christ. In Chapter VII. the doctrine of the Cross in its "judicial" aspect, or "the sin-bearing of Christ," is re-stated so as to show how Christ "bore our sins" and manifested the Divine Righteousness, in the way in which His Cross actually came to Him in the sequence of the Divine Moral Order, and apart from any arbitrary transfer, substitution, or suggestion of penal infliction on Christ. The Cross is also shown to be the Supreme manifestation of the Love of God.

v

Above all, the desire has been, at a time when many are finding it difficult or impossible to receive the old forms of doctrine, to bring out afresh the reality of the *Gospel* as the proclamation of the universal and unconditioned forgiving and saving love of God in Christ. We believe that, rightly apprehended, it is the only power that can really save the world of men, individually or socially, because it is "the Wisdom and the Power of God" to substitute for the reign of *self* that of God in His Love in human hearts. The Gospel of Reconciliation is therefore set forth in both its individual and social aspects.

The present outlook in a large portion of Christendom is, in the words of Lord Rosebery, "most ominous," and it presses on the Churches the question whether they have been faithful to Christ and His "Gospel of God," the effect of which is Love and Righteousness and Peace.

Fernihirst, Shettleston,
Glasgow, *June* 1909.

CONTENTS

I

THE GOSPEL AND THE CROSS

CHAPTER I

THE GOSPEL AND THE CROSS

ALTHOUGH the Gospel was first preached by Christ Himself, it was through the Cross that it went forth to the world. The Gospel of Christ therefore involves a doctrine of the Cross. But the Cross cannot be separated from the life and teaching which preceded it and of which it was the crown. All that Jesus said and did, whether in His life or by His death, had one great object. Like the garment that He wore, the work in which He clothed His spirit was one seamless whole. In His teaching He sought to bring men to God, to their true life of sonship toward their heavenly Father, and of brotherhood towards each other. In His own phrase, it was to make "the Kingdom of God" a reality in the world. To the same end He accepted His Cross, believing that it would be effectual to accomplish what His life and teaching had failed adequately to do. He was sure that after His death the Kingdom of God would come. As His confidence is expressed in the Fourth Gospel: "I, if I be lifted up from the earth, will draw all men unto Me."

It is the same thing that is meant by God's sending

forth His Spirit in order to raise men into their true spiritual life as His children. That Calvary was followed by Pentecost was no accident. The one was necessary in order to the other. Pentecost, or the going forth of God's Holy Spirit for man's salvation, was the designed sequence of Calvary. It was the result of the Divine manifestation there. Strictly, indeed, the one was the means of the other. The Spirit of God must come to us clothed in some word or deed or personality, and it was through the Cross of Christ that the Spirit went forth in the fulness of Divine saving power.

It is as bringing the power of this Spirit to us that any doctrine whatever is of value—as bringing Divine influences to operate on our hearts to save us from self and sin to the love of God and our fellow-men—to become itself the principle of the life of Love in our hearts. Christ was full of this Spirit, and through His Cross He poured it forth on the world. Of what avail are our doctrines if they promote not the practical life of Love in the world? It is the want of the Divine Spirit of Love that is the real source of evil, and its absence or the feebleness of its manifestation on the part of professed Christians furnishes the strongest argument against Christianity. All moral wrongs are rooted in that self-centred, self-loving, self-seeking principle which occupies the place that Love should fill. It was this that was the source of sin in both Jew and Gentile. And it is this that is the deepest cause of the separation between man and God and between man and man to-day. It was *this* that needed to be broken up, removed and changed to Love, if men were really to be brought into oneness with God and with one another. And the same need exists wherever men are found. If a Divine power is to operate on the world for its salvation, it must be one that can change the natural self-love of the human heart into the love of God and man. It must be a power that can *regenerate* and quicken quite a new life within the soul.

Not that there is no natural good in men or no love towards their fellow-men, or towards that Highest and Best that may stand for them as God. Far from it. But there is still, even in the best, at bottom, a principle of self-love which is never wholly overcome. It asserts itself in many ways in even the maturest Christian, and has to be constantly fought against and kept under. And it takes the most insidious forms. But in the new life the principle of Love to a personal God and Father, and to all men as brother-men and children of the one heavenly Father, is accepted as the dominant principle. Given this new life, developed and rightly directed, and all removable evils that curse the earth would disappear.

That the Gospel which was preached through the Cross of Christ was effectual to the quickening of this new life in the case of multitudes, is a matter of history beyond dispute. It led those at whose instance Jesus had been crucified to feel the enormity of their crime, and to cry, "What must we do to be saved?" It convicted many others of the reality of sin, and moved them to repentance. It enabled them at the same time to believe in the forgiving love of God, to realise the burden of their guilt removed, to have peace with God and the assurance of Divine acceptance. It was so used by the Spirit as to shed abroad God's love for them in their hearts and to quicken an answering love, the principle of the new life, within their souls. It moved them to die with Christ to self and sin, and to rise with Him to a new life of love and righteousness. And it broke down the barrier between Jew and Gentile, taking away "the Law" that separated them, "making of twain one new man in Christ." Many questions may be raised concerning the New Testament Scriptures, but these are facts of ordinary history. The Gospel proved itself to be "the power of God unto salvation to all who believed." In short, the expectation of Jesus was justified: after His death and by means of it, the Kingdom of God began to come in its true spiritual power.

Although causes soon appeared which checked the Gospel in its early march of victory, yet throughout the Christian centuries the Gospel of the Cross has shown itself mighty to accomplish similar results under a great variety of circumstances and with many different theories held concerning the Cross. So that we cannot doubt that its *central purpose* is to bring men into a union of Love with God and with one another. Whatever theory we may hold of its relation to God, this is certainly its relation to man. Whatever theory can

most effectually aid in the accomplishment of this great
end is the truest theory. And whatever stands between
the Cross and its Divinely-intended end must be
removed.

It is because the Gospel that entered the world
through the Cross of Christ has this Divine power that
it is of supreme importance for men to-day. Many are
still living in separation from God and from each other,
and, because of the isolation of self in its own earthly
interests, men are suffering in countless ways, and the
eternal life is being missed. Because God is not reign-
ing in human hearts, the inevitable consequence is
wrong and suffering. If this Gospel can still do its old
work, there is nothing so important for men. If it can
save the world from its self-centred life to the life of
Love, the duty of holding it forth is paramount. If it
be, as Paul believed and as results proved it to be, " the
Wisdom and the Power of God " for man's highest good,
to ignore it is as unwise as it would be to ignore the
beneficent forces of Nature.

For effective belief in or preaching of the Gospel of
the Cross we need to have some understanding of it.
It is quite possible that no perfectly complete and
adequate doctrine of the Cross may be within the power
of man to formulate. Like all the works of God, it may
be so deeply grounded and so many sided that no one
mind nor any number of finite minds can comprehend
or even see the whole. Its many-sidedness, and the fact
that we always feel that there is something still hidden

from us, is a proof of its Divineness. As with the Moon, we behold only one side at one time and another at another, and it is only one side we can ever see at all. There is a Godward side of the Cross which we cannot behold as we can its manward side. More than one theory, therefore, may be true, or, rather, there may be some element of truth in all reasonable theories. We are not justified in setting up any one theory and saying that this alone is evangelical and true. In doing so we are going contrary to history and everyday experience, and are arrogating to ourselves a function that belongs only to the ever-teaching Spirit. One fact stands sure and is founded on by all Christians. Jesus certainly accepted His Cross for our sakes, and we owe to Him our salvation. As Dr. Jowett wrote long ago: "All or almost all Christians would agree that in some sense or other we are reconciled to God through Christ —all would join in saying that He is the way, the truth, and the life. And had the human mind the same power of holding fast points of agreement as of discerning differences, there would be an end of the controversy." And he asks, "If our Saviour were to come to earth again, which of all the theories of atonement and sacrifice would He sanction with His authority? Perhaps none of them, yet perhaps all may be consistent with a true service of Him" (On Atonement and Satisfaction; *Essays*, pp. 498, 504). Dr. Denny also in his latest book remarks that a doctrine of Atonement arises out of Christian experience and is not a condition of faith. It is well known that in the post-Apostolic Church some very fantastic forms of doctrine concerning the Cross were held, yet God's love in Christ shone through them and wrought towards men's salvation. The great thing was to feel the love of Christ, and under that influence be drawn to God and the true life. This must ever be the essential thing. At the same time, a right understanding of the Cross is far from being a matter of indifference. The Cross will certainly be to us what we believe it to mean, and the truer our conception of its meaning the more effective will be its power.

But many of the theories which have been formed of the Cross, many of its doctrinal interpretations, are such that not a few are quite unable to receive them in the light of present-day knowledge and feeling. The Cross itself has become in some minds so identified with certain theories concerning it that it is practically left out of account, and with it the Gospel for which it stands. It is regarded as something which served its purpose but it is now obsolete. The doctrines that have prevailed concerning it are believed to have rested on misconceptions and on ignorance of the conditions of thought in Apostolic times. By some modern writers much ingenuity is shown in explaining away what has hitherto been regarded as the Apostolic teaching. Certain quite incidental beliefs entertained by the Apostles as men of their time are said to explain their whole doctrine. In a recently published *Handbook of*

Early Christianity, by Professor Slack, of New York, he gives the standpoint from which we must view the Apostle Paul as being that stated by Wrede: " Paul believes that without Christ mankind is in the power of potent spirits, demons, and angelic powers. In our own day, angels are regarded as the property of children and poets; for the Apostle and his time they are sober realities." This is how the English-reading million are asked to view Pauline Christianity. Apart from such extremes, there is a wide agreement amongst recent critics that Paul's doctrines are to be explained by his previous Jewish opinions. Not to believe this is to be behind the times. There is in this, of course, a measure of truth; but to give it as a complete explanation is to confound the *form* with the *substance*. Even many Christian preachers and Christian people feel the want of such a doctrine of the Cross as shall enable them to hold it with confidence, or to preach it and the Gospel it declares with the power that can only proceed from personal conviction, and in such a manner as will make it credible to the minds and effective in the hearts of the men of to-day. The old doctrines of satisfaction, substitution, and penal endurance are felt to be incredible or inadequate. By many the Cross is regarded as the manifestation of the Love of God, but it is not seen to be at the same time the manifestation of His Righteousness. Some are seeking refuge in the conception of a *Confession* of man's sin by Christ as our Representative, but still it is felt that there is much in the New Testament which this view does not cover. In short, not a few are seeking such a statement of the Cross as shall be true to fact and experience, and as shall make it a living and influential reality to the mind and conscience of the present. Nearly all thoughtful Christians feel the need of this.

The importance of the Cross, however, is in its relation to the Gospel of God's Love and to what that Gospel is meant to effect. By many the Cross is identified with the Gospel, and because they cannot believe certain theories of the Cross the Gospel itself is rejected or ignored. God as revealed in Christ is therefore unknown. It is this absence of the knowledge of God in His truth that keeps the world in spiritual darkness and hinders the operation of the Divine Power upon it. It is only *God* who can truly bless men and save the world. But if His Presence in the Love in which He revealed Himself in Christ and His Cross is unknown, it is the same thing with respect to the spiritual and higher interests of men as if the sun suffered an almost total eclipse. What the world so greatly needs to-day is what it has always needed, the light of God's gracious Presence to shine upon it, His pitying and saving love to be realised so that it may also live in us. It is this, not any merely doctrinal or theological interest, that calls for the endeavour to remove misconceptions and to set forth the truth concerning that Cross in which the revelation of God to men culminated. The Cross rightly viewed brings men

to God and God to men. For long the cry has been
"back to Christ"; now it is "back to Jesus, the prophet
of Nazareth": the Gospel of the Cross leads men not
only back to Christ and back to Jesus, but, through
Jesus Christ, back to *God*. We do need to return to
Jesus, in whom God was manifested as man—thorough
loyalty to His teaching, His life, His Cross, is just our
great want. But for this we do not need to forsake
"Christ" or Paul in those essential truths in which he
was at one with Jesus and the continuator of His work.
And for an effectual return to *Jesus*, we must first be
baptized in His Spirit.

II

NOT ATONEMENT, BUT AT-ONE-MENT

CHAPTER II

NOT ATONEMENT, BUT AT-ONE-MENT

THE whole subject of the Cross has been obscured and rendered difficult by the introduction of words and phrases which either have no place in the Scriptures or are taken in a wrong sense. But the chief source of error and confusion lies in the use of the word *Atonement* in a sense quite different from that warranted by the New Testament. No doubt this has been often pointed out; but it has been done most frequently in support of the idea that the reconciliation was wholly on the human side. As the use of the word Atonement in the sense referred to continues on the part of many of the most recent writers, it is necessary to be explicit, and to show the true meaning of the word in the New Testament, and its bearing on an *evangelical* conception of the Cross. This is necessary, even though it may cause us to say things that "every one knows," but which, if known, seem to be constantly forgotten. Adherence to the New Testament sense of "Atonement" will, we believe, more than anything else, help us to the understanding of the Cross. It will at least clear away the most formidable obstacle to an understanding of it and the most potent source of misunderstanding. It is true that the use or non-use of a particular word or term cannot determine such a great subject; but the unwarranted sense which has been imported into this particular word has given the very name by which the work of Christ on His Cross is commonly described— the familiar everyday term "the Atonement." Hundreds of learned volumes and laboured treatises have been based on this misleading word, and, as already remarked, we find the error constantly repeated. This is true of both English and German theological writers, whatever their theological opinions may be. The consequence in Germany as well as in Britain is that, as Rothe remarks, "our dogmatists consider that it is a matter quite self-evident that the atonement for sin is a satisfaction for sin through expiatory endurance of its punishment" (*Still Hours*, E.T. p. 206).

The word "Atonement" occurs only once (Rom. v. 11) in the Authorised Version of the New Testament; it is not to be found in the Revised Version at all, the Greek word so rendered in the A.V. being in the Revised correctly translated *Reconciliation*. The word "Atonement" is right enough if it be used in its original and proper sense of At-one-ment. But, as it is commonly employed in theology, preaching, and controversy, it is used in the sense of atoning *for* sin, making an atonement or satisfaction for sin, or expiating it. Christ's "Atonement" is represented as something offered to or done before God which expiates

sin or satisfies the Divine Justice or Holiness in view of
sin, so that it can be forgiven.   By some quite recent
writers Atonement and Expiation are used as equivalent terms.   Some who seek to avoid this implication
still use the misleading word without explanation.
Such implications are by no means contained either in
the original Greek word used by Paul or in the English word "Atonement" in that older and proper sense
which it bore about the time when the Authorised
Version was made, but which was also the time of
transition to its later significance.

The Greek word used by St. Paul is καταλλαγή,
(*katallagē*), meaning a *change* or *exchange* of any kind ;
hence, in the New Testament, a change in the position
or condition of parties, *e.g.*, from enmity or opposition
to friendship, a reconciliation, a becoming at one, or at-
one-ment.   Therefore in the Revised Version we read
in Rom. v. 11 (where the A.V. had "Atonement"),
"Through whom we have now received the *reconciliation*."   So in Rom. xi. 15 we have, "If the casting of
them away be the *reconciliation* of the world."   With
special reference to the Cross, Paul speaks in 2 Cor.
v. 18 (as in both A.V. and R.V.) of "the Ministry
of Reconciliation," and his designation of the Gospel
that thus came to men is "the word of Reconciliation."
These are the only occurrences of the noun.   In several
places the verb (καταλλάσσω) is used in the sense of
to reconcile, as in 2 Cor. v. 18, "But all things are of
God who has reconciled (or atoned) us to Himself

2

through Christ." So Rom. v. 10. In 1 Cor. vii. 11 we read, "Let her (the wife) be *reconciled* to her husband." It occurs in no other sense. If we are to found on Scripture, then, there can be no doubt that "the *Reconciliation*" is the proper term, or "Atonement," not in the sense of expiation, but of being at one, or At-one-ment.

This was also the original sense of the English word "Atonement" (originally "onement"), and it is possible that it was in this sense it was used in Rom. v. 11 by the translators of the A.V., although Dr. John Owen, writing not long after the time of the translation, says, "which (Reconciliation), I know not by what means we have translated 'Atonement'" (*Works*, x. 263).

Many examples of the usage of atone and atonement in their original sense of at-one-ment might be given from early writers. In Shakespeare we have,

> "He and Aufidius can no more atone
> Than violentest contrariety."

> "I would do much
> To atone them, for the love I bear to Cassio."

> "He desires to make atonement
> Betwixt the Duke of Gloucester and your brothers."

From Murray's *New English Dictionary* one or two further examples may be given. Milton writes in 1643, "The king and Parliament will soon be attoned." Bayne, on Ephesians, has, "Now God is atoned and reconciled through Christ." We have an illustrative example in Queen Catharine Parr, who writes in 1553, "To reconcile himself and make an onement with God." Tyndale in 1526 translates 2 Cor. v. 18, "God hath given unto us the office to preach the Atonement." Kyngsmill writes (in *Man's Estate*), "If God did vouchsafe to make atonement with us." Here it will be observed it is *God* who is said to make atonement. As late as 1650, S. Clarke has in his *Ecc. History*, "We must not come to make an attonment with God—before we make an attonment with our brothers."

The word, however, came also to be used of "the propitiation of an offended or injured person by reparation of wrong or injury, amends, satisfaction, expiation," and in this sense it has been adopted by theology. This leads a theologian very ingenuously to remark, "The old word atonement has by true instinct deepened into the idea on which it rests, and has come to carry with it the idea of propitation or expiation." But this is just what is so greatly open to question, and, as the article in Murray's Dictionary notes, "The word is not so applied in any version of the New Testament."[1]

Of course, it will be said that what is meant by the

---

[1] As Dr. Trench remarks, "The notion of *satisfaction* lies now in these words (atone and atonement) rather than that of *reconciliation*. An atonement is the *satisfaction* of a wrong which one party has committed against another, not the *reconciliation* of two estranged parties. This last, however, was its earliest meaning, and, if the word may be rightly divided at-one-ment, as probably it may, is in harmony with its etymology" (*Select Glossary of English Words*). "Tell your scholars," he says elsewhere, "that Atonement means *reconciliation*" (*Study of Words*, p. 335).

term in its modern theological sense is that what Christ did on the Cross is that which leads to the At-one-ment or Reconciliation. It is true that it was in Christ and His Cross that God was atoning the world to Himself; but if we understand this in the sense of Christ making satisfaction, etc., it ignores, or, rather, contradicts the fact that, according to the Scriptures, the Atonement originated with *God*; it was "God" who "was in Christ at-on-ing the world to Himself." Into what Christ is believed to have done has been *imported* the idea commonly expressed by the modern use of the word atonement, namely, satisfaction or expiation. But this sense is not conveyed by the word that Paul uses, which means simply *Reconciliation*.

The use of the word Atonement in its modern theological sense is no doubt partly due to the influence of Anselm's "satisfaction theory," and partly to a belief in the nature of the Old Testament sacrifices which is now widely discredited. The expression "to make atonement" is frequently employed in the O.T. to translate the Hebrew verb *Kipper*, which means "to *cover*." We have there the institution of "atoning sacrifices," the oft quoted statement that "the blood maketh atonement for your souls," the great "Day of Atonement," and certain special sacrifices by means of which Moses and others "made atonement for the sins of the people." This language has been carried over into Christian theology *with the assumption* that these sacrifices were strictly propitiatory

sacrifices, expiating or "atoning for" the people's sins.
But this by no means follows. It is now generally
held that the Hebrew word means simply "to cover."
The great passage in Lev. xvii. 11, with reference to the
Blood, says simply, "I have given it to you to *cover*
your souls." As Schultz remarks, "the idea of expiation has been put into the word 'cover' without
any justification." What is stated is that the Blood,
being the seat of life and as such peculiarly holy (if not
even Divine), *is given by God* to them as a covering in
relation to certain offences, so that by offering it before
Him in a way prescribed they may continue in
Covenant relations to Him. So with the other sacrifices, even the sin-offering and the guilt-offering (*Old
Test. Theology*, vol. i. p. 385 f.). Dr. Davidson, in his
Theology of the Old Testament, remarks that "while
stating the fact that the life thus given atones, the
ritual law offers no explanation. The traditional explanation has been that the victim was a *pœna vicaria*
for the sin of the offerer. And it is probable that this
idea did become attached to sacrifice. It is questionable,
however, when all things are considered, if it be found
in the law" (p. 353). As for the prophets, "none of
the prophets, not even Ezekiel, refers to sacrifice as the
means of atonement for the sins of the people. God
forgives of His grace and mercy alone" (p. 330).

Finally, to quote a *Jewish* authority, Dr. Kohler in
The Jewish Encyclopedia defines "Atonement" as
"the setting at one, or reconciliation of two estranged

parties." There was a gradual spiritualisation of the idea. Sin meant estrangement of the life from God. Hence (as all Jewish interpreters agree) the blood was offered as representing *the life*. " The life of the victim was offered, not, as has been said, as a penalty in the judicial sense, to avert Heaven's punishment, not to have man's sins laid upon it as upon the scape-goat of the Day of Atonement, and thus to have the animal die in his place, but as a typical ransom of ' life by life,' the blood sprinkled by the priest upon the altar serving as a means of renewal of man's Covenant of life with God."

That none of these sacrifices of the law had in themselves, or in the fact of their being offered, any actual expiatory character, is evident from the words of the writer of the Epistle to the Hebrews : " For it is impossible that the blood of bulls and goats should take away sin ": the law having " only a *shadow* of the good things to come." That none of them was meant to propitiate God (after the manner of heathen sacrifices) or to make Him willing to forgive, is clear from the fact that they were all of Divine appointment and provision. They were ceremonial observances ordained by God Himself in His merciful regard for the people by observance of which they, in spite of their sins, might be " covered," or continue to stand in acceptance before Him. The sacrificial system was " an institution provided by God for sins committed *within* the Covenant : sins done with a high hand cut a man off from the covenant

people" (Davidson, *Theol. of O.T.* p. 310). As Dr.
Dorner (who himself held a doctrine of "atonement")
remarks : "That the blood of beasts of itself, or the
mechanical offering of the same, has expiatory force
for men, is not only expressly repudiated by the
Psalmists and Prophets, but contradicts the institution
of the sacrificial service; for it is only through God
that the sacrifice can avail for the reconciliation of
man" (*System of Christian Doctrine,* iii. p. 405). It
was really At-one-ment in the sense of Reconciliation
—proceeding from God—that these sacrifices provided
for. By means of them *God* was atoning the people
to Himself as members of His community. It was
God who gave them to this end, not man that devised
them as atonements for his sins. They were a manifestation of the Divine *long-suffering,* and had not the
power to purify the conscience. The atonement was "for
individual offences, to which the sacrifices apply, not
an atonement for *the sin,* for the guilt-burdened state.
For this reason the full and proper forgiveness of sins,
the atonement for the entire man, is reckoned in the
Old Testament itself among the blessings of the New
Covenant which was to be looked for" (pp. 408–9). By
their use, Atonement in the sense of Reconciliation was
always open to the people. What Paul says in the
third chapter of Romans throws light upon the method
of the Divine procedure. He says that God "passed
over in His forbearance the sins of the past," instead
of strictly punishing them. But if these sacrifices had

been real propitiations for sin he could not have spoken thus. It is quite clear, therefore, that we have here to do with At-one-ment or Reconciliation, not with Atonement in the modern sense. These sacrifices had no intrinsic value or virtue "to atone for sin," "to propitiate an offended Deity," or "to avert His just wrath." Whatever we may believe concerning the origin of the O.T. sacrifices, they were never intended to have any such virtue or value. Later Jewish theology may have ascribed it to them, but without warrant; indeed, as the result of lower conceptions of God. Such atonements can have no place with the God of Truth. And, as a matter of fact, for downright, high-handed sin or transgression no reconciling or covering sacrifices were provided. Death was the doom of the wilful transgressor. But, at the same time, At-one-ment with God through penitence and confession was proclaimed to all sinners by the prophets, altogether apart from sacrifices. "The sacrifices of God," said the Psalmist, "are a broken spirit; a broken and a contrite heart, O God, Thou wilt not despise." In the suffering Servant of Jehovah we have the picture of one who bears the sins of his people, enduring what is due to their sins with a redeeming effect on the people. But it does not follow that he was "making atonement for them," or that his sufferings were really expiatory, although they should issue in at-one-ment for many.

The importation of the sense of expiation into the English word Atonement (the German word *Versöhnung*

also means both Expiation and Reconciliation) has, we
cannot help thinking, often led theologians far astray
in their endeavours to interpret the Cross, a source of
error from which adherence to the word actually used
by Paul would have saved them. A man may desire
to make atonement to God for his sins, or to his brother
for the wrong he has done him. He is anxious to do
or endure something that will show his sorrow and
wipe out his fault, or to make some great sacrifice
which he thinks may "atone" for the injury or offence.
When such a feeling is rooted in a real sense of wrong
done or of sin, it is, of course, a commendable one. It
was doubtless necessary that man should be led to feel
that sin, morally conceived, real sin, was injurious to
man and heinous before God; that it deserved to be
punished, or in some way expiated if that were possible.
It was a necessary preparation for the coming of God
into man's deepest nature. Whatever external form
the earliest sacrifices may have taken, the feeling of
something standing between the man and his god was
doubtless of Divine origin. The study of Comparative
Religion bids us see God deepest of all in all religions.
But, owing to his sensuous nature, the Divine education of man has been very slow, and has been strangely
perverted. The desire to propitiate the gods, as characteristic of the earlier forms of religion, was not moral in
its character. It was a transfer to the deity of human
relations and feelings, founded in ignorance of the true
God. It was expressive of a feeling deep seated in the

animal nature (we see the same thing even in some domesticated creatures in relation to man), and no pages of human history are more sad and terrible than those which record the developments of propitiatory and expiatory sacrifices wherein, not only animals, but little children, weak, trembling women, captives, slaves, strong men in their prime, sometimes in holocausts, were immolated on the altars of sacrifice. It was *self* that was strongest in it. As Dorner remarks : " An Egoism, although unconscious, lies at the foundation of heathen acts of worship ; they are means of bribery and flattery." The Deity is not conceived as *holy*. Even when a sense of sin was in some measure felt, the disposition was " either to transfer the guilt of evil outside self, or at least to seek an expiation outside one's own person. But where the expiation is taken upon one's own person, the guilt is at least discovered outside the soul itself—in the body, and attempted to be erased by means of negative, lacerating or life-destroying ascetic practices ; or the lusts of the flesh put on the garb of devotion, and require or present the sacrifice of innocence in pretended honour of the gods " (ii. 256, 257). Therefore we say that as it entered the human purpose, it is, in Pauline phrase, " of the flesh," not of the spirit. It is for selfish satisfaction. And if a man could persuade himself that he had done or suffered enough, it would tend to a self-satisfaction or self-righteousness inimical to the higher life, it would lead, in short, to that parody of true religion contained

in the cry of Louis XIV. of France in the face of his
troubles—"After all that I have done for God!"

True religion, therefore, does not adopt the principle
or the practice. It was in order to separate the
Israelites from those heathen sacrifices, so fraught with
evil, and ultimately to deliver them wholly from them,
that the Mosaic Legislation was instituted and a system
of provisional sacrifices in view of a Divine Law
appointed and provided as a means of reconciliation,
not by the offenders, but by the supreme Lawgiver.
And, side by side with these sacrifices, there were the
prophets, telling the people how vain and empty these
were in themselves. It was a preparation for the full
revelation yet to come that the Reconciliation must
proceed, *not from the offender, but from the offended One,
not from man, but from God,* that it was God alone who
could propose or provide a real propitiation for man
in view of his sin. Certainly, that propitiation was not
likely to be provided after the manner of heathen
sacrifices of human life or the death of innocent victims.
If the blood of animals could not take away sin, no
more can "a sacrifice of richer blood and nobler name"
do so if it be materially and not spiritually regarded.
The desire to atone is commendable as between man
and man, and it may often, as with Sidney Carton,
manifest itself in noble action; but as between man
and God the old question of the prophet remains un-
answerable: "Wherewith shall I come before the Lord,
and bow myself before the high God? Will the Lord

be pleased with thousands of rams, or with ten thousand rivers of oil? shall I give my first-born for my transgression, the fruit of my body for the sin of my soul?" And still it is true: "He has showed thee, O man, what is good; and what doth the Lord require of thee, but to do justly, to love mercy, and to walk humbly with thy God?" In returning to God without any atonement, the prophet proclaimed that the way of at-one-ment was always open to men. We cannot atone for our sins before God, but we can turn unto Him and be forgiven. The sense of guilt, however, is real, and it needed to be deepened. Where a deep consciousness of sin is felt, God's forgiveness can only be assuredly and savingly received where it is recognised that God's righteousness in relation to sin has been adequately manifested, as it has been in the Cross of Christ.

What we have in Christ, however, is on the same lines as those followed in the Old Testament. It is not the movement of man towards God, but that of God towards man. It was God who in Christ made and declared the way of at-one-ment. As Paul said, "God was in Christ reconciling (at-oning) the world to Himself."

We do not for a moment question the validity of trust in what Christ did for us on the Cross. But it is very desirable that we should endeavour to understand what it was that He did. The description of the work of Christ as "atoning for man's sin to God" has tended to hide His actual work from many. It has also

introduced an element opposed to the higher life of
man as it is designed to be by God and as it is set
before us by and in Christ. While it is perfectly true
that Christ suffered on account of our sins, and that He
"bore our sins," *atoning for them* is another matter
entirely. Atoning for anything implies that something
has been done that *needs* atoning for. How could
Christ atone for the sins of generations yet unborn, for
all the dreadful crimes of men before ever they were
committed? There is a true sense in which the work
of Christ was *Eternal*, but this does not affect our
present objection to the interpretation which has been
given of it. An eternal atonement embraces past,
present, and future.

The idea that sin has been already atoned for
(although it is often counteracted by other considera-
tions) tends to give quite a false conception of the
relation of men to God and to sin with its consequences.
If all my sins have been really *atoned for*, how can I
be treated as a sinner? If my sin is a fact, so also is
the adequate atonement for it. If strict justice is to
rule, the sinner has nothing to fear, whether he accepts
Christ or not. Here, surely, we are going against the
Divine Holiness or Righteousness, and suggesting
something to the sinner prejudicial to his highest
interests. One often wonders to see how indifferent
to certain forms of sin, and even to the knowledge of
what *is* sinful, some who say they are accepted by God
on account of Christ's Atonement can be, and at what

a low level many holding this form of faith are content
to live. We need not wonder. For here is an element
which, all unconsciously, may work disastrously: " I
am a sinner, but all my sins have been atoned for by
Christ,"—if I rest in this, am I not in very real danger
of taking sin lightly, of cherishing a merely selfish
satisfaction in the fact of *my* salvation, and a false
contentment with myself as I am and with the world
as it is? I may be told to think of what it cost Christ
to make that atonement. But this is just what those
of whom we speak do not think and cannot realise.
Indeed, we must ask in all seriousness whether the
belief that my sin has been expiated or atoned for by
another, especially by another's suffering, does not tend
to perpetuate or to carry men back to that old selfish
egoism which characterised so much of pre-Christian
religion with its substitutionary sacrifices?

Again, to rest our confidence on the ground of an
atonement made by Christ for our sins, is to fail to
realise the fulness and freeness of the Divine forgiving
Love as Christ proclaimed it and manifested it. It
causes a serious limitation to our sense of the love of
God—the Love that God is—and, consequently, to the
possession of our souls by that Love. And this accounts
for that undue self-centredness which still remains in
many Christians, and for the absence of a larger
measure of that broadly Divine and human, universal
and brotherly Love that showed itself in Christ, the
want of which, in the measure in which it ought to be

present, is the greatest defect of modern Evangelical Christianity.

But although Paul did not use the word " atonement," did he not really teach that what Jesus did was to atone for our sins, and that it was this which made the At-one-ment or Reconciliation actual? Let us ask now, therefore, what St. Paul's doctrine of the Cross really was.

III

PAUL'S DOCTRINE OF THE CROSS

CHAPTER III

PAUL'S DOCTRINE OF THE CROSS

PAUL'S doctrine of the Cross has both a *judicial* and an *ethical* side or aspect. It had necessarily a judicial aspect, because he had to show how the Cross of Christ met and ended "the Law." He had to vindicate the Cross in the face of that Jewish opposition which based itself on "the Law" as a Divine institution which could never be set aside, which separated them from and raised them above the rest of the world. He did this by showing that under "the Law" righteousness, entitling to acceptance with God, was impossible; that the Jew under the written law was equally guilty with the Gentile to whom the law of God was witnessed in his conscience, so that under no form of Law merely could man attain to "the glory of God," that is, to the Divine approbation. But *now* God had opened for all men a new way of righteousness and salvation through faith in Jesus as the true spiritual Christ. In His death God's own righteousness had been so manifested that Reconciliation or At-one-ment had been made for the whole world, so that those who, because of their sins, had been in the position of "enemies" could be received into favour, "accounted righteous" in Christ, blessed with God's peace, and made partakers in that spirit of true life and real righteousness which went forth to the world in Christ.

Stated briefly, his doctrine on its *judicial* side, as given in Rom. iii. 21–26, was this: that God, who was drawing nigh to men in His forgiving love, gave up Christ His Son to death as a manifestation of His righteousness, in view of His passing over sin in the past, and of the proclamation of Forgiveness and acceptance now being made in the Gospel. There was, however, a deeper *ethical* element in his thought of the Cross which must yet receive our special attention. But, meanwhile, let us observe some features of Paul's *judicial* conception as here stated, which show that certain theories of "the Atonement" do not find support therein.

First, be it noted that the whole procedure *originated with God*, not with Christ considered apart from God. It was God who took the first step; it was God who was drawing nigh to men in His Grace. The Cross, therefore, could not possibly be an atonement offered *to* that God from whom the whole proceeded and who Himself made the sacrifice,—"who spared not His own Son, but delivered Him up for us all." It could not be to induce, or even to enable God *to forgive*; for God was already forgiving men, and it was *because* He was forgiving them that He gave up His Son to die for them. It could not be in any real sense to *propitiate*

God. The idea of God propitiating Himself, or atoning for sin to Himself, is forced and unnatural. Besides, it is out of keeping with the historical facts which show us Christ accepting the Cross as the will of His Father, and dying with the cry of desolation on His lips. God can neither die nor feel Himself forsaken by Himself. It was Christ, His Son, *in human form* as true *man*, that was given up by God so to suffer and die.

But does not Paul attribute our justification to "the blood of Christ"? does he not speak of the death of Christ as a sacrifice,—a propitiatory sacrifice,—and is not Christ elsewhere described as "the propitiation for our sins; and not for ours only, but also for the whole world"? The "Blood of Christ" simply means His sacrificial death, although some prefer to take it in a spiritual sense as in John vi. 53–56. The meaning of the word (*hilastērion*) in Rom. iii. 25, rendered in the A.V. "propitiation," is doubtful. It is rendered by some, *Mercy-seat*, since in the Greek version of the Old Testament it is used to designate the lid or cover of the ark on which the sacrificial blood was sprinkled, and over which the Divine Glory appeared, speaking peace to the people. This is the meaning of the word in the only other place in which it occurs in the New Testament, Heb. ix. 5, "overshadowing the mercy-seat." It is easy to understand how Christ on His Cross is the meeting-place between God and man; where the Divine mercy descends in its supreme manifestation. Others, how-

ever, prefer "propitiation" or "propitiatory sacrifice."[1]
A similar dubiety applies to the phrase in Rom. viii. 3
(*peri hamartias*), rendered in the R.V. "as an offering
for sin." It will be noticed that the words "as an
offering" are not in the original text, but simply "for"
or "concerning sin"; but the phrase is used in the
Septuagint to denote a propitiatory sacrifice. Paul, no
doubt, had the Jewish sacrifices in view. His manner
of speaking of *the blood* of Christ suggests this, although
"blood" was also a familiar synonym for life taken, or
a violent death. And if we bear in mind what we have
already seen with respect to these sacrifices, the sense
in which Christ is the propitiation for our sins will be
manifest. It is in the same sense as that in which these
sacrifices were propitiations. They were not actual propitiations *of* God, but means *provided by God*, whereby
men by using them might, in spite of their sins, be
accepted by God, at-oned to Him, and abide in the
community of His people—in Christian language, "in
fellowship with God." So, in a similar way, God, not
man, has provided in Christ a propitiation (or a propitiatory sacrifice) for sinful men. It is by no means

---

[1] Deissmann concludes a learned inquiry into the meaning of the word
by maintaining that it means simply "the propitiatory thing," "the means
of propitiation," and holds that in Rom. iii. 25 the general sense "means
of propitiation" is quite sufficient : Christ, the exalted spiritual Lord, in
whom the believer lives, moves, and has his being, is, as faith in blood-
communion with Him proves Him to be, given to us by God as our
ever-present propitiator, our continual propitiation (*Ency. Bib.*, article
"Mercy-seat"). See also 1 John i. 2, where, however, we have a different
word.

implied that the death of Christ actually propitiated
God in the sense of gaining His favour. What Paul
says concerning the necessity for that sacrifice we shall
see immediately. But that God so gave up His Son,
not to propitiate Himself, but to be an ever-availing
propitiation for sinners, is the very foundation of Paul's
Gospel. It was this—not merely the fact that there
was a sacrifice for sin, but that God Himself made the
sacrifice of giving up His own Son for us all—that called
forth the note of wonder and kindled the flame of love
in the heart; and this fundamental fact must rule in all
interpretations of the Cross. Just as those Old Testament sacrifices were not, like those of the heathen world,
meant in themselves to propitiate God, but were provided by God for the people, in order that by their
bringing them into His Presence they might have the
consciousness of the remission of their transgressions,
and of abiding in His favour as members of the
community of His people, so is it with the great sacrifice
of Christ. It is something provided by God in view of
which remission of sins can be realised by all, something
that man can always look to and place his confidence
in. Therefore, of Christ, Paul says, "Whom God set
forth (or put forward) as a propitiation through faith in
His blood." Why "whom *God* put forward," if it was
to propitiate God? It will not do to say that in Christ
God gave humanity the means of making propitiation,
but that the propitiation was actually made by Christ
as representing man. What the Apostle says is that

God set forth Christ as a propitiation. It is *this*, not merely the gift of Christ to men, that is attributed to God. It will not do to turn it round to say that Christ made propitiation *to* God. And why "through faith in His blood"? Through man's faith in its sufficiency, as the Israelite found a propitiation through faith in the blood of the animal sacrifices which God provided for him. As Weiss remarks in his *New Testament Theology* (i. p. 428), "In the blood of Christ He set forth to the world a means of propitiation through faith."

Again, Paul says that God has provided "a righteousness of God *through faith in Jesus Christ unto all them that believe.*" It was only "unto them that believe" that Christ was a propitiation, just as the ancient sacrifices were only propitiations to those who accepted them and relied on them—in *faith.* God provided these for all who would accept them; so He has provided in Christ the complete and final propitiation for all who will accept Him.

Men do not need to understand it in its Godward aspect; it is sufficient that it has been provided for them by God. It is in this sense, then, that Christ is "the propitiation for our sins." As it is put in the First Epistle of John: "If any man sin, we have an Advocate with the Father, Jesus Christ the Righteous One: and *He* is the propitiation for our sins: and not for ours only, but also for the whole world." That is, although we sin, there is an abiding propitiation provided for us by God, so that we need not any other sacrifices,—a propitiation, in virtue of which, "if we confess our sins, He is faithful and just (in view of the propitiation which He has Himself provided) to forgive us our sins and to cleanse us from all un-righteousness."

In virtue of that Divinely-provided propitiation we can abide in fellowship with God. This is very different from the idea of the Cross as a propitiation made by Christ *to* God.

2. What the Cross was in the view of God—what it was meant by Him to be in relation to sin—Paul also tells us, still from the standpoint of something done *by God*. It was the *manifestation*, setting forth, or *demonstration of God's Righteousness* in view of His having passed over sin, and of His forgiveness and acceptance of sinners. The Apostle's words deserve all attention: "But now, apart from law, a righteousness of God (a free gift of acceptance) has been manifested—being made (or accounted) righteous freely by His grace, through the Redemption that is in Christ Jesus; whom *God set forth* a propitiation (or a propitiatory), through faith in His blood, in order to *show forth* (or demonstrate) His righteousness, because of the passing over of the sins done aforetime, in the forbearance of God, for *the showing forth* (or demonstrating) of His righteousness, at the present time, in order that He might Himself be righteous (or perhaps, "shown to be righteous")—and the Giver of righteousness to him

who has faith in Jesus (or, "who is of the faith of Jesus"), Rom. iii. 21–26.

It is now almost universally agreed that "righteousness" in vers. 25 and 26 means God's moral righteousness. But the point to be noticed here at present is that the Cross was provided by God Himself *in order to demonstrate His Righteousness* in view of His merciful passing over of sins in the past and His gracious gift of justifying righteousness to sinners in the present. The word is *endeixis*, which meams a pointing out (properly with the finger; *index* is from the same root). As he had said before that Christ was "*set forth*" (*proetheto*) by God to be a propitiation. It was not to satisfy the Divine Justice or holiness, but to *demonstrate* it, to show it forth to the world. This is the important thing to grasp.

In this way, Paul says (2 Cor. v. 19), "God was in Christ reconciling the world to Himself," that is, at-oning it, making it at one with Himself in His righteousness. Just as by means of the propitiations provided by Him under the Law, offenders were at-oned to Him. This was something done *by God* in Christ once for all and completely for the whole world. It was something provided by God for man as man of which all could take advantage. It was not merely that God in His Love was seeking men to be reconciled to Him. He *was* doing this in Christ, and through the Apostles as Ambassadors for Christ; but He had first of all actually in Christ reconciled the world to Himself,—the world as represented by Christ,—and it was this that was the basis of the Gospel message and appeal. On His side all was done that needed to be done; it was now for men individually to enter into the Reconciliation. What God did in Christ made a true and lasting At-one-ment or Reconciliation for all sinners. God declared Himself reconciled to them in Christ, it was for them to be reconciled to God. The Reconciliation was *first* on God's part, provided by Him for man. It was something which, Paul said, God had done in Christ for us "while we were enemies," something for men to "receive" or take advantage of by their laying aside their enmity to God who had in His Love provided this Reconciliation or At-one-ment for them. "We entreat you," he says, "that ye receive not the grace of God in vain."

If we ask next, *How this was done?* there is no doubt that it was in the death of Christ on the Cross, or, as Paul states it more definitely in 2 Cor. v. 21, by His being "made sin for our sakes." The meaning of this we may best consider in a separate chapter.

IV

CHRIST "MADE SIN FOR US"

CHAPTER IV

CHRIST "MADE SIN FOR US"

BY many of the older interpreters the expression
"made Sin" was on the ground of supposed
Septuagint usage explained as meaning "made a
sacrifice for sin." But this is rejected by modern
expositors. The question, however, is immaterial,
because even if we interpret it in the sacrificial sense
contended for, the sacrifice would represent *sin*. A
common interpretation is that Christ " took the sinner's
place," died in the sinner's stead the death which the
sinner was doomed to die. This is also the interpretation adopted by those who explain the Cross (and
ultimately explain it away) as having exclusive
reference to "the Law," and who regard the death of
Christ as the suffering by Him of that penalty of death
which the Law declared, but which had not been
inflicted on sinners. We shall have to return to this.
But Paul does not say that Jesus was made or treated
as a sinner, but that He was "made *sin*"; just as in
Gal. iii. 13 he says, He was made *a curse*, not an
accursed person. He seems purposely to avoid the
suggestion that Christ was made or treated as a

sinner by using the abstract terms "sin" and "righteousness": Christ, he says, was made *sin*, that we might be made the *righteousness* of God in Him. We thus give to "sin" the same sense as in the previous sentence, which says that "Christ knew no sin." The idea of *exchange* in the "Reconciliation" is also thus suggested. Elsewhere, also, sin is personified by Paul. In the sixth chapter he tells how *sin* entered the world and what it has wrought, contrasting it with righteousness in Christ. And in the seventh chapter, sin is represented as an enemy which wrought in him all manner of coveting, and slew him. "Apart from the law," he says, "sin was dead," but with the law sin "revived"; beguiled him and doomed him to death. He was sold under sin as a hard master or owner, so that it was no more *he* (the real man that he was) that did the evil, but *sin* that had seated itself in him and held him captive. Again, he says in chap. viii. 3 and 4, that "God, sending His own Son in the likeness of *sinful flesh* (literally, 'flesh of sin') and for, or on account of, sin, *condemned sin in the flesh*; that the requirement of the law may be fulfilled in us who walk not after the flesh, but after the Spirit." The point here is that it is as standing "in the likeness of *sinful flesh*" that he thinks of Christ, and that it was "sin in the flesh" or the sinful flesh, not "the sinner," that was condemned and died before God. To say that *sin* was condemned in the flesh is very different from saying that the sinner was represented as con-

demned and judged in Christ, or that Christ took the
sinner's place, while it remains wholly true that Christ
died "for our sakes" and "for our sins." It was our
sins that caused or necessitated His death, and it was
in order to show forth God's righteousness in relation
to sin that He died.

No doubt He represented the sinner also, *if the sinner
cannot be separated from his sin*; and, as man cannot
of himself free himself from his sin, Christ's death, in
Paul's view, represents the death which we must all
have died. But Paul explicitly teaches that the sinner
is *not* to be identified with his sin. While sin is
inseparable from "the flesh," it is not inseparable from
the man. Sin is something foreign to the true man,
"the man within," the man as God conceives him, the
man as he knows himself in his true being. It is a
tyrant foreign to his true self that has got seated in
him, from whose dominion Christ dies to free him.
It was that false usurping power, which had hitherto
dominated men, that was judged, condemned, and
rendered powerless by means of the Cross of Christ.
As, according to the Fourth Gospel, Christ Himself
said, " Now is the judgment of this world, now shall the
Prince of this world be cast out." It was not directly
the sinner, therefore, but *sin*, and God's judgment on
sin, that was represented by the Cross of Christ.

How does Paul think of Christ as being "made sin"
for us? No interpretation, of course, can be correct
which says that Christ was actually made *sin*—a thing

4

impossible. It must therefore have been in some *representative* sense. It was, he says, in order that the righteousness of God in His relation to sin might be demonstrated. The natural meaning is that Christ on His Cross suffered what *sin* deserved to suffer, died as sin (or "the sinful flesh," from which in Paul's view *sin* was inseparable) was doomed to die. In this way the righteousness of God in view of sin was set forth. It was shown that, although God had passed over sin and was now forgiving it, sin was not lightly regarded by God, but was doomed to death. Such a manifestation was necessary, says Paul, that God might be seen to be just, and the justifier of him who believes in Jesus. Such was Paul's *judicial* doctrine of the Cross, whatever we may think of it. But before discussing it further, let us note how, at this point, it passes into an *ethical* doctrine.

It was as representing sin or "sinful flesh" that Christ died ; and Paul teaches that, *as so represented*, man in the flesh died before God. Christ's death was a death *to* sin, and in that death all men died representatively. They did so in the very fact that the sinful flesh died utterly in Christ's death. Man died completely in Christ as regards the old life, and arose in Him in His resurrection a new creature. In the sixth chapter of Romans this aspect of the Cross is emphasised. "We who *died* to sin, how shall we any longer *live* therein—all we who were baptized into

Christ were baptized into His death—that like as Christ was raised from the dead, through the glory of the Father, so we also might walk in newness of life." It was not in baptism that they so died, but in the representative death of Christ. "Our old man was crucified with Him, that the body of sin might be done away, that so we might no longer be in bondage to sin: for he that hath died is justified from sin (freed from it); the death that He died, He died unto sin once for all, but the life that He liveth, He liveth unto God. Even so reckon ye also yourselves dead unto sin, but alive unto God in Christ Jesus." "You died," he says elsewhere, "and your life is hid with Christ in God" (Col. iii. 3). "The love of Christ constraineth us," he says again, "because we thus judge that if one died *for* all, therefore all died; and He died for all, that they which live should no longer live to themselves, but to Him who died for them and rose again" (2 Cor. v. 15). The death of Christ was thus a death *to* sin, and represented before God the death of all men to sin or "the flesh." *Sin* died in Him. It had an *ethical* significance to God, and it comes with an ethical inspiration and power to men. And Paul hesitates not to say that if this ethical significance of Christ's death be not realised by men, Christ will have died in vain. Notwithstanding Christ's death "for our sins," he says plainly that if men continue to live after the flesh, they shall "die"; only if they follow the Spirit shall they live. In Christ nothing avails but "a new creature." "If any man have not the Spirit of Christ, he is none of His."

Again, the death of Christ is with Paul inseparable from His *resurrection*. Both were representative acts; and apart from the resurrection, the death would have been insufficient. The death might vindicate God's passing over sins and His proclamation of forgiveness, but God in the Gospel does more than forgive. He "justifies" the sinner, reckons him "righteous," accepts him as His son and heir, imparts to him His Spirit. This is because in Christ man not only dies in the flesh, but rises to a new spiritual life of righteousness. Therefore, he says, "Christ was delivered up for our trespasses, and was raised for our justification." He represented before God a new, redeemed, spiritual Humanity. Men in Him could be, not only forgiven, but justified, even "glorified" (Rom. viii. 30). As we read in Ephesians ii.: "God, being rich in mercy, for His great love wherewith He loved us, even when we were dead (justly liable to death) through our trespasses, quickened us together with Christ (or in Christ), and raised us up with Him, and made us sit together with Him in the Heavenly places in Christ Jesus." Christ in His death, therefore, was "made sin," as representing the death which sin is doomed to die, and which the sinner must die if he cannot be freed from his sin; but He also represented the death of sin, or of man *to* sin, and his uprising into the new spiritual life of righteousness.

This representative character which is given to the death of Christ, and the union in it of the judicial and the ethical, gives quite a peculiar complexion to Paul's doctrine of the Cross, and forbids its interpretation after any merely human analogies. What he sees in it is something wholly unique and Divine, impossible to be found in the case of another. And not only does he lay at least equal stress on the ethical and the judicial aspects of the Cross, but it is in the realisation of its ethical significance alone that man's actual salvation is to be found.

V

PAUL'S DOCTRINE CONSIDERED

CHAPTER V

PAUL'S DOCTRINE CONSIDERED

THE modern mind finds no difficulty in accepting the ethical aspect of the death of Christ, especially if He be regarded as the Head and Representative of Humanity. But great difficulty is often felt with respect to the judicial aspect of His death, and it is often misapprehended. The problem of the present may be said to be how to conceive and state the judicial aspect of the Cross, so that it shall be credible and vital for us to-day. Let us now, therefore, give our careful consideration to Paul's doctrine. We are by no means *tied down* to Paul's teaching: the Cross is there for each man to interpret for himself. But we must believe that Paul was Divinely taught, and made the instrument of the liberation of Christianity from Judaism, so that through him it went forth as that universal world-saving religion Jesus meant it to be. That Christianity was further developed by means of Paul, is no reason for placing Paul in opposition to Christ. If we claim for ourselves Divine teaching and progress in the truth, we must not deny it to Christ's first followers. What we have to do is to separate the *substance* from the temporary *forms* which contained it. By most Christians, Paul's teaching has been accepted as the foundation of the evangelical faith. Paul, therefore, cannot be lightly regarded ; and if, as we must believe, he was led by the Spirit of God, there must be lasting truth, deeper than such forms of thought as were to him the necessary media of the Spirit's teaching, and the means whereby the special necessities of the time were met. Paul had, as we have seen, a particular work to do in the first instance in relation to those who stood for the old religion of "the Law," and for the idea of a temporal Messiah who should come for their special behoof. He had to show that those who boasted themselves of that law were, judged by their law, sinners before God as truly as the Gentiles whom they despised ; liable, therefore, to the doom of sin under the law, and only redeemed therefrom by the death of Christ.

Hence much in Paul's writings has reference to *redemption from the Law,* and to the opening of the door of God's Kingdom to the Gentiles through that Cross which ended the separating Law. In the Epistle to the Galatians the Cross is regarded almost exclusively in its relation to those who were under the Jewish law. "Christ," he says, "redeemed us from the curse of the law, having become a curse for us," that the promise of righteousness through faith—which was prior to the law —and that life in the Spirit to which faith in Christ leads, "might come upon the Gentiles." Again, he says that

Christ was "born under the law, that He might redeem *them which were under the law*, that we might receive the redemption of sons "—the Jews themselves being thus raised to a higher standing. It was to meet the demand of the law that he says, "the Son of God loved me, and gave Himself up for me." So in 1 Cor. xv. we read, " The sting of death is sin, and the strength of sin is the law"—which dooms man as a sinner to death. In Ephesians and Colossians also, the stress is laid on the work of the Cross in relation to the law, leading to the "reconciliation" of Jew and Gentile: "But now, in Christ Jesus, ye that once were afar off are made nigh in the blood of Christ. For He is our peace who made both one, and broke down the middle wall of partition, having abolished in His flesh the enmity, even the law of commandments contained in ordinances, that He might create in Himself of the twain one new man, so making peace" (Eph. ii. 15, 16). See also Col. ii. 13, 14.

In the first portion of the Epistle to the Romans the thought of the Law and its claims is predominant, and it may be fairly said that, when the Apostle speaks of the death of Christ in chap. iii., he has *primarily* before his mind the doom of death under "the Law." Even in the spiritual emancipation described in chaps. vii. and viii. 4, it is still redemption from the Law—" the law of sin and death "—the law which only revived and increased sin—that he has in view. Deliverance from that law, with the hopeless life under it, meant much more to Paul and his fellow-Christians than we can well realise;

and that Cross which, he held, freed them from it, at the same time broke down the barrier between Jew and Gentile, doing thus a redeeming work for the Gentile as well as for the Jew. No wonder, then, that Paul magnified the work of the Cross as freeing men from "the Law."

It is held by many modern writers that this reference to "the Law" sufficiently explains all that Paul says with respect to the Cross of Christ : that his doctrine of the Cross is simply an adaptation of Jewish theology to his purpose of showing how Christ's substitutionary or representative death met the penalty which the Law demanded, and thus adequately manifested the righteousness of the Lawgiver, so that, its ultimate demand having been met, the law was ended. His reasoning was, in short, an *argumentum ad Judæos*, which served a necessary purpose, but has now lost its value. That is, indeed, a commonplace of much recent theology, and it may be questioned whether evangelical writers have sufficiently faced and met this position. Certainly, some of Paul's arguments have no force for us to-day. *We* were never under the Jewish law, or needed redemption from it. As Gentiles, we share in the benefits of its removal, but that would be for us a much too distant motive of devotion to the Saviour. Moreover, we cannot look upon that law to-day as the Jews of St. Paul's time did, as being a direct and inviolable Divine institution or revelation, on the fulfilment of every requirement and threat of which the righteousness of God Himself was staked. Nor can we see, perhaps, how the violent death of Christ could really meet the demands of a righteous Law. It is impossible for us to-day to believe, *e.g.*, that "cursed is every one that hangs on a tree," altogether irrespective of the merit or demerit of the sufferer.

But to affirm that this meets all that Paul says about the Cross would be far too sweeping a statement. It is not merely with "the Law" that Paul is concerned, but with *sin*—real, universal sin, and want of righteousness before God on the part of both Jew and Gentile. Besides, it must be remembered that it is not Paul alone who asserts that Christ "died for our sins"; it is the universal Christian belief. In much that Paul has written and in his practical doctrine of sin and spiritual salvation the place given to the Cross goes far beyond any reference to the Jewish law. Even in the Epistle to the Galatians there are hints of a wider reference, as where he says that Christ "gave Himself for our sins, that He might deliver us from this present evil world" (or age), and that by the Cross of Christ he was "crucified to the world, and the world to him." In Ephesians also, where he speaks of the union of Jew and Gentile, he says they were made one, that Christ "might reconcile them *both* in one body unto God through the Cross"; and, writing to them as Gentiles, he says, "as Christ also loved you, and gave Himself up for you an offering and a sacrifice to God for an odour of a sweet smell" (Eph. v. 2, etc.).

In the Epistle to the Romans the *universal* reference of the Cross is made quite clear. The Gentiles, he shows, were under a law to God as well as the Jews, to which their consciences bore witness, in view of which they were sinners "worthy of death"; *all* came short of righteousness; for none was it possible under any "law"; for *all*, therefore, Jesus died. In His death, therefore, Jesus met a universal necessity, and became the Head of a new spiritual humanity. The soundness of his argument may be questioned, but certainly his view of the Cross was not restricted to its relation to the Jewish law. And although we may not be able to view it exactly as Paul did, it is possible that we may yet see that there was a real and abiding Divine significance in the death of Christ "for our sins." Instead of hastily brushing aside Paul's reasoning, we ought to inquire what lasting truth there is in his doctrine, and how we can apprehend it to-day. We have already seen that there do not enter into it any of those ideas of "atonement for sin," "expiation," or "propitiation of God" which are commonly attributed to Him, and that the Cross was God's own provision in order to set forth His righteousness in view of sin and its forgiveness. Let us return, then, to the consideration of the essential elements of Paul's doctrine. These are:

1. The necessity for a manifestion of the righteousness of God in view of sin.

2. That sin is doomed to death.

3. That Christ was made sin for us, or died for our sins.

1. When Paul says that the death of Christ was necessary as a manifestation of God's righteousness in view of His passing over, in His forbearance, the sins of the past, his statement is, of course, open to the objection that it is based on a too external conception of the relation of God to sin and its punishment. It seems to rest on the idea (that of " the law ") that such a punishment must be a violent death or some openly manifested infliction. This, of course, we cannot believe. Sin does not go unpunished although it is not openly visited by such Divine retribution as we may feel it deserves. God does not *really* pass over sin, although in His mercy the sinner does not suffer at once the ultimate penalty. It is in *this* that His forbearance is shown : He is " not willing that any should perish, but that all should come to repentance." But just because of this *apparent* passing over sins, just because of man's misconception of God's ways, a demonstration of His righteousness in relation to sin was needed by the world. Especially was this necessary in connection with a Gospel which proclaimed universal forgiveness.

Here, however, an element in Paul's gospel, not always recognised, must be taken into account. It is often objected to the Cross that in the Old Testament God's forgiveness was always freely extended to the penitent ; that the teaching of Christ, *e.g.*, in the parable of the Prodigal Son, followed the Old Testament in this respect, that, prior to the Cross and quite apart from it, Christ proclaimed the Divine forgiveness.

But the gospel of Christ goes beyond the Old
Testament teaching. Christ did not merely repeat the
teaching of the prophets. If John the Baptist was
"more than a prophet," much more was Christ. What
He proclaimed was the fulfilment of that which the
prophets had foretold,—the drawing nigh of God in
the Grace of *wholly free and universal forgiveness* unto
the salvation of His people, "for His own name's sake"
—in order to lead them to repentance and salvation.
It was not the old announcement of pardon to the
penitent merely, but the proclamation of a gospel of
Divine grace to the nation and ultimately to the world,
in order that God's reign might be really and permanently established in their hearts. As we have seen,
it was *because* God was forgiving sin that, as Paul
taught, He gave up His Son to death in order to
demonstrate His righteousness. In view of the Divine
forbearance in the past, and especially in view of this
newly declared movement of universal Grace, it is
evident that the righteousness of God must be at the
same time manifested if men are really to be saved
from their sins. For Forgiveness to have been limited
to "the penitent" would have been no advance on the
past, and would have failed in respect of that attractive
power which the Gospel was meant to possess. It
would have left out the chief motive which was designed
to lead men to God, namely, His forgiving Love going
forth to all without exception through the Cross of His
Son; and it could not have produced in man that glad

confidence in God which the Gospel was designed to produce, and which it did produce. On the other hand, to have simply proclaimed forgiveness would have failed to produce in men's hearts a due sense of the evil and danger of sin; it would have created quite a wrong conception of God as a Being of mere good nature, instead of that Holiness on which the world's hope rests; it would have tended to increase sin, instead of to save the world from it. It is not on this head that Paul's doctrine is open to objection; on the contrary, he has here seen and stated a great truth.

And here be it noted that this central element of Paul's doctrine, that what Christ suffered on the Cross on our behalf was a sufficient manifestation of God's righteousness in view of sin, so that sinners are forgiven and accepted by God,—this, apprehended under many forms, has ever been the *essence* of the distinctively evangelical faith.

2. That sin must *die* is a Divine necessity, quite apart from any positive Law; and it is a necessity that holds good for any nature from which sin is inseparable. It is quite impossible that sin can enter Heaven or be perpetuated in an eternal life. The relation of God to sin and its necessary doom of death have been obscured by mistaken views of sin's nature and source. Hence a revolt has arisen against the theological conception of sin which is dangerous in its tendency and untrue to fact. Sin is not that absolutely mysterious and un-

5

accountable thing which it has often been represented as
being.   It is the action of the self in disloyalty to the
true governing principles of life.   It is the outcome of
the animal nature in man failing to rise to the higher life
of the Spirit.   Every form of sin, in thought, word, or
deed, can be traced to its root in the self-loving, self-
seeking principle which is necessarily that of the animal
nature considered in itself.   It is inseparable from that
nature, though separable from the man as he is thought
by God and meant by God to become.   The animal
nature had to come first; but man is more than an
animal; ideally, he is a son of God; Love, not self,
God, not the world, is the true principle of his life.   It
is often said that sin is the great problem of the world,
and it is asked, Why did God permit sin?   Or, Why
should sin appear in the world of a *good* Creator?   The
appearance of sin is always possible in a world where
finite beings are endowed with a *self* of their own ; and
apart from such endowment, *man* could have had no
existence.   A *good* being cannot be externally created ;
and, as Dr. Caird says most truly, " the very consciousness of *self* carries with it the assertion of self and the
seeking of self; and in a finite being such self-assertion
and self-seeking have in them the germs of all that is
evil " (*The Evolution of Theology in Greek Philosophy*,
p. 341).   The source of sin is seen still more clearly
when we take into account man's slow emergence from
a lower condition as science has revealed it to us.   That
which becomes sin in man was not *sin* in the purely

animal creation. As Paul says, "Where there is no law, sin is not imputed." Where the law of a higher life does not make itself felt in the Conscience, or does not in some way claim man's obedience, such a thing as sin has no existence *as sin*. The law of man's higher life must be *freely* obeyed; he cannot be good or righteous mechanically, or under compulsion. Sin is simply the result of man's failure, in his freedom, to comply with the higher law of his life.—This is true whatever theory we may hold of his origin. Sin, in its essence, is life for *self*, instead of for *God*.

Paul pictures the condition graphically in the seventh chapter of Romans. The man, awakened to hear the call of the higher law, inwardly approving of it and even desiring to obey it, yet finds himself unable to rise to the occasion. Sin is seated in him as it were a usurping tyrant, so that in spite of his better self that has become awakened, he finds himself ever coming under sin's dominion and condemnation. It is truly *seated in him* in that self-pleasing principle of his lower nature from which he cannot by any effort free himself. Sin in him must die, if he is to rise into the higher life. But that means that man after the flesh merely must die. He cannot in that lower nature be a son and heir of God: "they that are in the flesh cannot please God." "In solemn truth I say unto you," said Jesus, "Ye must be born anew. That which is of the flesh is flesh, and that which is of the Spirit is Spirit."

"The flesh"—not the body, but the lower animal

nature—is the seat of sin, and it is certain that sin
cannot be perpetuated. It cannot "inherit the Kingdom
of God"; its place is "the outer darkness"; its doom
is death away from God. The flesh had to come first,
but its rule in man was not meant to last, it was to
be changed into that of the Spirit. The flesh had a
necessary purpose to serve in the evolution of humanity ;
but, having served that purpose, it must *die* if man is
to rise into his true, God-intended life. Just as the
flora and fauna of earth have had again and again to
die for the sake of higher orders of life, so man in the
flesh must die, to be succeeded by man in the Spirit.
If we think of this and of the necessity for preventing
sin's entrance into the eternal life (if such a thing be
even conceivable), we shall see that the doom of death
on sin is an absolutely necessary one. It is not the
sentence of a hard and stern Lawgiver, but the ordering
of the Love of God in the fulfilment of His creative
purpose. But this must be kept quite separate from
the idea of an arbitrary penalty externally inflicted, or
such as could be endured by a substitute.

3. It is with our third head that we shall encounter
the greatest difficulty. In what sense can we credibly
say to-day that Christ "died for our sins," was "made
sin for us," "bore our sins," or endured their consequences ? In what way can we see this to be true
apart from the idea of "atoning for" or "expiating" sin ?
Here it is evident that we must leave aside or get

beneath those differing interpretations of the Apostle's language which men of equal learning and conscientiousness are led to give. It is clear that on those matters where such differences of interpretation are possible, Paul's teaching cannot be meant to be normative. How can we tell whether we accept Paul's teaching or not, if we cannot be certain as to what he says? We must view the subject broadly in the light of his essential position *that Christ died in order that God's righteousness might be manifested*, and that in so dying He died for, *i.e.*, on account of, our sins, showing forth in His own person what sin entailed on sinners in the righteousness of God. As such a broad statement we could (if " wrath " be rightly taken) accept that given by Dr. Stevens in the course of his criticism of Paul's doctrine: " Christ was ' made sin ' on man's account, that is, He so came under the action of the Divine Wrath against sin, that God's Justice is thereby vindicated and satisfied " (we would omit " and satisfied," for that is, we think, going beyond Paul), (*The Christian Doctrine of Salvation*, p. 60). But is it so certain that, as he proceeds to say, " it is unquestionably true that the juridical elements in Paul's theology as seen in his doctrines of expiation and justification are survivals of his Pharisaic training "? Is Paul's judicial doctrine of the Cross *only this* and nothing more? We have already seen that the ideas of " expiation " and " atonement to God " are foreign to Paul's doctrine. They cannot with fairness be imputed to him: and perhaps it will yet appear that, underlying his judicial representation of the Death of Christ, there is something more broadly human and Divine, something Christian as well as Jewish, something lastingly true, although it may need to be stated differently.

Let us suppose for the moment that this is so, that in some real sense the death of Christ was "a death for our sins," or that Christ was "made sin for us," the accident that Paul apprehended and stated this in the forms of thought or speech with which he and his readers were familiar does not affect *the fact* in the slightest degree.   How else *could* he have apprehended and stated it?   The men of Paul's day apprehended many things — even the commonest things — in a different way from ourselves, and gave them other names than those we apply to them, but *the things themselves* are the same for us all.   The real question is, was there *a truth* apprehended by Paul under these forms, and what is that truth?

There is wide agreement to-day in the rejection of anything *penal* in the death of Christ.   So far as an external legal penalty is concerned, and so far as the thought of Christ suffering punishment directly at the hand of God, or any idea of satisfaction by suffering, comes into theories of the Cross, the rejection is to be justified.   That conception of the death of Christ to which Pfleiderer, for example, seeks to tie down Evangelical theology cannot be received.   Nor do we think that it can be fairly ascribed to Paul. According to this, Sin up till then had not been duly punished. This required a proof of the Divine Justice. This could only be given—since death is the wages of sin— by a bloody penal death. In order to show grace to the guilty, God, instead of inflicting the full penalty of death as His avenging justice required on all who had deserved it, inflicted it on one who had not deserved it, and thus set forth this one in His blood that was shed as the victim who suffered (vicariously) the punishment due to others, and so expiated their guilt. And this He did in His own interest (*proetheto*, middle voice) in order to cause the recognition of His own justice, which recognition had been endangered by the previous impunity of sin.

This is said to be the only view that accords simply and naturally with Jewish notions, according to which justice is the exact requital of actions and consequent punishing of every instance of guilt; but in whose person the guilt was punished, whether in that of the guilty person himself or vicariously in that of another, was of no immediate concern, all that was required was that the penalty should be inflicted.

Now in this, of course, there would be no real manifestation of the *righteousness* of God, but the reverse. It was a strange doctrine this even for "the Jews." [1]

---

[1] Jewish scholars repudiate the assertion of Christian writers that Paul represented Rabbinic Theology. Dr. Kohler, writing in the *Jewish Ency.*, says, "There is no indication in Paul's writings that he had received the rabbinical training ascribed to him by Christian writers ancient and

It would be still more strange if Paul, with his sound judgment, Christian feeling, and high regard for real righteousness, believed that such an example was set by God before the world ; and preached it as the means of man's salvation.[1] It would be a very peculiar mode of getting that freedom from " the law of sin and death," in which he gloried,—by an act of the strictest and most literal legalism on the part of God, thus at once satisfying and doing away with the law,—a law which Paul regarded as having only a *temporary* value. To think of the righteous Father for the sake of that temporary law, inflicting " a violent death " on His Son, or setting Him forth to suffer it in order to maintain His Justice, is quite repellent, and we cannot but believe that Paul viewed the matter in some other way than this. If such were indeed the only legitimate interpretation of his reasoning, we should not hesitate to regard it as being only an *argumentum ad hominem* in which he adapts himself to the Jewish view of Law and penalty for the sake of proving to the Jew how, on his own principles, the Law has been met and satisfied. But the way in which he extends his doctrine to the Gentiles as well as to the Jews, and the place which the death of Christ holds in his gospel generally, suggests

modern, least of all that he was a disciple of Gamaliel." The representations of Weber, Bousset, etc., are not accepted.

[1] While his Jewish training naturally influenced his forms of thought, was Paul the Christian so completely under the power of " Jewish notions of justice " (if such these were) that he could only conceive the Cross which *freed him from Judaism* in terms of them ?

that Paul saw something more in the Death of Christ. It was something occurring in the Divine moral order; only thus could he be so confident that *God* was in it. And, as we have seen, it was the death of *sin*, or of "sinful flesh," that Paul had in view; he carefully avoids the suggestion that Christ was treated as a sinner.

Paul certainly teaches that "Death" is the "wages of sin"—the penalty of sin under the Law of God, and we are compelled to ask, What did he mean by "death" in this connection, and what warrant had he for his assertion? By some Evangelical writers the death which happens to all in physical dissolution is regarded as the penalty of sin. "Death," says Dr. Denney, "is the word which sums up the whole liability of man in relation to sin, and, therefore, when Christ came to give Himself for our sins, He did it by dying. It does not occur to Paul to ask how He could bear the sins of others. The death that He died was the only death that we know." But if it did not occur to Paul to ask how Christ could bear the sins of others, there are many to-day who are anxiously asking that question, and also, how physical death can be regarded as the penalty of sin? It can only be so on the unsupported supposition that had not man sinned he would have lived for ever on the earth, or have been gradually spiritualised and translated. These we may imagine as possibilities, but we have no ground for saying that they entered into the Divine thought of man's creation. We cannot look upon bodily death as being a penalty for sin, although it is, doubtless, made to serve a wise and good purpose under God. Death, we are told, must be interpreted through *conscience*. But it must be also interpreted through *intelligence*. Physical death has often been accepted by one person for another; it is constantly faced by some in the pursuance of their profession, and in the fulfilment of their duties it is often vicariously endured. The most unselfish and heroic conduct frequently entails it on men, and surely we cannot think of it as coming upon them as a doom from God. Such a conception tends to make both God and sin very unreal. Such theology, though no protest may be voiced against it, carries no real conviction. And if the Cross meant nothing more than the acceptance of physical death in a shameful and cruel form, it would doubtless be something that ought to arrest the attention and move the heart in some measure, but it would not possess that unique value in, not merely temporal but eternal relationships which it had for Paul, and which has given it such a power over human hearts. It is easy, in a way, to defend the Cross if no more than this was involved in it, but it is a Cross bereft of its highest power.

Science will not allow us to regard physical death as the penalty of sin. The energy of every finite organism must sometime become exhausted. Death is just as natural as life, and is absolutely necessary if humanity is not to be a narrow and restricted thing, both numeri-

cally and in its character. Had it not been for Death
making room for us we should not have been here
to-day. Science shows us that Death came in to
further the evolution of living forms. And had it not
been for Death, man would have remained on a much
lower level, with far inferior endowments.

What valid *scriptural* grounds are there for saying
that physical death is the penalty of sin? Doubtless
Paul included it in his thought of "Death," but he
shows us that he founds on the Genesis narrative,
which cannot in the light of our present knowledge be
regarded as direct Divine revelation.

In the teaching of Christ, physical death was not the
punishment of sin. His teaching is here quite distinct.
Man, He said, could inflict bodily death, and, therefore,
His disciples were *not to fear it*: there was something
else beyond man's power to inflict—and it was *this*
they ought to fear. The final consequence of sin was
exclusion from the Kingdom of God, which certainly
does not mean physical death. All die, saint and
sinner alike. The death that comes to all cannot
possibly cover our Lord's representations of exclusion
from the Kingdom, of the outer darkness, of Gehenna,
of æonian punishment. Did Paul mean nothing more
when he said, "If ye live after the flesh, ye shall *die*"?
Was this really the death which he said Jesus died for
us in order that we might live unto God and *not* die?
There is no correspondence between the two things.
Paul does not say that it was in order that we might

not die "with a bad conscience" or "with fear," but
that we might not *die*. We all do die physically, and
the sinner often dies with ease and comfort, welcomes
death as a blessed release, seeks it for himself. When
Paul speaks of Christ being "made sin for us," he does
not think merely of His physical death. How could
that be any manifestation of God's righteousness in
view of His having passed over sin? *All men had died*,
and if bodily dissolution be the penalty, sin had *not*
been passed over. If this be all that Christ did for us—
what many a man has done for his fellows—it is no
wonder that the preaching of the Cross should often
seem so powerless, and that it should have so little real
influence on some modern believers.

But although Paul may sometimes seem to have
simply physical death before his mind, much more was
included under his conception of "Death." This is
clear from the passages already referred to, *e.g.* when
he says to the Roman believers, "If ye live after the
flesh, ye shall *die*." They were certain to taste physical
death whether they lived after the flesh or not. The
death which "the law" enjoined for high-handed
transgression—for real sin—was *off-cutting from the
community*, violent death, "destruction," says Davidson.
So with the Prophets. When Ezekiel says, "The soul
that sinneth, it shall die" (xviii. 4), it is this off-cutting
that is meant,—in v. 13 the Hebrew is "shall be put to
death." (See also Isa. i. 20, "If ye refuse and rebel,
ye shall be slain with the sword," etc.) It was not

mere "natural death," nor "eternal death," but a violent
death from God in punishment of their wickedness.

The truth is that Paul accepted the Hebrew conception of death, not as a part of Pharisaism, but as
contained in the Old Testament Scriptures. This
included physical death, but it was not the mere act of
dying; it was the *entering on death as a state*, and from
that state, to the sinner, there was *no resurrection*.
Death in itself was the worst of evils. As the end and
antithesis of *life*, it meant cessation of that inspiration
of the Divine Spirit that made man man—separation
from God, though not extinction of being. Even the
righteous shrank from it, and their only hope was in a
redemption or resurrection. As Dr. Davidson remarks:
"To die was to become separate from God; to be dead
was to continue in this state of separation. This is the
meaning of death in the Old Testament. Hence the
terrors that gathered around dying" (*Theol. of O.T.* p.
520). Death, then, in Paul's view meant, not an act,
but *a state* of separation from God, out of which there
was, to the sinner,—and in his view we were all sinners,
—*no resurrection*. We can now understand how solemn
was the warning, "If ye live after the flesh, ye shall
die"; we can see what is meant when it is said that
"Death is the wages of sin"; how "sin, when it is fully
matured, bringeth forth death," and how much more
than His passing through physical death is involved in
the statement that "Christ *died* for our sins," "was made
sin for our sakes," "loved me, and gave Himself up

for me." He gave Himself up to enter a state which, in itself, involved separation from God. We fail to see this, because we throw back upon it the light that has come to us through the resurrection of Christ.

It is death in this sense of continued separation from God that is the ultimate doom of sin, its necessary consequence indeed. But we cannot think of it as being *an externally inflicted penalty* which may be endured either by the actual sinner or by a Substitute. We shall see immediately in what sense Christ "bore our sins," etc., but the affixing and exacting of penalties in such an external way is quite inconsistent with the Christian thought of God as the Father of men. It belongs to the older thought of God as a Sovereign and Judge. There is an externality and legality in it which are out of keeping with the idea of Fatherhood. We must ask reverently—Could God do nothing more for His incomplete, if sinful, children than sum them all up under this hopeless doom of death? And, if strict Justice is to rule, so that the sinner must die, how would the suffering of death by Christ meet the demand of justice on the actual sinner?

Even the idea of "Grace"—although true for individual sinners — suggests Sovereignty rather than Fatherhood. We plead for no "mere good-natured Fatherhood"; but we do plead for real *Fatherhood*. Grace is favour shown by a Sovereign, not a Father's loving, sympathetic, and righteous regard for his children. It suggests a relation of God to man which is different from that revealed in Christ, and a conception of sin and guilt which neither Christ's teaching and attitude towards men nor modern knowledge bears out.   Sin and guilt are both sadly real, but man is not just the subject of a Sovereign Ruler, amenable to His Justice and doomed to Death if he offends, but, at the lowest, a creature of God destined to become His child, for whose presence in the world and entire nature as man God in His Wisdom and Love is responsible.   In man the animal nature had to come first: he is a growing being, weighted by the inevitable "flesh," for whom God had a higher life in view.

We should greatly err, however, were we to exclude from our thought all idea of *penalty*, in the sense of consequence and punishment.   Every conscience witnesses that sin deserves to be punished, and there are consequences of wrong-doing which must be regarded in the light of punishment.   What we have to avoid is the conception of a penalty affixed to an external law under which man has been placed, which must be rigorously executed on him or else on a substitute, and which is executed as from without.   But the whole experience of life bears solemn witness to the fact of penalty or evil consequences following sin and wrong-doing.   The entire Universe is under Law, with its inherent, self-acting penalties.   It is quite conceivable also that the final consequence of sin persevered in, or with which a man identifies himself, is separation from God, exclusion from the kingdom, as Christ teaches.

This, indeed, we have seen must be the fate of sin and the doom of that "sinful flesh" from which sin cannot be separated.

Paul certainly teaches that the doom or just desert of sin was set forth in the death of Christ "in the likeness of sinful flesh and on account of sin," and that in this the "righteousness of God" in view of sin was manifested. It was in some sense a judicial act, and something which Christ endured instead of sinners. Although Christ did not actually take the sinner's place, He took the place of sin in the flesh, or of sinful flesh, and died as man's Representative the death which sin must die. He was "made sin" for us. The question that now confronts us is, what is the truth underlying this teaching? How was Christ's death on the Cross such a manifestation of God's righteousness?

Whether Paul represents Jewish theology or not, it cannot be denied that he has *the Law* with its penalty of "death" primarily in view in his argument. But it is impossible to believe that it was really to vindicate His righteousness in having declared this penalty, or His veracity in connection with it, that God had to sacrifice His Son. When Evangelical theologians so represent the necessity for Christ's death, we must ask, with our altered conception of Inspiration, *where* has *God* so pledged His word to inflict this penalty on sinners that Christ had to die in order to show Him veracious? We do not now believe in *verbal* inspiration, and no such word was ever directly spoken from Heaven. It is true that in the nature of things sin must die: but we are here getting on to different ground.

But does not Paul's *ethical* view of the Cross come here to our help? Was it not really in the ethical dying of Christ to sin, which Paul so emphatically declares must be realised in us also if we are to be truly *saved*, that the manifestation of God's righteousness consisted? This, however, with Paul was founded on the *judicial* conception of the death of Christ. It is not, as is sometimes said, a view of Christ's death standing side by side, unconnectedly, with the other. It was not because he saw Christ in the ethical sense dying to sin in our name that he enunciated the ethical aspect of his doctrine. It was because Christ's death was a *complete death* of " the flesh," of " the old man," and His resurrection a rising out of that death into an entirely new life of the Spirit. As he says in the sixth of Romans: " He that hath died is freed from sin "; and of Christ, " The death that He died, He died unto sin once for all." One who has *died* is freed from all pertaining to the flesh and the former life. So, he argues, this complete death to the past and the old man having been represented in Christ for us all, we all died completely before God to all that pertained to the old life and rose to a new life, which it must now be ours to realise practically through the power of that Spirit of Christ which is the Spirit of the true life for us all. It

6

was *thus* that the judicial death of Christ came to have for Paul an ethical value and power.

If, however, we go to the Gospels, we shall see that, in itself, Christ's death was an ethical death to sin and to all that was of the flesh. We shall see how, in His complete obedience to the Will of the Father even unto death, in spite of all the natural solicitations of the flesh in the midst of all that could try it, and under the utmost that man can suffer, "the flesh" did in Christ die utterly and ethically and representatively for us all.

The question thus arises: Was not this representative ethical death *in itself* a sufficient manifestation of the righteousness of God in view of His passing over the sins of the past, and of His proclamation of Forgiveness and acceptance in the Gospel? Was not God's righteousness in view of sin demonstrated, inasmuch as it was here made manifest that in due time sin should be conquered in man, that the sinful flesh should utterly die, and man rise to a new life of the Spirit and of righteousness? This was the Divine purpose from all eternity, although only in due time could it be realised and manifested. Was it not in view of this that the Heavenly Father bore with His weak, imperfect, and sinning children as He did? Was not this a real reconciliation or At-one-ment of God with man; and is it not because now man has been set forth in Christ as dead to sin and risen to righteousness that the Gospel Message of Forgiveness and acceptance goes freely forth to all? In this deeper view of the representative death of Christ to sin it would certainly seem that we have a real At-one-ment of God with man, and such a manifestation of the Divine righteousness as appears to be necessary in connection with the going forth—not the procuring—of the Divine Forgiveness.

But it by no means follows that the "*judicial*" aspect of the Cross has no truth underlying it. We cannot believe that its statement by Paul was a mere accommodation, or *argumentum ad Judæos*, or a mere inheritance of Paul's Jewish training: still less that the general Christian faith rested on nothing real when it held the confidence that "Christ died for our sins." It must indeed be seen in a deeper way; but were we to leave it out altogether, we should omit an important aspect of the manifestation of the Divine righteousness in the death of Christ, and we should deprive the Cross in large measure of its power to produce in men the ethical fruits of Christ's death.

We need to bear in mind *what* it was that God was doing in Christ. He was reconciling the sinful world to Himself in His righteousness *with a view to save men from sin and make them His children in spirit and truth*. The Cross was not a mere setting forth of His righteousness in view of sin: it was this in order to the *salvation* of the world—in order to the salvation of men from sin to their true life in Himself. It is not merely something that men can intellectually perceive done in their name that can move them as they need to be moved. It must be something that they *feel*, so that it shall become an inspiring and soul-winning power—something that shall make them realise at once the actuality and the evil of sin with its consequences, and, at the same time, the greatness of the forgiving love of God. They must see Christ, not merely dying *to* sin, but dying *for* their sins; in some very real way "bearing the iniquities of us all." It was necessary that sin should be set forth in all its hideousness and in the evil that it works for man, if men were to be saved from it. And this could only be fully done by one who could *die* in our name and who could come forth again from death to be the power of a new life in men. It was necessary that such a manifestation of the evil of sin and of the love of God should be made as should move sinners to repentance, give them confidence in the Divine Forgiveness, and kindle an answering love to God in their hearts. History has shown that from the Cross viewed in this light have proceeded the most powerful motives to lead men to God and salvation. Therefore God "spared not His own Son, but gave Him up for us all." It was not merely, as it is sometimes represented, the sense of the world's sin that was the element of suffering in the experience of Christ. He bore our sins in the sense of suffering the consequences that come upon man through sin.

We here reach the question which so greatly needs to be faced and answered to-day: How can the death of Christ, in the circumstances in which it came to Him

at the hands of sinners, be seen to be His bearing the
sins of men in the sense of suffering that which comes
on man as the consequence of sin in the righteousness
of God? In other words: Can the judicial as well as
the ethical aspect of Paul's doctrine be still maintained?
We believe that it can. But, just as Paul's ethical view
of the Cross must be reached in a deeper way, so his
judicial conception of it can only be vindicated by
viewing it in a wider light. Paul teaches that God's
righteousness was set forth by His giving up His own
Son to bear the consequences of man's sin. This may
be stated in such a way as to be repellent. But it may
also be shown to contain a great truth. It can, we
think, be shown that in the same sense as that in which
the righteous servant of Jehovah bare the sins of his
people, in the Divine moral order of the world, the sin
of the world came upon and was borne by Christ. But
this must be set forth in such a way that it shall be
seen to be no mere arbitrary representation or external
transfer, or taking on Himself of the world's sin, but
that which actually came upon Him in the sequence of
the Divine moral order, in the historical circumstances
under which He endured His Cross, and in harmony
with both the righteousness and the love of God.

But first let us consider for a moment the Cross in its
actual historical setting, when we shall see more fully
the reality and value of that *ethical* aspect of the Cross
of which we have spoken.

VI

THE CROSS IN ITS HISTORICAL SETTING

CHAPTER VI

THE CROSS IN ITS HISTORICAL SETTING

HOW did the Cross come to Christ? It came in the course of the fulfilment of His mission to bring in the Kingdom of God. The Gospels give no ground for the assertion, often made, that He came into the world to die. He came preaching "the Gospel of God" to His people, asking them to receive Him, believe the good news, and, turning to God, rejoice in His salvation. It was only their rejection of Him that made His death necessary. Doubtless, long before the event He anticipated it; but the Gospels show us a hopeful beginning with a Divine message which ought to have gladdened the hearts of all who heard it. We see Christ *grieved* because of their unbelief, and wondering at the little faith of His disciples. Even as late as Gethsemane He could pray that if it was possible the cup might pass from Him. The idea that He came just to die, and that before ever He went forth to preach He was convinced that His preaching would be rejected, makes His whole life and pleading with men quite unreal. How completely opposed it is to the opening words of St. Mark's Gospel: "The beginning of the Gospel (the glad tidings) of Jesus Christ." Jesus Himself was the first Preacher of the Gospel: He did not merely "make it possible for a Gospel to be preached." Ignoring the fact that Jesus Himself first preached the Gospel, has created much needless difficulty. In various ways it has been sought to explain how the Gospel came to be preached by the Apostles, who are supposed to have proceeded on quite different lines from those pursued by Christ, so that we need to come back from them to Christ Himself; while it is the simple fact that what they preached was really the completed form of the Gospel first preached by Jesus Himself.

Jesus came preaching "the gospel of the Kingdom of God." That with Him meant the drawing nigh to men of the Heavenly Father in His forgiving love, in fulfilment of the promises of the prophets. Therefore He said, " The time is fulfilled, and the Kingdom of God (so long looked for) has come nigh to you; the promised acceptable year of the Lord has dawned." It was a *spiritual* Kingdom that He preached, one that should be realised when men were brought nigh to God in spiritual sonship and in brotherly love to one another; the Kingdom of God, He said, was first of all *within* men. But this was not the kind of Kingdom the people in general were looking for. They believed that they were God's chosen people, His children already by natural heritage, and they expected an outward dominion to be set up, in which they, as God's people, should be supreme. Therefore all but a few not only rejected, but resented, the spiritual preaching of Christ, and at length the Heads of the nation determined that He should die.   For some time He had seen this dark shadow brooding over His future ; but although He shrank from entering it, He accepted it as His Father's will, believing that it should do what His life and preaching and gracious works had failed to accomplish, namely, bring in the Kingdom of God, make His Gospel real and effectual to men's salvation.   Although he met His death at the hands of wicked men, it was not because *they* had decreed it that He died.   The Gospels show us that His acceptance of death was wholly *voluntary*.   That He need not have died, so far as man's action was concerned, is clear from their records.   He knew His danger, and, humanly speaking, there was no need for Him to enter into it.   He had looked forward to His suffering, and had spoken to His disciples of it repeatedly.   He felt that He "had a baptism to be baptized with," and was "straitened till it was accomplished."   He was to give His life a ransom for many.   His Body should be given for their sakes ; His Blood should be to them that of God's saving Covenant.   After His death He should "drink the new wine" with them in His Father's Kingdom.   Surely it is absurd to believe, as the method of interpretation of such sayings of Christ by some modern critics would lead us to do, that Jesus looked forward to a literal drinking of new wine along with His disciples after His death : He surely meant that His death would

be the means of bringing in the spiritual Kingdom.
The wine which He looked forward to drink in their
fellowship was the wine of joy in the accomplished
saving purpose of God. Yet, as the event became
imminent, He shuddered, and He only accepted it
when, after earnest prayer, He was convinced that
nothing else could meet His Father's will. He rebuked
His disciples' well-meant attempt to save Him : " Think
ye not," He said, "that I could pray to My Father, and
He should give me twelve legions of angels "—wherewith to scatter His foes. He went forward to His death,
not because He was helpless before His enemies, but
because He gave Himself up to that Will of His Father
which sought to accomplish man's salvation—moved
to this by the Father's own Spirit within Him. This
deliberate giving of Himself up to death for the spiritual
salvation of men gives an altogether unique significance
to His self-sacrifice. While it places it in line with
that of the suffering servant of Jehovah in Isaiah, the
immediate purpose of that sacrifice was rather the
temporal salvation of the people than their spiritual and
eternal salvation. He goes " as it has been written,"
and, according to Luke's Gospel, that embraced what
had been written concerning the servant of Jehovah :
" For I say unto you that this which is written must be
fulfilled in Me, ' And he was reckoned with the trans-
gressors' : for that which concerneth Me hath fulfilment " (xxii. 37). As that suffering had the effect of
fulfilling Jehovah's good purpose, so He felt sure it

should be with respect to His own.   It was also as "the Son of man" that He should die, which gives to His death a representative aspect.   If He said also that it was "for the remission of sins," that might be true in more ways than one.   It would be true if His death led men to repentance and so to forgiveness.   His more express teaching concerning His death will yet be considered.   But we may say here that He nowhere says anything that clearly and unmistakably suggests that He regarded His death as an atonement for sin, or a satisfaction to God's justice, or a penal infliction.   The way in which His death came upon Him seems to forbid such conceptions of it.   While He accepted it voluntarily, it yet came upon Him at the hands of His enemies.   He was to be "killed," "put to death" by them.   It was "the hour and power of darkness."   His blood was to be violently "shed," like other "righteous blood" that had been unrighteously shed : all of which should come upon "this generation."   He by no means died as bowing to Justice in human law, but was deeply conscious of the injustice and wickedness of those who compassed His death.   It were "good for the man who betrayed Him that he had never been born."   "If they do those things in the green tree, what shall be done in the dry?"   His murderers knew not what they did : "Father, *forgive* them," He prayed.

Why He should not only suffer but pass into that state of death which to the pious Jew was one of separation from God, relieved only by the hope of a resurrection, was *possibly* not made clear even to Himself. But we cannot doubt that He who had told His disciples not to fear them who could kill the body but could not touch the soul, surrendered Himself to it with confidence in God. His cry on the Cross cannot, therefore, be interpreted as one of despair or of failure, as some would interpret it. It cannot mean that He lost His faith in God. If we interpret it in the spirit of the Psalm from which it was taken, it was the cry of one passing through such suffering as might have suggested Divine abandonment, but underneath which was the confidence that it had a gracious purpose to effect in His own experience and in that of others (Ps. xxii.). It is really a *question* with the answer implied. Had the disciples understood it as a cry of despair, or failure, or loss of faith, it is impossible to conceive how they could have maintained their faith in their Master. As we shall see, the experience it indicates may have had an important part to fulfil in relation to the perfect obedience of Christ.

So far as we have gone, the simple truth may seem to be that Jesus accepted His Cross with all that might come upon Him, even death itself, in order that, through the influence of His suffering thus for our sakes, the evil of sin on the one hand, and the Love thus displayed on the other, might bring men to God, and so making them members of God's kingdom, save them with a spiritual and eternal salvation. No explanation is given of *why* He should die, save that His death was for the sake of others and should have a saving issue.

Nothing is said from Heaven either in explanation of this death of the Son of God in those solemn circumstances. His disciples at first simply could not understand it. But that Cross stands there before men. *It* speaks, and it is for men to listen and try to understand what it says as something that came to Christ by the will of the loving and righteous God and Father. A *Spirit* goes forth from it, and it is for men to feel and receive that Spirit's influence. In the light of that Spirit's suggestion the Cross must be interpreted, and so become effectual for its purpose. If there is any reality in Divine spiritual teaching—if God by means of what He does can speak to man—we must be loyal to the Spirit's teaching. This does not mean that that teaching will come to every man in the very same manner. We shall see only what we have been prepared to see. And the Spirit's teaching is not limited to one aspect of the Cross, or to one generation of men. There is ever "more light and truth" to come to us. It does not imply that we must accept the very *forms* in which the teaching of the Spirit was first apprehended and expressed. The Spirit of God does not teach in the words of men, but in deeper convictions, impressions, excitements, and suggestions than can perhaps be expressed in any human language. Of this Paul, for one, shows himself to be well aware. But if we believe in the reality of the Spirit's teaching at all; if we claim

that teaching for ourselves and for the present generation, if we would have really progressive Divine teaching,
we must be careful not to deny the coming of that
illuminating Spirit to Christ's first disciples and Paul,
and, however far we may advance, we must hold fast
the *substance* of that which was taught them, which
they apprehended and expressed in the forms of their
own time. Otherwise, we virtually deny that there is
any such thing as Divine spiritual teaching, and man
is left to make himself " the measure of all things " in
heaven as well as on earth.

If we can trust the Gospels and the Book of Acts,
the first Christians were led to interpret the Cross in
the light of those Old Testament Scriptures which
had been a guide to Jesus Himself. According to
Luke's Gospel, Jesus, after He was risen, had expounded to two of His followers " the things in the
Scriptures concerning Himself," showing them that
it was necessary that the Christ should suffer and
enter into His glory. In that glory they believed He
was to come again to judge the world and set up the
eternal Kingdom of God. His crucifixion is regarded
as a notorious criminal act, which, however, served a
high Divine purpose. He whom the Jews had crucified, God had raised from the dead and made Lord
and Christ. Although the narrative of Philip and the
Eunuch shows that the fifty-third of Isaiah was before
their minds, there is no mention of an atoning sacrifice.

The stress is laid on the *resurrection* of Jesus by God. Repentance and Forgiveness of sins are preached in His name. All who believed in Him should be saved. Paul, in his preaching at Antioch, still lays the stress on the Resurrection. The "glad tidings"—the *gospel*— was, that God had fulfilled the promise made to the fathers "in that He had raised up Jesus," "and through this man is proclaimed to you remission of sins; and by Him every one that believeth is justified from all things, from which ye could not be justified by the law of Moses." The *ground* of this justification is not stated, but it is implied that there was such a ground. In his later speech before Agrippa, Paul again refers to the fulfilment of all that had been written in the Scriptures, that the Christ should be a suffering Christ, and "that He first, by a resurrection from the dead, should proclaim a message of light to the Jewish people and to the Gentiles." We see here why the stress was laid on Christ's resurrection from the dead. Thereby, Paul says, He brought a glad message of *light*. What was that light? It was the light of "eternal life" for mankind. His emergence from that "death," which is the doom of sin, was the proclamation in "this man" of man's justification before God—a justification in which all who believed in Him should share. Nothing whatever is *said* of the relation of Christ's *death* to this justification; but it was natural to believe that it had *some* relation to it. Paul's entire doctrinal system may very well under-

7

lie this preaching. For the Christians generally, with
their familiarity with animal sacrifices, and in view of
the significance these were believed to have, it would
be a most simple and natural thing to interpret the
death of Christ as "a sacrifice for sin." As Peter says
in his Epistle, "Christ suffered (or died) for sins once,
the righteous for the unrighteous, that He might
bring us to God"; "who His own self bare our sins in
His body upon the tree, that we, having died unto
sins, might live unto righteousness." Hence the first
word of the Faith as it was delivered to Paul was
"that Christ died for our sins." The essential matter
here is that, as we must believe, under the Divine
Spirit's guidance they *did* so interpret the death of
Christ; and therefore, although we may not be able
to view it in the same simple manner, we seem to be
bound to believe that there was a truth underlying
their belief. It was this belief that brought to them
the saving Power of the Gospel.

We know how the meaning of the Cross came to
Paul. It "pleased God to reveal His Son in him";
but he had to be prepared for the revelation by a
deep and trying spiritual experience. He had been
striving for a sense of acceptance with God, endeavouring to work out a righteousness in which he should
stand "justified" before God and an heir of eternal
life. Was it not by observance of that Law which
God Himself had ordained that righteousness was to
be found? And now the followers of the Nazarene

(such as Stephen) were preaching that the Law and
the Temple worship were to be ended, and that Jesus
who had been crucified had been raised up by God,
who had even brought Him back from the dead, in
the power of a new and endless life, to be their Leader
to a truer worship and a more real righteousness.
They were affirming that all had failed to keep the
law, and could only be justified by faith in " the
Righteous One," whom God had approved as such by
His resurrection from among the dead.   But certainly
they were wrong: God would never abolish His Law
like that, and He would never have suffered His Son
to be crucified.   And yet! we know not what pangs
of conscience Paul already had—how far, even now,
he experienced that condition of the awakened soul
which he afterwards described so well in the seventh
chapter of Romans.   He had probably begun to feel
that this might be the way after all; that all his efforts
had not brought him peace with God or assurance of
His acceptance.   And when Christ showed Himself to
him in the way to Damascus, he felt sure of it.   He
saw the Christ risen into that very life for which
he was hoping, the life of the justified—a life wholly
free from the power of that " flesh " which he already
knew within himself to be the seat of sin, the ambush
in which the enemy lurked that was constantly gaining
the mastery over him.   To be done with the old life
entirely, to be raised with Christ into that new life of
the Spirit which was in Him stamped with God's

approval,—*that* was the way of salvation. He felt himself to be a sinner before God, needing His forgiveness. The way of man in the flesh, the struggle after righteousness under the law, was a hopeless one: henceforth he would be done with it and seek the way of the Spirit. Trusting no longer to his own righteousness, he saw and accepted God's provision of righteousness for man made in Christ, the righteous One. God had provided a new way of righteousness "apart from Law." Christ "was the end of the law for righteousness." What part did the Cross play in this? It, said Paul, for one thing at least, marked the end of the law. The death to which the law doomed sin was met by Christ. The righteousness of the Divine Lawgiver was thus manifested in the death of Christ, so that the law was ended and God could justify men freely out of His grace in Jesus Christ. It was an amazing revelation that thus came to him. In that Cross which he had deemed a sure proof that Jesus was *not* the Christ, he now saw an unspeakable manifestation of the Love of God for sinful men, a Gospel of Forgiveness going forth to the world, and a new way of life made manifest for Jew and Gentile alike. "God," he said, "was in Christ at-oning the world to Himself, not imputing their trespasses unto them. For Him who knew no sin He made sin for our sakes, that we might be made the righteousness of God in Him."

It was undoubtedly this interpretation of the Cross

that sent the Gospel forth into the world as a Divine saving power.   But we have seen how, while a judicial aspect belongs to Paul's doctrine of the Cross, he seems to carefully avoid saying that Jesus atoned for man's sin in the later Jewish sense of Atonement; how impossible it is to give this meaning to his teaching, seeing that it is founded on the fact that it was *God* who gave up His Son to die.   Hence Paul regards the Cross as a setting forth of God's righteousness in view of sin by Jesus dying "in the likeness of sinful flesh," representing the death of the sinful flesh in all men.   We have further seen that, while this is susceptible of a judicial interpretation, there is a deeper ethical thought in the mind of Paul.   He saw Christ dying, not only *for* our sins but *to* sin, and rising to a new life in the Spirit—representing the death of all men to sin and their resurrection to the life of righteousness.   The essential thing with him was the *new life of the Spirit.*   It was the sinful flesh that died before God, not *the man.*   It was this death to sin and life to righteousness that had to be realised in each man's experience.   In Paul's view "the flesh" died in Christ because Christ's was a *complete* death in the flesh.

If we now go back again to the actual circumstances of the death of Christ, we will see how fully, in a deeper way, this ethical interpretation of the death of Christ is borne out.   We see Jesus, a true man—stand-

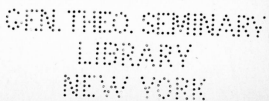

ing in the likeness of sinful flesh, but at the same time the Son of God entirely at one with His Father, accepting the Heavenly Father's will to the uttermost, even to the complete sacrifice of Himself, *whatever* that sacrifice might involve. As we see in the agony in Gethsemane, the flesh shrank from the ordeal, pleading with strong crying and tears that, if it were possible, He might be saved from it: there was thus even in Christ a will of the flesh that *might* have refused that cup. But He accepted it in obedience to the Divine Father's will, and drank it to the bitterest dregs. If we regard the cry from the Cross as indicating a temporary loss of the consciousness of the Divine Father's presence, we may gain thus an ethical interpretation of it. It was *His final testing*. He was left completely to Himself—to His simple manhood— in order that He might prove the complete conquest of the flesh by the spirit—its utter death in Him—and the entire oneness of man in Him with God. If, in the absence of everything beyond Himself (as that self had been formed under Divine influences), He persevered in His obedience, then the human will showed itself wholly one with the Divine will, and man in Christ was made entirely at-one with God. The cry from the Cross we may regard as the cry of the flesh in its bitterest experience. Yet, in all the spirit conquered.

The Divine Man who so atones our Humanity to God becomes in that very fact the source of a new life

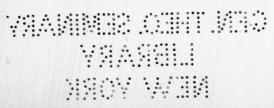

to men, even that life of the Spirit which wholly possessed Him and showed itself so triumphant in His experience—the life of God in man.   Humanity has now in Christ entered on a new epoch; man after the flesh has completely died, and out of that death man after the Spirit has arisen.   " Old things have passed away": there is a new Creation.   Before God, the old Humanity is dead, and unto Him a new Humanity has been born.   God's righteousness in view of His merciful forbearance in the past is vindicated in this conquest of sin and oneness of man with Himself.   The old, therefore, can be allowed to pass wholly away,

> " To die forgotten as a dream
> Dies at the opening day."

A Gospel of free, divine Forgiveness can thus go forth to men.   God can deal with them no longer as under stern Law, but as under " Grace," "not imputing their trespasses unto them."

It is obvious that the Cross is in this way also brought into harmony with that *Fatherhood* of God which is the Christian revelation of God.   God was chiefly known to Israel as a Sovereign, but to us He has been revealed as the tender and loving Father of men.   Judaism was no doubt reaching after that thought of God, but it was Christ who made it real.   Christianity is not an extension of Judaism, but, while arising out of it, it is a new religion which transcends it, as truly as new creative epochs transcended those which had preceded

and prepared the way for them.   It is not as the stern
Ruler and Judge, exacting penalty, that God is revealed
in Christ, but as the loving Father, yearning over His
children, seeking to raise them to their true life in union
with Himself.

The Cross is thus also brought into line with the entire
life and work of Christ.   It is seen to be the culmination of that at-one-ment of man with God which was
increasingly manifested in His life.   And it is not a
new Gospel that the Cross proclaims, but the old Gospel
which Jesus preached, sealed and made effectual
unto us.

Is there then, we are led again to ask, no truth
underlying Paul's *judicial* conception of the Cross?
Is there no sense in which it can be rightly said that
Jesus was there bearing the sin of the world in the
sense of enduring for our sakes the consequences of
sin, which "the bearing of sin" in Biblical phraseology
means?   If we reject Paul's judicial conception of the
Cross, shall we not be ignoring the way in which the
Cross actually operated on men to bring them to God?
It was the love of Christ in enduring what He did for
their sakes, His actually bearing their sins in His own
body upon the tree, that moved the heart so mightily
and quickened love within it.   It was not because men
reasoned out how the righteousness of God was
ethically manifested by Christ, but because they saw
Christ dying for their sakes under the righteousness of

God, that they were moved to repentance, to faith, and to love.   We still need to see the Cross in such a light as shall bring home to our hearts the love of Christ in what He suffered as bearing *our* iniquities for our salvation.

It is true that there was another side to this view of the Cross.   In after times the love of God tended to be obscured by the love of Christ.   The heart in going out to the Christ who died for men did not always go out to *God*.   The Cross was not always seen to be the manifestation of the love of *God*, it was rather the expression of the love of *Christ* who "interposed His precious blood" between men and God to save them from His wrath.   God was regarded as the stern Judge rather than as the loving Father.   He was not known as the Cross ought to have made Him known.   Dark thoughts concerning the Best came to fill the minds of men, and in time Christ Himself became to them the awful Judge instead of the loving Saviour—one with whom His Mother had to intercede for sinners.   All this was, of course, unworthy, untrue, and unwholesome. The bad effects have not yet wholly passed away, and they have not a little to do with the present wide-spread indifference to religion.

Yet there is, we believe, a deep truth underlying the judicial conception of the Cross which we cannot afford to leave out of account.   Of course, even in a purely ethical aspect of the Cross, it was *because of our sins*, "for our sins," that Jesus had to pass through all His suffering and

die.   But the ordinary mind does not readily grasp this,
and we shall see that it is also true that He bore our
sins in the sense of enduring their worst results in the
righteous judgment of God; that in His death we have
the actual lighting on Him of the consequences of the
accumulated sins of the world; and that this was an
essential element in that manifestation of the righteousness of God in which He was reconciling the world to
Himself, which Christ had to endure for our sakes.   To
show this in such a way as shall be free from all taint
of suffering Divinely inflicted on the innocent and
operative on God, free from all arbitrariness and artificiality, and in keeping with the way in which the Cross
actually came to Christ, yet so as to manifest at once
the evil of sin and the righteousness and love of God,
is, we think, one of the most imperative requirements of
the present, if the Gospel is to retain the fulness of its
power.

VII

HOW CHRIST BORE OUR SINS

CHAPTER VII

HOW CHRIST BORE OUR SINS

ONE objection to the doctrine of the sin-bearing of Christ as it is commonly stated, and to the Pauline representation of the manifestation of God's righteousness in His death, is that the Cross seems something arbitrary, thrust into the course of this world's life as it were from without, not coming in the natural sequence of human action, in the way of cause and consequence. A second difficulty is, How could the punishment of *sin*, in any sense, fall upon or be endured by one who was wholly sinless? A third objection is that Paul's doctrine is an individual interpretation of an historic fact which, viewed in its actual connection, appears in a very different light. Christ's crucifixion, as it came upon Him, was a human crime, the crowning act of man's unrighteousness,—how, then, does His suffering under man's unrighteousness become at the same time the supreme and sufficient manifestation of God's righteousness? We must emphasise this question, for it is so generally ignored by Evangelical writers. The fact that Christ suffered voluntarily does not meet the case. It is under *God's* judgment that sin is punished.   But Christ died at the hands of wicked men, not of God.   It was God's will, no doubt, that He should die: God gave Him up to this, and He died quite voluntarily.   Still, it was sinful men who condemned Him and put Him to death.   The question which needs to be answered is, How was the righteousness of *God* shown in this—the righteousness of God in His judgment on sin?   Sinful men were not the executors of God's justice.   In other words, How was Christ, who was put to death at the hands of sinners, at the same time " bearing their sin "—that is, the punishment of the sin of man?   And if we were to think of *expiating* sin, we should have to ask (if we may put it bluntly without offence), How could that crowning sin—that murder of the Son of God—become the expiation of the sin of the world?   We cannot think of God as in an arbitrary or external way " laying our sin " or " its doom " on Christ, saying, " Be Thou Sin; all that is done to Thee shall represent its punishment."   If we are to get at it at all, it must be in some other way than this.   And we *must* get at it, or else give up the judicial aspect of Christ's death entirely.   Because it has not been made plain, many *have* given it up, thus (often unconsciously) implying that there was an element of untruth in the original Gospel

We may see something of the truth which underlies Paul's judicial representation if we bear in mind (1) that God is Law as well as Love; (2) how, under the

Divine Law, sin in man is actually punished; (3) the Solidarity of the Humanity represented by Christ; and (4) the mode of action of the principle of vicarious suffering; (5) we must also bear in mind that the method of Divine Revelation is not by means of words, but by events and experiences in the Divine moral order, to be interpreted by man's Reason and Conscience quickened and enlightened by the Divine *Spirit*.

1. God is Law as well as Love: lawless Love would be no true Love: God is at once Reason, Righteousness, and Love. The Divine Law is not something external to God, enunciated in a Code, such as that given to the Jewish nation: it is one with the holy Love that God is, and is for ever operative. An approximation to the knowledge of the Divine Law was made by the Jewish and by other peoples, but the Law itself resides in God and is one aspect of God Himself. There is a *Divine* moral order, higher, juster, far more searching, and surer in its operation than any law or order that man has formulated; a Divine Law by which all human law is judged. That Law man often fails to discern. Its operation is hidden from him. Human life on earth is not so long that it can always, or even often, work itself out in the experience of individuals. Its action is more clearly discerned in the case of nations and of Humanity as a whole. On a wide view of the world's history it is manifest that there is "a Power Eternal, not ourselves, that makes for righteousness." The ever-operating Divine Law entails without fail on all sinners

the just and necessary consequences of their sin. It never turns aside for any person, or for any reason: it is identical with Reason itself, with Causation, with God. Throughout both Jewish and Roman history that Law had been acting, and it was under its operation that the Cross came to Christ, came to the Righteous One in the midst of the self-loving, sinful world. The Law that brought it could not be turned aside even for Christ. It was not possible for the cup to pass away from Him who was so identified with this sinful Humanity. But His openly drinking it could be made the means of the world's redemption. For the manifestation of His righteousness, God gave up His Son to die under the action of the Law which brings the consequences of man's sin on man's own head, and which here lighted on and was voluntarily endured by man's truest Representative for the sake of man's spiritual salvation.

2. We shall understand that Law and its working better if we ask, in the light of actual fact, *How does God punish sin?*

We know how man's judgment on *crime* falls on the offender by an external act of punishment. But this is no true analogue to the Divine mode of action. Man's moral order is not identical with God's; on the contrary, it often embodies much that is really immoral. Man's law can only deal with what man accounts crime, social or political; *sin* it cannot touch, and may not even recognise. God's Law deals with *sin*, which is not always, by any means, externally expressed in action.

While God transcends the world, His action on it is not from without, after the manner of human action. Apart from the influences of the Divine Spirit on man, there is no external Divine action manifested in the world. We cannot, therefore, think of God as standing simply above or over-against Christ, and by an act of Divine determination causing His righteous indignation at sin to fall upon His Head. God is *in* the world by His Law or Order, and He was *in* Christ pre-eminently in His holy, saving Love. Whatever was done on the Cross in relation to sin was done, not by a wholly external Deity, but through a Divine Spirit which dwelt in Christ, with which He in His humanity was wholly one.

"The *history* of the world," it has been most truly said, "is the judgment of the world." According as men have lived or have failed to live in harmony with the Divine Law of their life, their experience has been. Not their experience of outward good and evil, but of real good and evil within the soul. There is no direct infliction of punishment or forth-going of wrath, as if from without, on the individual sinner. The wicked may outwardly prosper in their wickedness, the good may suffer, and no God *seem* to care, so that "the fool says in his heart, There is no God." But God is there all the same, at once Love and Law, Mercy and Judgment. *Sin is made to become its own punishment.* Its just reward is reaped by the unrepentant sinner in his increasing sinfulness and widening distance from God

8

which may be accompanied by a growing hardness and insensibility to all that to *him* would savour of punishment. The wickedest man may be the least troubled within or without. The climax is reached when it can be said, "Ephraim is joined to his idols, let him alone"; when the conscience becomes "seared as with a hot iron." Then the man is, for the time at least, wholly away from God, dead to God and to his true self, not far from moral self-destruction. This is how Paul in the first chapter of his Epistle to the Romans exhibits the working of "the wrath of God." That wrath is not something that strikes out at the sinner; it does not act by outward inflictions. God punishes sin by suffering the sinner constantly to fall into deeper sin, till, it may be, the deepest and most unnatural depths of depravity are reached, and the consequences are, as far as may be, reaped in his own body and by those with whom he is associated in even this present world. As Olshausen remarks on Rom. i. 32, "Into this flood of sins the holy God permitted unholy men to sink; not by means of any special influence tending to make them bad, but according to the necessary law of the moral order of the world. For where God and His holy Being is not, and therefore the vanity of the creature's self is the ruling power, there sin begets sin, and punishes itself by sin. In this law Divine love shows itself as plainly as Divine justice; for the frightful consequences of sin are intended to awaken in man the germs of those better feelings that slumber there." The principle is summed up in that solemn saying of St. Paul's: "Be not deceived; God is not mocked: for whatsoever a man soweth, that shall he also reap." It is only of some sins, however, that their punishment can be thus made manifest.

In the case of a community we can witness the action of the Divine punitive principle more clearly. While there is still no direct Divine infliction, the consequences of their sins may come upon them in a manifest external manner, through the action, it may be, of those who are as great, or, possibly, even greater sinners than themselves, but who are stronger, more cunning, or more powerful. And, while the consequences of the individual evil-doer's sins may not light on himself in any external manner, the consequences of his sins, or those of "a multitude of them that do evil," may fall very heavily on those associated with them in an organic or more or less close capacity—who may themselves be the most innocent and righteous in the community. The sin of a people goes on in increasing sinfulness, but sooner or later it brings suffering, it may be disaster, upon them; and such suffering or disaster will fall quite as heavily (it may be more heavily) on the good as on the evil-doers.

We have a striking modern illustration of this in the American Civil War as a consequence of slavery, when, as the poet-prophet predicted, the exodus of the slave was "through a Red Sea whose surges are of gore," when righteous and unrighteous suffered alike. "Careless seems the great Avenger," but His judgment neither slumbers nor sleeps. The French Revolution, the terrible doom that fell on Jerusalem and the Jewish nation, the self-destruction of civilisations in which righteousness did not rule, afford illustrations of the principle. We might take in illustration, indeed, the result of fostering the war-spirit in nations. For many years, it may be, all seems well. Armies and navies go on increasing, and the people congratulate themselves on their wisdom and security. But it is a *wrong* spirit that has been fostered, and, sooner or later, actual war breaks out and the innocent suffer with the guilty. The man who at such a time—when national passions are inflamed—would speak out and stand for the right, might be made to suffer most of all.

3. These results are owing to the national *solidarity*. But there is also a wider, *human* solidarity—a oneness of humanity. It is ideally an organic unity. Humanity is as one man before God. It is "the world" as a unit He is said to "love." Jesus is "the Saviour of the world." It was "the world" that God in Christ was reconciling to Himself. He was dealing with *the race*. We all share in *one* life. We are all so bound up together that, just as in the physical realm there cannot be a blow struck or even a movement made which does not, to some extent, however infinitesimal, affect the entire material universe, so the good or evil that men do influences, more or less, all their kind, according to the force of the influence and the nearness or distance

of the relationship.   Nor does it die with them, but may go on gathering fresh force as it proceeds.   A righteous man may thus suffer for the sins of his fathers and mothers, of his brothers and sisters, of his nation, of his race, owing to this principle of solidarity. In the words of Dr. Dale: "It is this law of inter- dependence, this vital union of men with each other, which underlies the darkest mysteries and the divinest glories of the moral universe.   We are not isolated individuals, but members of a race.   We cannot dis- solve our relations to mankind.   It is not true, without qualification, that we have our life and character and destiny in our own hands.   We are involved in all the sins and follies of past generations, and their wisdom and virtue are ours. . . . Christian theology has steadily refused to acknowledge that there can be any real separation between the individual and the life and fortunes of the race" (*Essays and Addresses*, p. 103 f.). This principle is at the root of Paul's doctrine of "the oneness of the race in its fall and in its redemption": All dead in Adam; all made alive in Christ.   When we see the innocent suffering, its explanation is to be found in this fact of *solidarity*.

4. When the suffering that falls on an innocent person as a member of a sinful community is accepted and endured by him as that due to their sins, and borne in order that God's moral order may be vindicated and others benefited, we witness *vicarious suffering* in its highest form.   The sins of others have lighted on the

sufferer ; they are accepted by him as justly due to the sins of his people, and are borne by him in the hope that his suffering will have a salutary influence on them. In what he suffers he is truly " bearing their iniquity " ; " the transgression of his people has lighted on him "—who himself was wholly innocent.

The classical example of such vicarious suffering is, of course, that of the Servant of Jehovah in Isaiah. We do not here raise the question whether our Lord had this in His mind in His acceptance of His own suffering. We believe that He did. But whether or not, there it stands as a luminous example both of how the punishment of sin comes on a people and of the vicarious suffering of the righteous. Their sinfulness had increased till it had weakened the national character, becoming a foolishness which brought upon them conquest and captivity. But the consequences fell heaviest of all, either on a prophet or on the most pious amongst them. In Isaiah they are represented as falling on a person. They could have come upon him only at the hands of the oppressor, or of the wicked amongst his own people. Yet it was *the Divine judgment on their sins* that he was bearing. He accepted and bore it all in order that God might be justified when He judged, that they might see what their sins had wrought, and, perceiving the evil of their ways, might turn to the Lord. It was a manifestation of God's righteousness. The sufferer was, so far, " made sin " for their sakes. If we interpret the picture as a representation of the suffering of Israel itself for the sake of the salvation of "the nations" who come to discern the meaning of that suffering, the principle is the same. The sufferer was truly bearing in his own person *the judgment of God on sin*, although it came upon him, not by an external transfer or laying on him of the sins of others, or by direct Divine infliction, but as the result of his relation to a people whose sin had gone on increasing, and had in this way brought this suffering upon him. "For the offences of my people am I stricken."

5. So was it in the case of Christ. Remember that He stood there as the "Son of man," the Representative of Humanity. He is not to be separated from those who crucified Him. He was identified with them, and He chose to remain so identified. Even as *a man* He belonged to the race. He stood there "in the likeness of sinful flesh," the representative of man before God, and on His head lighted the worst consequences of the sins of Humanity in the working out of the Law that punishes sin by increasing sinfulness. It was not the punishment of his *own* sins that the suffering servant of Jehovah endured, but that which came upon him *as the consequence and the punishment of the sinfulness of his people.* So, in the case of Christ, what He suffered was that which came upon Him as the consequence and punishment of human sin in the Divine moral order. It was the ever-increasing sinfulness of men that made such an act as His rejection and crucifixion possible,

and in that ever-increasing sinfulness the real self-entailed punishment of sin, issuing in suffering and " Death," consists.

(1) In this act sin reached its climax; it proclaimed its own utter badness in the presence of the Divine righteousness, and made manifest the justice, nay, the necessity of its doom of death. In its judgment of God's Son it judged itself. God simply allowed things to take their course without interference, and He did this for our sakes, that sin might be seen to be exceeding sinful, and that His righteous judgment on it might be witnessed to by every man's conscience. As His enemies judged Christ to be worthy of death, so every enlightened conscience judges worthy of utter death the sin that could commit such a crime.

(2) God's judgment on sin was seen in Christ's death, inasmuch as He accepted that which had come to pass through sin, bringing suffering and death on the Son of man, as arising in that moral order and will of God to which He submitted Himself. It was not that He bowed to the *human* order that condemned and crucified Him,—with respect to that He said, " They know not what they do." As we have seen, He always regarded His death at the hands of men as a crime: " The Son of man shall be delivered into the hands of men, and they shall *kill* Him "; " the Son of man is delivered into the hands of *sinners*"; " now is the hour and power of *darkness*." But deeper than the human, there was the Divine moral order,—the will of the

Father,—to which He referred all that came to Him— the Divine moral order making sin its own punishment till it became manifest in its destructive consequences. That law must work on; and its reality must be made manifest to men oblivious of it. Christ in His self-identification with Humanity must be given up by God to suffer under its action in order that God's righteousness in relation to sin might be manifested and men saved from the sin which has such results. Owing to the method by which sin is punished by God, in increase of sinfulness tending to death, it was *only in this way*—by letting sin work its worst on Christ— putting to death the Best, the true Head and Representative of Humanity, that God's righteous judgment on sin *could* be revealed. Not by speech from Heaven; but by the deed that sinners were left to do in the natural sequence of the moral order. Therefore, although He saved others, Himself He could not save. It was not for any abstract reason or for some satisfaction to Himself that God gave up His Son to the Cross, but in order to save men from sin. "Its operation was not to be on God, but on man." The Cross did not make any "change" in God or in His attitude to man; it was the complete revelation and expression of the Divine forgiving love, and the means by which it went forth to the world in its saving power.

Humanity as represented by those who crucified Christ was really acting self-destructively. As *they* represented the worst, *He* whom they crucified represented the highest and best in the race—*was* indeed *man* in his highest and best. He was truly, as Paul taught, the Head of Humanity and the Representative of man before God. His crucifixion was the work of "sinful flesh." Sin in the flesh was thus shown to be destructive of Humanity, as there represented in its Head, in its highest and best. The judgment that ultimately comes on sin—God's condemnation of sin— was thus shown, not by anything that God inflicted on Christ, but by His giving up His own Son to sinful men — that is, not interfering with the natural sequence of events—in order that sin should be suffered to work itself out and there, once for all, manifest itself as that self-destructiveness which it is made to become under the Divine righteousness. Here it was shown how truly "sin when it is fully matured bringeth forth *death*." Had Jesus been simply a man after the flesh, like other men, His crucifixion would have been the ruin of the world. That death of Christ would have been the utter death of *man* in the higher aspects of his being. What is true of the individual is true of the race. "Selfishness," says Sir Oliver Lodge most truly,—"selfishness, long continued, must lead to isolation, and so to a kind of practical extinction : it is like a disintegrating or repulsive force in the material cosmos; while unselfishness is like a cohesive and con-structive force" (*Hibbert Journal*, vol. ii. p. 474).[1]   This

---

[1] This is quoted also by Mr. Lofthouse in his *Ethics and Atonement*. "Then it was made clear to mankind," he says, "that sin was 'exceeding

effect of selfishness in its worst form—in the guise of religion—was seen in the death of Christ at the hands of men professing a zeal for God. Had the evil there manifested really triumphed, had Christ continued under the power of the death then inflicted on Him, it would have been the moral and spiritual destruction of Humanity. Evil would have gone on its baleful way unchecked; it would have seated itself on the throne of the world instead of God, and death in the darkest sense would have been the fate of man.

Does this seem too strong a statement? Not if the Christian conception of Christ's personality and of man's true ideal and destiny are sound. It may be said that we are unwarrantably extending to the world what was realised in the experience of one person in one corner of the globe only. It may be asked, was God nowhere save in Christ; was there no morality and religion outside of Palestine; although Jesus might have been crucified and silenced for ever, would not the race still have made progress? *But to what goal?* Where else was man on the way to realise his ideal as a son of God—as a being whose self was surrendered to God that God might live in him? In what person other than Christ had this been reached? Jesus was truly the "second man"—man wholly after the Spirit; and if He was put to death by those who ought to have

---

sinful,' and that it contained within itself the seeds of dissolution, which, unchecked, brought forth death. Thus, in the death of Christ, man not only felt but saw his own punishment; the sword hanging over his own head had fallen on Him who knew no sin."

been the best fitted to recognise and receive Him, did
not Humanity, as represented by those amongst whom
the Divine education of the race had been carried to
the highest point ethically, repudiate its true life as it
was designed by God, and choose for itself a lower life
which, to whatever intellectual, moral, and material
advance it might lead, meant really the death of man
as he was meant to become by his Creator? There
would have been not only failure to rise as God meant
man to rise, but the downward-tending influence would
have gained in power. " Not this man, but Barabbas,"
—the representative of self-centred, self-serving *force*,—
would have become the Ruler of the world. There
were certainly great thinkers other than Christ, and
religious Leaders besides Him ; but where has there been
one who has led man to His true life in God, apart from
Christ? What philosophy, what religion has accomplished it effectually, however near they may at times
have come to it? What lasting value to man in the
highest aspects of his being has there been in it all,
save as it has been taken up into Christianity, or as
Christianity has entered it? Where is the path that
has led men onward as spiritual beings, save that on
which the revelation of God in Christ has shone, and on
which the Spirit of the Crucified has descended? That
which we behold in Christ was the culmination of all
God's working in the world, with the view of raising
man to his true life in Himself. It was *there* that God
was in His complete entry into Humanity. Christ was

filled with the Divine Spirit of man's true life, and it was this which men refused to receive. It was only after they had crucified Christ that the reaction came, that men saw their sin and began to receive the Spirit of the Saviour, which is that Spirit of God which alone can make man partaker in his true life and God-intended destiny. If we are to maintain Christianity in its power, it must be in no half-hearted manner. We must see and assert that God was in Christ for the salvation of the *world*, and that "there is none other name given under heaven wherein we must be *saved*."

It is in this view of the Cross that we behold the marvel of the Divine Wisdom and Power, that we see how truly *God* was in it. For, while Christ stood in the sinful flesh, He knew no sin. The *Spirit* was the real principle of His Life: in the power of that Spirit He arose out of death, and His death thus became "the death of death," the redemption of the world. Through His voluntary acceptance of it, that death of man in the flesh became the death of *sin* in the flesh and the life of man in the Spirit.

In a word, it was *Humanity* that was there represented both in Christ and in His murderers—Humanity that, in its members, had failed to rise above the self-centred lower nature, and whose sin had, in the righteous retribution of God, gone on increasing and deepening, till it inflicted on Him who represented Humanity in its truth, a death which, had He not been man wholly after the Spirit, would have meant its own destruction. And this all came about under that "righteousness of God" which makes sin its own punishment. The Righteousness of God in its relation to sin was thus *manifested* in that crucifixion of Christ by sinners.

In all this we see Christ literally "bearing our sins," "dying for our sins," "made sin on our behalf," "manifesting the righteousness of God in view of sin," and making it possible,—not for God to forgive sin,—but for the Forgiveness that was in His heart, and wherein He was visiting men, to go forth to the world so as to save it. He was the world-sufferer on whom lighted the world's sin, the sin which would have been the moral and spiritual, and, ultimately, the utter death of the world, had it not been met by one in whom the power of the Spirit was mightier than that of sin in the flesh. As has been well said: "What slew Him was sin conspiring under many forms against its Divine Adversary; it was the general selfishness directly attacked by His word, and put under constraint by His life; it was hypocritical formalism (the Pharisees), it was servile traditionalism (the Scribes), it was sacerdotal pride (the priests), it was frivolous or selfish politics (Herod, the Sadducees, Caiaphas), it was religious scepticism (Pilate) which coalesced finally to overwhelm Him" (Réville). These evil influences all have their roots in that "flesh" which is *common to man*. And it was by letting these evil influences which here came to a head do their natural work on the Best that the self-destructive nature of sin, as it has developed under the righteous Law that makes sin its own punishment in that increase of sinfulness that works death to man, was set forth. It was thus that God's righteousness in relation to sin was *judicially* manifested in the death of Christ, in order to the world's salvation.   In this manifestation of the result of sin in the complete working out of His righteous Law ; in its acceptance by Christ in our name and endurance of its consequences, God at-oned the world to Himself in His righteousness, so that He might save it.   It was in this way *only* that Christ bore the punishment of man's sin.   Not as inflicted on Him by God, nor as representing man in His sinfulness : He represented man at His highest and best.   But He suffered to light on Himself the worst consequences of man's sin as these came to Him (Himself wholly sinless) in that moral order and righteous judgment of God, which makes sin its own punishment, which is made manifest in what men through increasing sinfulness are left to do, and which unchecked would have proved the destruction of Humanity.   It was God's condemnation of *sin*, not of Christ as representing men.   His Cross thus became the manifestation of God's righteousness in that self-acting punishment of sin of the reality of which, because it did not fall upon them in any open manner, men were oblivious, and at the same time reversed the action of sin by bringing a new principle into operation in virtue of which the world might be saved.

As we have seen, while Christ was truly bearing the

consequences of our sins,—before God, it was really *sin* in man that died. As Paul says, "The death that He died, He died unto sin once for all; the life that He liveth, He liveth unto God." With Paul, the judicial death became an ethical death of sin in the flesh. Man was represented in Christ as dead unto sin and alive unto righteousness. Therefore, all who accept Christ and His life-principle as theirs are accepted by God as His sons and heirs, justified, glorified.

The death of Christ in its relation to sin was necessary, let us say once more, not to propitiate God, nor to atone for man's sin in the sense of making expiation or reparation, nor to satisfy Divine Justice by bearing a certain penalty, still less to meet a personal wrath in God; but, as Paul states it,—although we cannot accept the *forms* of his representation, —*to demonstrate God's righteousness* in view of His forbearance and forgiveness of sin, and to manifest His Love, in order that men might be saved from sin into that life of Love which is the life of God in man.

It was *this* that Christ did for us on the Cross: He endured the worst that sin could bring on man for the sake of the manifestation of God's righteousness and for our salvation. His death at the hands of men showed what sin, continued in, brings on man. He so died, by the will of God indeed, but at the hands of sinful men, in order that what sin works in the righteous retribution of God might be manifested. It was necessary that the righteousness of God in relation to sin should be *manifested* if the world was to be saved from sin. On account of the Divine forbearance, it had not been adequately manifested. Men did not realise it as it needed to be realised, especially in view of the Gospel proclamation. The necessity was met, we have sought to show, not by any arbitrary intervention, but by the Divine action continuing to proceed along those lines on which both the Love and the Law of God had been always moving—Law and "Wrath" reaching their climax in the self-acting punishment of sin in the case of those who put the Divine man to death, and Love reaching its supreme expression in God's giving up His Son to endure the worst consequences of man's sin for the sake of man's salvation. The requirement of the Divine Righteousness was met, we have sought to show, in a twofold manner: *ethically*, by the perfect obedience of Christ unto the death of the Cross, and *judicially*, if we may use the term, by Christ suffering to light on Himself the cumulative results of the sin of the world. Yet these two aspects are *one*. It was in His acceptance of the death of the Cross in obedience to the Father's will—in the working out of the Divine moral order—that "the flesh" died ethically in Him. Paul, we have seen, has both a judicial and an ethical conception of the Cross; and although we cannot accept the form in which he states either, yet in the light in which we have sought to place them both are true. Neither aspect can be omitted and yet the Cross retain

9

the fulness of the Divine Wisdom and Power for the salvation of the world.

We cannot look upon the death of Christ as being an arbitrary substitution of Christ for sinners, or a representative act in which an external penalty was laid upon Him. The ethical righteousness of God, the sinlessness of Christ, and the manner in which His death came to Him, all unite to make such conceptions impossible. But we see Christ standing in such a vital relation to Humanity that there light upon Him, and are vicariously borne by Him, those consequences of human sin which are also its punishment in the righteousness of God. Viewed thus, there is indeed a sense in which we may speak of both substitution and representation. For He endures in Himself that last consequence of sin which would otherwise have proved the destruction of Humanity, in order that we may be saved from it. This is the truth *underlying* the Pauline and later forms of evangelical doctrine.

The tendency to-day is to reject the " judicial " aspect entirely. But in that case the real evil and the certain, self-destructive doom which sin brings on man are not seen and felt, and the greatness of the debt that we owe to Christ and to God is not sufficiently recognised. The power of that Divine Love which identifies itself with us even in our sin, even at its worst, for our salvation, does not adequately reach and win the heart ; the self is not so humbled before God as to renounce itself and have the dying and living again of Christ repeated in its experience.

All that was done on the Cross was, we shall endeavour to show, the manifestation of the love of *God*. But the view of the sin-bearing of Christ which has been here presented is best seen in the light of His Headship of Humanity. We shall therefore devote a short chapter to the statement of this truth, after which we shall test the whole by an appeal to Christ's own teaching.

VIII

CHRIST AND THE RACE: THE HEAD
OF HUMANITY

CHAPTER VIII

CHRIST AND THE RACE: THE HEAD OF HUMANITY

WHAT has been said in the preceding chapters, in common with all forms of evangelical doctrine, implies that Jesus held the unique position of being the true Head of Humanity. By this we mean that the Divine ideal of man in the ethical truth of his being was realised in—not an Ideal "Christ," but Jesus of Nazareth.

This unique and representative position of Jesus is rejected by not a few to-day, and with others it constitutes a difficulty. Of course, for those who really believe that in Christ God was incarnate in human form, no question of His Headship can arise. They can see the truth of the teaching ascribed to Him in the Fourth Gospel: "I am the true Vine, ye are the branches." But for those who approach Christ on the human side it is different. To speak of the Headship, unique, or representative character of Christ, savours to some of theological artificiality, tends to make His person a needless mystery, and to remove Him out of real relation to ourselves. They remind us that Jesus was not the only God-inspired man, that His Cross is not the only atoning Cross in human history, and that the work of at-oning God with man and man with his brothers is being carried forward by a means of all the crosses of sacrifice and suffering voluntarily accepted and endured in the world.

It is highly desirable to drop all that is arbitrary and artificial in our conception of Christ and His Cross; there has been too much of that kind of thing in theology. But in affirming the Headship of Christ we are simply asserting that Lordship of Christ which all Christians acknowledge. We do not regard that Lordship as being His in any arbitrary manner, or for any external reason; nor do we represent Him as a Being abruptly introduced, out of all relation to those who have gone before Him or who have followed after. On both sides of His Person we see Him issuing from out of our Humanity, and at the same time from God as He has been progressively expressing Himself therein. We see thus in Him, not only man, but God as man.

We sometimes fail to see the uniqueness of Jesus—the real incarnation of God in Him—because we expect too much; we look for the impossible. We lay down, as if we had all knowledge, *a priori* conditions which must be fulfilled if God is to be incarnate; and because we do not see these all met in Christ, we refuse to believe in Him: we believe so strongly in ourselves. But if we think carefully and modestly, we will see that it is contrary to the very idea of man as a finite, limited being that all the infinite perfections of God should be manifested in any human person. Such a person would be no longer man, but wholly God in human disguise. Yet there is an aspect in which the Infinite *can* be revealed in the human—in its ethical truth—which is that which is deepest and most essential in God. If we can say "God" at all, He must be essentially *ethical* Being. And so truly is man in the image of God, that we can behold in a human life a righteousness and love which are perfect, to which we can put no limits or conceive of aught that could be added. Such a perfect righteousness and love we do behold in Jesus Christ. To look for Omnipotence and Omniscience in a human being, for the display of all manner of Divine riches, or even for such knowledge and teaching as would have been unnatural in a true *man* of that time and place, is to look for the impossible, and to overlook the actual presence of the essentially Divine. It is just the absence of such features that makes Christ's humanity real. It is not the absolutely complete *teacher* in even the ethical field—attacking every form of evil and giving instructions for every sphere of action—that we can expect to see. It is one who has as the deepest principle of His life, and who expresses in the actual circumstances in which He finds Himself placed, that which is the *one* principle of all morality and of all righteousness. To see this in the lowly man of Nazareth, in *Jesus* apart from all subsequent "idealisation" of Him, is part of that wisdom that is "hid from the wise and prudent and revealed unto babes"—to the childlike spirit. To-day, as of old, the Greek seeks for "Wisdom" and the Jew craves "miracle," and so they fail to discern the truly *Divine* in that true *man*, under the limitations which necessarily conditioned His life.

To say that Christ does not stand absolutely alone, or that in His Cross we have the highest example of *all* vicarious suffering, is no argument against the uniqueness of His Person and Cross. The Head of the body is not the less a member of the body because it is the head. But it is *the Head*, and as such occupies quite a unique position in relation to the other members. All that the other members experience is carried to the Head; there alone is it felt and interpreted, and from the Head the directions come which guide the other members, as well as the energy which enables them to act. Apart from the Head, the other members would be quite blind and unknowing; and if they were to refuse to acknowledge and trust the Head, or fail to follow its guidance, the life of the Body would become impossible. While belonging to the one organism, the Head is *above* all the other members. The distinction between Jesus Christ and others may therefore very well be that between the Head and the other members of the Body.

In another aspect, the distinction is that between the incomplete and the complete, the imperfect and the perfect, the sinful and the sinless, the striving and the attained.   The distinction between the incomplete and the complete "makes all the difference."   It gives us just that uniqueness which we claim for Christ.   To make this plain, let us borrow an illustration used in another connection by the late Professor Le Conte.   Here is an even surface of water ================.   From this we may imagine portions being gradually raised till the complete drop is reached ================.   There is identity, yet a very real difference.   The complete drop, although consisting of the same water, represents something *new*—something which stands out from the rest and can exist by itself: it is unique in its completeness.   So with the various members of humanity in relation to Christ.   The completely formed, perfect humanity is seen only in Him.   There had been approaches to that which was attained in His birth and life: He alone was from the first man *wholly* after the Spirit.   And in the culmination of His life He was man in whom God in His essential, Ethical Being was wholly incarnate.

To Paul, Jesus was "the second man," "the new man," the perfect Son in whom the Divine and the human were one, who was therefore at once "the man Christ Jesus" and the "image of God," the representative of both God and man.   The Gospels bear out this conception of Jesus Christ.   He so represented *God* on the earth that He could forgive sin.   Yet it was as the "Son of *man*" that He did so.   Explain the

origin of that name by which He ever called Himself
as we may; say that it means in the Aramaic only
"man" or "the man," we cannot get away from its
representative significance as it was used by Christ.
As Professor Schmit acknowledges at the close of his
learned discussion in the *Ency. Biblia*: "When Jesus
declared that man is lord of the Sabbath, and has the
authority to pardon sin, he no doubt thought of man
as he ought to be as the child of the heavenly Father."
And, we must add, He must have been conscious that
He was *that* man, or else He could not have taken upon
Himself those functions. But it is not the name only
that gives it. His whole attitude and teaching imply,
and, indeed, directly claim, such a position. His consciousness of Himself in relation to men was one of
universality. The recognition of Jesus as Lord is based
on His own claim: "Ye call me Master, and Lord; and
so I am," He could truly say. As we have it in St.
Matthew's Gospel, "*One* is your Master." He knew
Himself to be such a Master as could claim of right
the trust and obedience of all other men, even to the
sacrifice of their earthly lives. Father or mother, sister
or brother were not so near and had not such claims
on men as He had. It was not a merely physical bond
that thus united Him to others, it was spiritual. There
was, He declared, a higher kinship than the earthly:
"Whosoever shall do the will of God, the same is My
brother, and sister, and mother." It was the presence
in Himself of the fulness of that Divine spiritual life

which is the truest and highest life of man that gave
Him this universal relationship. The fulness of that
Divine ethical life which is the essential life of both
God and man was centred in Him. He, therefore,
stood forth as the Representative of man as God's
child, claiming for man the freedom, the good, the
sonship which God meant him to possess. *He* was to
be seen and served in all men ; in the little child, in His
suffering brethren. He who received a little child in
His name received *Him*. " Inasmuch as ye did it unto
one of these the least of these My brethren, ye did it
unto *Me* ; and inasmuch as ye did it not to such, ye
did it not to *Me*." These and similar sayings, His call
for unreserved faith in Himself, and His attitude
generally, bespeak, not an individual, but a universal
relationship. In a word, *He* was *man* before God, the
true Head and Representative of Humanity.

That Humanity should have its Head is necessary
according to the analogy of all life. What Nature long
strove to produce was a *head*. When the first head
appeared there was an immense ascent in life. The
head was at first very humble, very small in its
beginnings, very simple in its nervous structure ; but
in that lowly *head* Nature first came to some faint
consciousness of itself. It was the dawning world-
consciousness. As the development of the head
progressed, Nature ascended higher and higher, till
in the human brain it reached its climax. Then
began the evolution of man in his spiritual nature,

as a child of God. It was the culmination of the Divine working towards the realisation of man's spiritual nature which was reached in Christ, and constituted Him the true Head of Humanity. The Nature - consciousness became in Him at once a completely human and a truly Divine consciousness. God's ideal of *man* in his true ethical being was realised and manifested in Jesus of Nazareth.

Every developed organism must have its *head*, which becomes its guiding and governing organ. Humanity itself is an organism, and as such must have its Head. Men and women are not a number of unconnected or loosely connected units, as it may seem to superficial observation. They are united as vitally as the branches and leaves of the tree, or as the members of a body. The want of acknowledgment of the true Head of our Humanity is just the cause of the anarchy and confusion which characterise society, and only in recognition of and obedience to its Head can that confusion be reduced to order. "The Head of every man is Christ."

This Headship of Christ is seen and accepted by His Church, "which is His Body," in the world; that is, those who believe in Him realise their true relationship to Him as the members of an organic Body of which He is the rightful Head. Their true life is, as Paul teaches, to be found by "growing up in all things into union with Him who is the Head, even Christ," from whom the whole Body receives its impulse and nourishment. It is just this that forms "the Church."

Christian thought has always recognised in Christ that character of completeness and universality which constitutes Him the Head of the race and gives Him His representative character. It has seen in Him a personality, neither exclusively Jewish nor Greek, Eastern nor Western, but simply and perfectly human, in the highest aspects of humanity. It united the strength of manhood with the tenderness of woman's heart. It was stern in its righteousness, yet full of mercy, combining in itself every virtue and grace, presenting an ideal for men and women alike wherever found. It was no more limited in respect of time than it was restricted in regard to place. It has shone before all the successive generations of mankind with the same lustre, and has appealed to the most varied temperaments with equal force. The desire of Paul's warm heart, in all things to follow Christ, has been paralleled by the dictum of the cold, clear intellect of the nineteenth century philosopher, John Stuart Mill, that we cannot find a better practical guide than "to endeavour so to live that Christ would approve our life." In the words of one whose utterance in this connection should carry weight, the life of Christ was that of "One in whom we see balanced and united the separate gifts and graces of which we catch glimpses only in His followers. It is a life which is mysterious to us, which we forbear to praise in the earthly sense, because it is above praise, being the most perfect image and embodiment that we can conceive of Divine goodness" (Dr. Jowett).

This unique relationship of Christ to us has also been realised in Christian experience. We know what Paul's experience was as he has expressed it in his writings. "There is," says the writer just quoted, "something meant by this language which goes beyond the experience of ordinary Christians, something perhaps more mystical than in these latter days of the world most persons seem capable of feeling; yet the main thing signified is the same for all ages, the knowledge and love of Christ, by which men pass out of themselves to make their will His and His theirs, the consciousness of Him in their thoughts and actions, communion with Him and trust in Him. Of every act of kindness and good they do to others His life is the type; of every act of devotion and self-denial His death is the type; of every act of faith His resurrection is the type. And often they walk with Him on earth, not in figure only, and find Him near them, not in figure only, in the valley of death."

If the men of to-day are ceasing to see all this in Christ, truly human, yet Divine in His humanity, *for* them, yet *above* them, calling them as the Head of the Body gives direction to its free members, their perceptions of the highest things must be becoming seriously impaired, and the loss will in some form or other make itself manifest to the hurt of all.

As the Head of Humanity in whom the fulness of its highest life was centred, Jesus could feel with and for men as none other could. If, as Paul said, in the body, when one member suffers all the other members suffer with it, how much more true is this of the Head. In Him all human experience centred. He wore our "flesh" and knew its power. The Spirit also in Him reached the fulness of its life in man. Our humanity was represented in Him on both sides of its being. In Him man could both die to sin and rise to righteousness. As the Head He could "bear the sins" of the members of His Body, that is, endure their consequences, in order that the evil of sin might be manifested and men saved from that which would otherwise have been their ruin. If we think of the Cross in its *judicial* aspect, as the manifestation of God's righteousness in relation to sin, we thus see that in crucifying Christ, men were really, so far as they could go, destroying the true Head and Representative of Humanity. How could the evil and enormity of sin as it deepens in sinfulness have been more effectually shown, or the Divine Judgment that makes sin self-destructive have been made more manifest?

The *Ethical* work of Christ as the Head appears with the same clearness. The Gospels show us how truly both principles—"the flesh" and "the Spirit"—were present in Christ potentially, although the lower principle was always subordinated to the higher. He had a self, a will of His own which *might* have opposed

10

itself to the Will of God. But, as in the keen struggle in Gethsemane, His whole life was governed by "not My will but Thine be done." Still, we see from the conflict there how truly He stood "in the likeness of sinful flesh," and could represent man in the flesh as well as man in the Spirit. In His acceptance of the will of the Father to the uttermost sacrifice of Himself, "the flesh" died completely *in* Him and *for* us all, through the power of that Spirit that was centred in Him and that proceeds from Him to us.

In short, as we have said, Christ before God was *man* before God. What He did in our name, man did in Him. Or, to state it from the Divine side, what was done in Him was done by God in man and for all men, because Christ was the true Head and Representative of Humanity. Therefore it was no mere flight of fancy or of unreasoned mysticism when Paul saw *all* dying in the death of Christ and *all* rising in His resurrection. In the great Body of Humanity there are many members—a multitude innumerable. But such would also be the plants proceeding from a single seed were they suffered to grow unrestrictedly. Yet they were all represented in that first single seed. To one with sufficient knowledge the possibilities of each could have been known and confidently reckoned on. So with Humanity in Christ : it can be forgiven, accepted, made the son and heir of God, because in Christ it has died as regards the flesh, and in Him there is the potency of perfect spiritual life for all who will consent to take up their right relationship to Him and from Him draw their life.

The conception of mankind as a unity, or the solidarity of Humanity, is one that is impressing itself on the modern mind with its growing social feelings and aspirations. Mankind are felt to be one Body with one common interest and aim. We are coming to realise the truth of that noble Stoic utterance which has been well called "the watchword of Humanity," but which for long stood in solitary grandeur: *Homo sum; humani nihil a me alienum puto.* The Spirit of Humanity is gathering force and seeking expression. But what the Body needs for its safe guidance and well-being is the recognition of its rightful *Head*. A body without a Head is a very imperfect and unsightly thing. If Christ were only seen to be really the Head and obeyed as such—if He were allowed to do for the body of Humanity what the head does for the physical body—our most clamant problems would be solved. They never can be solved till the Head is recognised. "Not holding the Head" was the source of error in Apostolic times, and it is the source of blindness and misery in our own day.

IX

RELATION TO THE TEACHING AND LIFE-WORK OF CHRIST

CHAPTER IX

RELATION TO THE TEACHING AND LIFE-WORK OF CHRIST

ANY interpretation of the Cross must be tested by its agreement with the teaching and life-work of Christ Himself. Primarily with His teaching concerning God and the Kingdom and His own death. His teaching concerning God is summed up under the word *Fatherhood*. God was the loving and merciful Father, rather than the strict, inexorable Judge. But He was a Holy Father, and, ultimately, also the Judge of all. While repentance and forgiveness were free to returning sinners, those who persisted in evil should be sternly condemned and banished from His presence. The door of the Kingdom stood open to all, but the unrighteous could not enter it; they should be cast out if they ventured in; their place was the outer darkness —away from God. This is manifestly the same fate as the "death" that Paul speaks of. If Christ dies to save men, it is *ultimately* from that doom. We cannot truly represent Christ's teaching if we ignore this sterner element; even if we think we can discern the glow of a hope beyond it. In the same way He speaks of the loss of the soul, of the life, of the self: "What shall it profit a man if he should gain the whole world and forfeit his soul" (or life), or "lose himself"? What is this loss of the soul or life, or of himself, but the death which Paul says is the wages of sin? Not necessarily annihiliation.

When, therefore, Christ says that He is "come to give His life *a ransom* for many"; while the word "ransom" in itself may have various applications, it is really, ultimately, from this death, as the consequence of sin, that He ransoms them by giving His own life for their deliverance.

But it is at the Last Supper that our Lord gives the most explicit teaching concerning the meaning of His death. The whole has been the subject of the keenest criticism, and we shall therefore keep to that which seems least open to cavil or question. By some, as by Bousset in his "Jesus," the Last Supper is left entirely out of account in this connection, because it seems to them hopeless to endeavour to ascertain its meaning. But with the three Synoptical Gospels and Paul all in substantial agreement in their account of it, and in view of the place which it gained in the early Church, it seems unreasonable so to treat it. That it was the Passover Festival, whether held on the proper evening or not, or, if not the actual Passover Feast, one substituted for it and suggested by it, cannot be questioned without overturning the whole narrative of these last days; and this fact must dominate in any interpretation of our Lord's utterances on the occasion. The sayings themselves have been much discussed, and are by some cut down to the meagrest measure. As they stand in St. Mark's Gospel, we read: "And as they were eating, He took bread (or a loaf), and when he had blessed, He brake it, and gave to them and said, 'Take ye: this is My body.' And He took a cup, and when He had given thanks, He gave to them; and they all drank of it. And He said unto them, 'This is My blood of the Covenant (some authorities insert, with Paul in 1 Cor. xi. 25, "*new*," the new Covenant) which is shed (or poured out) for many'" (Mark xiv. 22, 24). Schmiedel remarks that "with the omission of 'Take ye,' this may be regarded as the relatively (not absolutely) oldest form of the words of the institution of the Eucharist"; and he regards them as referring to His sacrifice "as an offering, not for sin, but for the immunity of His followers, after the manner of the Passover lamb in Egypt, or for ratification of their Covenant with God, as in Gen. xv. 10, 17; Jer. xxxiv. 18; Ex. xxiv. 1–8" (*Ency. Bib.* ii. col. 1887). By Hollmann the words of the institution are restricted to "This is My Body," and "This is My Blood," which is surely the least we can have if we are to have anything at all. Well, let us accept this provisionally, so as to keep on the surest ground. The words were spoken in the course of the Passover Feast (or a substitute for it), in commemoration of the deliverance of the fathers of the nation from Egyptian bondage, previous to which the blood of a lamb that had been slain was sprinkled on the lintel and doorposts of their dwellings that they might be covered or sheltered from the Angel of Death who smote the first-born in all the houses of the Egyptians. Whether historical or not, this was their belief. When Jesus in these circumstances gave His disciples the Bread and said that it represented His Body, and the cup of Wine saying that it should henceforth represent to them His Blood, was He not telling them quite plainly that He was to give Himself for their deliverance as the lamb had been given to their fathers in Egypt in order that its blood might be shed and used for their protection? Was He not saying that His blood should fulfil on their behalf a function similar to that which the blood of the lamb had fulfilled for their fathers in Egypt? He was manifestly substituting *His* Body and Blood for those of the Paschal lamb. If it was not the actual or regular Passover Feast, the substitution would be all the more impressive. His reference to His *Blood* in this connection suggests the language of sacrifice. For in the death that He looked forward to, no actual blood would be shed. But "the blood" of sacrifice had a commonly recognised meaning for all Israelites. It was given by God to be a *covering* for them. The blood of the lamb slain in Egypt was a covering for all on whose dwellings it was sprinkled—a covering from the Judgment that at midnight visited that land. So, Jesus meant them to understand that His Blood (the shedding of which would seem so strange to them) would be a covering to them in the Day of God's Judgment on the sinful nation. His life had been given to them by God to that end as that of the lamb had been given to their fathers in Egypt.

The full force of our Lord's saying here is not always realised, because it is taken out of its eschatological setting. Jesus was thinking and speaking to them of *the coming of the Kingdom,* when He should drink with them the *new* wine. But the coming of the Kingdom had a *Judgment* side to it, as He had taught in many of His sayings and parables. The darker side of Christ's teaching needs to be here kept in view. When the King should come in the glory of His Father, it should be to universal Judgment — the righteous should be welcomed to the Kingdom : on others doom should fall. But just as their fathers had been "covered" in Egypt by the blood of the Passover lamb, so should they be covered by *His* Blood in the coming Judgment Day. It implies that His death should avail to protect all who were His. Not because He should be punished by God instead of them, but because (as we saw in a previous chapter) He let the full consequences of the national and of universal sin fall on Himself, and it should operate to their salvation. It did so save them, and it would have saved the whole nation from the awful judgment that came upon it, had it been suffered to have its due effect on its Heads and Guides. It saved His disciples by separating them, as a new spiritual people, from the carnally minded Israel, and it is mighty to save all men by separating them in their spirit from the sinful world, in response to its influences.

If, as it is probable, He spake of His Blood as that "of the Covenant," the meaning is the same. For the Passover was "the sacred Covenant Supper" of which none could partake save those who were rightfully in the sacred community. "The sacred act of Covenant-consecration, as described in the oldest narrative, the sprinkling of the people with the blood of the Covenant, the acceptance of 'the words of the Covenant,' could never in the nature of things be repeated. But in memory of God's mighty act of deliverance, of the blood with which, on that occasion, the holy community was marked and protected from the wrath of the angel of death, in memory of the hasty exodus and the affliction of those days, the supper was to be observed as a symbolical act of worship" (Schultz). It is widely held that the blood of the Paschal lamb had an atoning, *i.e.* a covering or cleansing, efficacy, so that those who sat down to the feast could feel that in spite of their sins they were in acceptance with God; and that this naturally suggests a like efficacy in the Blood of Christ. But in any case, we see that the Covenant Blood was a "covering" Blood for those who accepted it. If Jesus spake specially of the *New* Covenant, the establishment of which was virtually identical with the coming of the Kingdom of God in its spiritual aspects, the meaning of "the Blood" would remain unchanged. His Blood would be the ratification of that New Covenant, or that which would make it effectual. The New Covenant was based on Forgiveness, and "the Blood" has always one well-understood sacrificial significance : it is always given as a *covering* to men. When we find Paul saying, "Even Christ our Passover has been sacrificed for us"; when we read in 1st Peter and in Revelation of "the Blood of the Lamb," and find in the Fourth Gospel Christ represented as "the Lamb of God that taketh away (or beareth) the sin of the world," and His crucifixion made to fall on the day when the Paschal lamb should be slain, with which in the narrative He is identified, we see how truly the Church had learned the lesson which its Founder sought to convey by His references to His Body and Blood, and how the Gospel representations agree with those of St. Paul. The Book of Acts shows us also that when Christ was first preached to men it was as one by belonging to whom men should be saved in the coming Judgment Day. We have the same teaching in the earliest of the Epistles —1st Thessalonians.

It is not *said*, indeed, in what sense His blood should avail for His disciples, that is, what precisely it should do ; but we seem bound to intrepret it as having some real analogy to the well-known efficacy of sacrificial Blood, especially to that of the original Passover lamb.

But it would surely be a great mistake were we to

interpret our Lord's references to His sacrificial death in a merely external and unspiritual manner. It was essentially a spiritual Kingdom that Christ preached, and the salvation He was bringing was primarily a spiritual salvation. Only as being such in the first instance could it become an external salvation. His Blood was not just like that of animal sacrifices. Such a comparison would be most odious and irreverent. A libation of the richest human blood could not be satisfying to God. Christ's life was given up to God in order to fulfil a high Divine purpose of spiritual redemption. It was the consummation of His life-work, the completion of the At-one-ment. In that act of supreme obedience, God and man were made wholly one. His " Blood " should avail only for those who belonged to Him, as the blood of the Passover lamb had availed only for those Israelites who sheltered themselves under it. But there could not be, as in their case, any literal blood in view, or any external sprinkling. It had to be received into the heart, which was perhaps symbolised by the words, " Drink ye all of it." St. Mark is careful to tell us that " they drank of it every one." As St. John has it, we must " eat the flesh and drink the blood of the Son of Man." It was *Himself* that He gave to us on that Cross, to be received as our Spirit and Life. It may be that this spiritual significance of His Blood, as we find it in St. John's Gospel, was only later revealed to His disciples; but we find it already in Paul, who teaches that it is only in spiritual union with Christ that salvation can be found.

At the same time, it was necessary in order to this spiritual union with Him that He should die as He did for our sakes. In that death He did a work on our behalf which no one else could have done, and which was necessary for our spiritual salvation. It is because He died for our sakes that we are invited to become united with Him in His Spirit; and it is through the influences that go forth from His Cross that the spiritual union is effected. His work *for* us cannot be ignored. We must receive His life to live in us *as He gives it to us*, and that is as giving it " a ransom for us," or, as Paul puts it, " dying for our sins "—the underlying truth of which we have sought to show. To think of coming to Christ, or of receiving His life, that is, His Spirit, to be our life, without any such sense of sin as feels the necessity for His Cross for the manifestation of the righteousness of that God in whose forgiveness we trust, is to propose something to ourselves that will not be realised in our experience. There is a measure of self-righteousness, or self-sufficiency, still in us that will make it impossible for us truly to receive Christ's life to be ours. The " natural " man is still asserting himself, so that the true spiritual man cannot be born. We still lack that very sense of human sin and of Divine Righteousness and Love which the Cross was intended to create—the want of which, in fact, made it necessary. The ground within has not been prepared so that the love that the Cross declares can, not merely fall on it, but sink into it, and become the power of the Christ-life within us. We forget that we are not, like Christ, born of the Spirit from the first. If Christ is to live in us, Self must die. We must be "born anew"—born "*of the Spirit*."

On the other hand, to trust in anything that Christ has done *for* us, without becoming spiritually united to Him, is sheer, inexcusable presumption, such as He tells us shall be disowned by Him in "that day." It is disowned by Him in this present day; for there is nothing more evident on the part of mere outward believers, whether "orthodox" or "unorthodox," than their want of the Christ-like Spirit. To enjoy the benefits of Christ's redemption we must belong to Christ, and this means cherishing and living in His Spirit of Love and self-sacrifice. For, "If any man have not the Spirit of Christ, he is none of His"; and, "If ye live after the flesh, ye shall die."

The Cross did not really *add* anything to what Jesus had taught and borne witness to in His life. All along He had declared both the Righteousness and the Love of God, both His judgment on sin and His forgiveness of sinners. The Cross was the final witness to both of these Divine principles. All Christ's teaching and all His life were here gathered up into one great word. Christ's dying *for* our sins and *to* sin was the culminating expression of both the Righteousness and the Love of God.

This is why in the Pauline doctrine attention is fixed on the death and resurrection of Christ, with practically no reference to His previous life and teaching. This those who would take us "back to Jesus," apart from the Cross, fail to see. The whole life and teaching of Jesus, His very innermost Spirit, are contained in the great act of the Cross, witnessed to by His resurrection. In that act Christ gives His very self to us that His death to the flesh and life in the Spirit may become ours. In that act we have a Christ entirely freed from all that was of the flesh. While He lived and taught under its limitations, local and temporal features might to some extent characterise His teaching, and men might lay hold on these outward features merely, as some of the early Christians did. But by His gift of Himself in that sacrifice of the Cross He passed entirely beyond all these, to come as an inspiring Spirit into the hearts of the men of all time and of all places according to their ever-growing and changing needs. The "ideal Christ," rightly conceived, is the real Christ of the Cross freed from all limitations of the flesh ; not a different Being from Jesus, or one to be vaguely conceived, but Jesus of Nazareth as He comes to us in the fulness and infinite inexhaustibility of the Spirit. Therefore Paul said, "I know not even Christ any more after the flesh."

It is the knowledge of Christ *in the Spirit*—in that Divine and human Spirit of Holy Love, of Righteousness and Truth, that so completely expressed itself on

the Cross, and from that Cross goes forth to the world
—that is the essential thing.   It is in this Spirit that we
are made individually truly at one with God.   In that
Spirit we have Christ Himself in us.   Wherever
Christ Himself in Spirit is really received, all that
is implied in His teaching, freed from the limitations of
time and place, will be expressed in life and action.
We are thankful for the record of His earthly life, but
we are not dependent on it.   The attention that is now
being given to the criticism of the Gospel records is in
danger of leading us away from that Christ of the
Spirit with whom we have to do, though it may end by
throwing us more completely on Him.   The Spirit is
ever deeper, greater and more important, than the
letter :

> "The letter fails, the systems fall,
>   And every symbol wanes ;
> The Spirit, over-brooding all,
>   Eternal Love, remains."

We sum up, then, by saying that we can get no better
interpretation of the Cross than that which was given
by St. Paul, if we view it in its *ethical* aspect in a more
direct manner, and see its *judicial* significance in a
wider way, both of which, however, are only expansions
of Paul's doctrine of the death of Christ to sin and of
the manifestation of the Righteousness of God in His
Cross.   In the suffering and death of Christ we have
the supreme example of that vicarious principle in
virtue of which a righteous person allows to light on

himself the consequences of the increasing sinfulness of those with whom he is associated as these show themselves under the Divine moral order,—himself bowing to that order for their sakes, in the hope that they will feel their sinfulness and, turning to God, be saved from what would otherwise be their fate.   But Christ holds such a relation to the race as its Head, and His acceptance of His Cross had such a direct relation to man before God, to the worst consequences of man's sin, to the manifestation of God's righteousness, in the doom that sin brings on Humanity, and to God's loving will for man's salvation, that, like His Person, His Sacrifice is unique and representative as that of no other person can possibly be.   It becomes the foundation of a universal Gospel, in which God, having thus in Christ reconciled the world to Himself in His righteousness, draws nigh to all with the word of Forgiveness, " not imputing to them their trespasses," but beseeching them to be reconciled, or at one, with Himself.

But as the universality of the Gospel and its absolute unconditionedness are not always fully recognised, and so the Gospel-message is thereby robbed of much of its Divine power, we shall yet devote a chapter to the setting of it forth.   Meanwhile let us seek to view the Cross, as far as we may, on its *Divine* side as the supreme manifestation of God and His Love, and in its relation to the Divine creative purpose.

X

THE MANIFESTATION OF THE LOVE OF GOD

CHAPTER X

THE MANIFESTATION OF THE LOVE
OF GOD

WHILE we see Christ on His Cross bearing the consequences of the world's sin as these come upon man in the righteousness of God and thus manifesting God's Righteousness, we must at the same time see in that which was done the supreme manifestation of the sympathy and love of *God*. One consequence of that view of "the Atonement" that has been so widely accepted is, that in spite of the verbal acknowledgment that the whole procedure originated with God and was the expression of His love, the love of Christ, as seen in what He endured for our sakes, has largely overshadowed that of God in Christ. When the Cross is represented as something suffered in order to satisfy God, His Holiness or Justice, it is impossible to realise in its fulness the great truth that it was *God* who was thus "in Christ reconciling the world to Himself." We may try to imagine something of the love of the Father who gives up His Son to endure all this, but the Divine so greatly transcends the human that our effort fails, and it is still the Son who is vividly before us as the actual sufferer: it was *Christ* who bore our sins; it was Christ who so loved us as to die for our sakes. No doubt, love to Christ ought to be love to God; but in actual experience it has not always been such, and in consequence there has always been something lacking. For it is *God's* love we must see, because it is to God we must be brought, and it is God's love that must possess us.

But to think of God as being wholly *outside of Christ*, giving Him up externally, as if separate from Himself, is quite out of keeping with the truth of the Incarnation of God in Christ, and with the truth of God as the all-inspiring Spirit of life. Christ was "God manifest in the flesh." What He did, God did in Him. The humanity was distinct from the Divinity, but it was *one* therewith. It was that Spirit of Holy Love that God is that was expressing itself in the whole life and work of Christ. If we see Christ bearing our sins, we see God in His great love taking them on Himself, and so reconciling to Himself the world in its sin and in its separation from Himself.

This is the most wonderful and the most affecting thing revealed in the Cross. The olden prophets could think of God as being afflicted in all His people's affliction, as bearing their sicknesses and sorrows, but they could not rise to the thought of God Himself bearing even their sins. Yet this was manifested in the Cross of Christ. We see God there taking on Himself, not only the sorrow, but the sin of the world. It is the revelation of what God has been bearing from all eternity, and is bearing now for our sakes. We think far too little of what *God* suffers and has to bear for the sake of His creation. We often lament our own suffering, and we see and deplore the suffering and sin of the world: the more holy and sympathetic a man is the more painfully does he feel the burden of the sorrow of the creation, the more repulsive is its thoughtlessness, selfishness, and sin; yet the more is his heart touched with sympathy for sinners. But does not God see it all, feel it all, sympathise with all, infinitely beyond anything that is possible to us? He could end it all; but then His loving purpose in His creation would be frustrated. Man must freely form himself and *become* God's child. So God denies Himself, restrains, limits Himself, in order that man may become man, and be, not mechanically, but freely, His child. It is the supreme, unsurpassable expression of this Divine sympathy and sacrifice on the part of God, originating with Him, moved and made actual by Him in Christ, that we behold in the Cross.

The life of God is for ever the same life of self-denial and self-sacrifice, because it is the life of perfect Love. Out of His overflowing fulness He is constantly giving of Himself in creation in order to find Himself again in those whom He has raised to participation in the Divine Life. This is that Eternal *kenosis* in which " the Son " is for ever passing out of " the Father " and again returning to the bosom of God. The Incarnation in

Christ was not that of a moment of time, and it was only completed by the Cross.   That Cross is the symbol and revelation of the Divine life.   We speak confidently now of the Divine Love, but it was only the Cross of Christ that made it known.   In some measure the Divine Spirit of holy Love moves in all men, and we can now recognise it in those who have become martyrs for the sake of their fellows, vicariously " bearing their sins."   They do this, not of themselves, but as moved by God's Spirit of Love.   They are not *alone* in their suffering : God Himself is in it.

> " Up from undated time they come,
> The martyr souls of heathendom,"

as we call it.   Deeper than all ignorance of men, *God* has been in it.   And in the fulness of the time all this suffering Love was revealed to man in the Cross of Christ as the very love of *God*.

We say reverently, therefore, that in the Cross of Christ we behold God taking on Himself the responsibility for His world in all its sinfulness.   Sin is very real, very awful in its consequences to man and in its actuality before God.   It is His great grief, His great burden, against it His holy Love inevitably operates in that which is so often misunderstood as " the Wrath of God."   That Wrath is nothing else than the necessary action of His holy Being against that which is contrary to Himself, to His children, and to His loving purpose, and which must disappear out of His creation.   But while men are rightly judged guilty and punished, inasmuch as they have not striven after righteousness as they ought to have done, but have yielded too readily to purely earthly influences and have cherished too long the desires of their lower nature of "the flesh," it is the fact of *their possession of such a nature* that is the real source of the world's sin. And their grounding in this nature was inevitable. First must come "that which is natural," and only after it "that which is spiritual." "The first man was of the earth earthy," and such is still true of all in whom "the second man" has not been born. Now, it was God who gave existence to the world and to man with this earthy, animal nature. He did this in His love, and He has never regretted it, because man should in due time transcend it. But it has caused Him to bear a very heavy burden. He knew that man could not be raised into his true, higher manhood in any mechanical way, or by mere creative force. To move man upward by an outward, uplifting Hand, or by some compelling force *in the very least degree*, would be destructive of his manhood. Therefore the long, sad story of struggle and of sin. Although man is a guilty being, a sinner before God, deserving of punishment, yet, practically, and in the sight of Him who knew the constitution of His creature, this sinfulness was something which was virtually certain to be manifested; because man, in order to *be* man, was gifted with a will of his own, and was initially weighted by "the flesh" or animal nature. The experience of

sinfulness may not have been necessary for his development and perfecting, although it is impossible to see
how he could otherwise have come to know the in-
finitude of the Divine Love, and so have that as the
principle of his life. But this implies the reality of sin
as sin, for which there can be no apology. But the
actual appearance of sin in man could not have been
unknown to God; it did not prevent Him from creating; must we not say with Paul, "Where sin abounded,
grace did much more abound?" It was all foreseen,
accepted, and provided for. Christ was "the Lamb
slain from the foundation of the world." The creation
was grounded in sacrifice, which should be given its
complete expression and manifestation in the fulness
of the time. As Peter says of Christ as the sacrificed
Lamb: "Who was foreknown indeed before the foundation of the world, but was manifest in these last times
for you, who through Him are believers in God, who
raised Him from the dead, and gave Him glory; so that
your faith and hope might be in God." Might be in
God, be it noted. The truth is that our hard views of
God's justice and man's punishment rest on the old
Jewish conception of Sovereignty instead of Fatherhood, and on the creation narrative in Genesis, where
man is represented as having been created wholly good,
"free to stand, yet free to fall," directly disobeying a
simple positive command which might easily have been
kept, given to one man, who by his disobedience
involved the race in sin and misery. Such a conception

cannot be entertained to-day. It does not consort with our knowledge of man's primitive condition, and we know that the narrative has no claim to be considered special Divine revelation. Man had to *rise* from the animal man to the spiritual man and child of God. Throughout all human history God has been seeking, not by force, but by means of spiritual influences, including the suffering of man for man and of Himself in man, to raise men to this higher life; and, when the world was best fitted to receive it, the supreme manifestation of His holy, sacrificial and saving Love was made in the Cross of Christ. God there seems to say: "Behold I take the responsibility of My world on Myself; I bow beneath the worst consequences of the sin which I condemn, that you may be saved therefrom; I show to you, O men, how truly I am in it all, suffering through you and for your sakes, in the hope that this My suffering will manifest My holy Love, and bring it to bear within you as My Power to your salvation."

Viewed in this light, we see how short those views of the Cross which regard it as something "to atone for sin," "to satisfy Divine Justice," etc., come of its Divine significance; how, in fact, they may be said to have sometimes been the very antitheses of the truth. And yet, as we have regarded it, we see God at once maintaining His inviolate Righteousness and revealing His infinite Love. All that sin suffers, all that it brings on man, is just and necessary; but Love is the source of the creation, Love will take it all upon itself so as to work out its loving purpose for mankind.

The purpose of God in the Cross was to bring us all into the same Spirit of holy Love as was there manifested. This is at once the creative and the redemptive Spirit, so that the great Deed of God in the Cross of Christ was truly *a fresh creative act*. It is in the power of that Spirit that God for ever acts. It is the only Spirit of true life. The creation itself, as we have said, is founded in sacrifice, and by sacrifice it is constantly maintained and carried onward and upward. By the sacrifice of the Cross God seeks to inspire, live, and act in men in this Divine Spirit. It is a manifestation of God in the truth of His Divine Life, to be *received* by us that we may thereby share in the one Divine and eternal life. As Mr. T. H. Green has said : " A death unto life, a life out of death must (in the light of the Cross) be in some way of the essence of the Divine nature—must be an act which, though exhibited once for all in the crucifixion and resurrection of Christ, was yet eternal—the act of God Himself. For that very reason, however, it was one perpetually re-enacted, and to be re-enacted by man. It is so far as the second man which is from heaven, and whose act is God's, thus lives and dies in us that He becomes to us a Wisdom from God which is Righteousness, sanctification, and redemption" (*The Witness of God*, p. 8).

The Cross was "the Wisdom and the Power of God, not only for the redemption of man, but for *the completion of the Creation*. It came as the culminating expression of the self-sacrificing love in which the Creation was founded and by which it had been continually elevated. It was God's purpose "in Christ to reconcile all things to Himself, having made peace through the blood of the Cross." It was to be the reconcilation, not only of man in his sinfulness to God, but of the Creation in its separateness to the Creator. Creation implies a going out of God from Himself again to return to Himself in the effected creation. Man, if God's loving purpose concerning him is to be realised, must exist as a separate personality, with a will of his own, and then be brought into oneness with God, not, of course, to lose thereby the personality that has been formed, but to find it perfected. In Christ as the Head of Humanity, that reconciliation—that return from separateness into oneness with God—was effected, actually in His own Person, and representatively and potentially, for all men. What Philosophy has sought to realise by thought, and Mysticism by ecstasy or intuition, was there realised in the moral and spiritual life, and it is only in that life that the world can ever become one with God. For that is the essential Divine Life. When the humanity in Christ entirely accepted the Divine Will in that complete sacrifice of the Cross, then, and then only, was the human entirely one with the Divine. In this perfect unity of Will and Spirit we behold that complete reconciliation which was, as such, the perfecting of the Creation. God and man were *one* in that self-sacrificing, holy love, which is the eternal life of God. The immanent Divine was one with the transcendent from which it proceeded. The Divine idea of the Creation was realised in that act in Christ in which not only did "the flesh" die that "the Spirit might live, but the finite was made eternally one with the Infinite—taken up into it. And it is when men realise the separation that exists between them and God, not merely the creaturely separation of the flesh and of finiteness, but the moral separation because of sin,—that is, self-love, self-will, self-seeking and pleasing, — and enter fully into the reconciliation effected in the name of all in Christ, that the life of God—the very life that God is—becomes their life also, and although the body of the flesh remains till death shall "rend the veil," all real separation is annulled and man in the Spirit is one with God.

That life of God comes that it may possess us fully through the Cross of Christ—through the holy love there manifested reaching us in our sinful separation and self-life. How else could the knowledge of it come to us so as to win us to itself?

Others have reached in thought the essential ideal oneness of God and man,—in Hindoo Philosophy, for example,—and have sought in various ways to tran-

scend all separateness. But only in Christ has the Way
been manifested; only in Him has it been fully
realised for all, and, therefore, where the knowledge of
His Cross has not reached men they are still in
ignorance of "the Way, the Truth, and the Life."
Here lies our Missionary obligation to the world—
"to the wise and to the unwise, to the Greek and to
the barbarian"—in taking up which we become "Co-
workers with God." God does not repeat Himself,
and it is in vain that we look elsewhere for that which
He has given to the world in Christ.

It is only through Christ's Cross accepted as ours,
on which we are crucified with Christ to *all* that is of
self and to all that separates our spirits from the
Infinite and Eternal Spirit of Holy Love, from God
and His unchanging Goodwill, however it may come
to us, that we enter into that complete reconciliation
or at-one-ment with God in which our true and eternal
life and peace are to be found. Paul had learned the
great lesson when he said, "I live; yet not I, but Christ
liveth in me." God in Christ is God in human form,
God as He has made Himself known to man, God as
He comes to live His eternal life in us. No mere
trust in an *external* Cross can really *save* us. We
cannot by any possibility be saved outside ourselves.
Christ must be "formed *in* us"; it is "Christ *in* you
the hope of glory." His Cross must be, as Paul saw
so clearly, and ever taught, the Cross within, whereon
we die with Christ to rise with Christ, or, to state it

12

differently, whereby self dies and God lives His own
life in us, and lifts us into eternal unison with Himself.
As many of the Mystics preached, and as Angelus
Silesius put it into rhyme :

> "Though Christ in Joseph's town
>   A thousand times were born,
> Till He is born in thee,
>   Thy soul is still forlorn.
> The Cross on Golgotha
>   Can never save thy soul :
> The Cross in thine own heart
>   Alone can make thee whole."

XI

THE GOSPEL OF RECONCILIATION

CHAPTER XI

THE GOSPEL OF RECONCILIATION

IN the preceding chapter we have been endeavouring
to state the highest aspects of the Cross; but the
whole is brought nigh to all in the simple Gospel-
message, if it be truly grasped and proclaimed. The
Evangel which proceeded through the Cross, however,
has not always been apprehended in all the freeness
and fulness with which St. Paul proclaimed it. Hence
God has not been known in all the greatness of His
love, and this has had much to do with the weakness
and imperfection which have too often characterised
the religious life, and with the growing indifference to
religion. Where God is not truly known, Religion
cannot really live. The great want of the world to-day
is a real belief in God as He has revealed Himself in
Christ—not in the mere words of a doctrine about Him.

With Paul, the Gospel was the very antithesis of
" Law," but with his successors there has too frequently
crept in a legal element. *Conditions* have been laid
down which men must comply with if they are to be
forgiven and saved. The tendency to a reversion to
legal conceptions has all along been the great foe to

Christianity.   The Judaism which contended with Paul
had dogged the Gospel throughout the centuries.   In
some cases it succeeded in quite transforming the
Gospel.   Nor did the Reformation wholly deliver men
from it.   This legalism is, as Paul said, "of the flesh,"
and therefore it is "natural," and readily finds favour
with men.

When the Cross is regarded as a sacrifice *demanded*
by God in order to satisfy His justice, sometimes even
to appease His wrath, or to enable Him to forgive, and
the Gospel or Grace as only coming to us as the
outcome of this, it cannot come thus in its Divine
freeness and fulness; it cannot thus affect our hearts
as the spontaneous outcome of God's love should do.
We do not really see God to be the Love that He is,
and, therefore, that Love does not come to possess us.
A doctrinal system like this soon becomes formal,
barren, and uninteresting.   It may be preached, but it
has little real influence; people get tired of hearing it
and ministers of preaching it.   It lacks reality.   But,
as we have seen, such representations are made in the
face of the plainest declarations of the New Testament
that the Cross represents the great sacrifice *made by
God* in His forgiving and reconciling love for the world.
It was the outcome and the supreme proof of that love.
If God had not been drawing nigh to men in forgiveness, why should He have given up His Son to suffer
and die for them?   Surely the great Gospel texts are
these: "God so loved the world that He *gave* His only-

begotten Son," and " *God* was in Christ reconciling the world to Himself, not imputing their trespasses unto them."

The *Gospel* as something new and in advance of even the highest prophetism has not always been apprehended. The difference between the forgiveness of individual penitent sinners previous to the Cross and that universal proclamation of Divine Grace and Forgiveness which goes forth to the world through the Cross, has not always been seen. All along in O.T. times Forgiveness had been freely proclaimed to repentant sinners: "Come now, and let us reason together, saith the Lord; though your sins be as scarlet, they shall be white as snow; though they be red like crimson, they shall be as wool"; "Who is a God like unto Thee, forgiving iniquity, transgression, and sin?" etc. Christ also proclaimed the Divine forgiving love for all repentant sinners. The father of the prodigal was ready to forgive his returning child. What true father would not be so? Some, as we have already said, have seen in these facts an argument against the necessity for the Cross. But this is because they have not understood the rich, free, universal Gospel which the Cross proclaims. It goes beyond the announcement of mercy for returning sinners. It is the proclamation of God's forgiving love to *the whole world* — His reconciliation of "the world" to Himself. The Cross shows us God, not waiting till His wandering children return, but going forth seeking them with the word of

forgiveness on His lips.   It is what Thomas Erskine
described as the "*Unconditional Freeness of the Gospel.*"
God freely forgives the repentant sinner.   But the
difficulty is that men will not repent.   The Cross was
designed to lead men to Repentance by the manifestation of the evil of sin on the one hand and of the love
and unbought Grace of God on the other.   Men will
not come to God, and God in His fatherly love comes
to them.   Not *waiting* till they do—what few would
ever do—return from the far country of sin, but going
after them in that surpassing sacrifice to draw them to
Himself: "I, if I be lifted up from the earth, will draw
all men unto Me," said Christ.   God comes to men in
Christ, Paul taught, as a reconciled Father, beseeching
His children to be reconciled to Him, freely and fully
forgiving those who had nothing wherewith to pay—
"not imputing their tresspasses unto them."   How
much there is in that last sentence "not imputing their
trespasses unto them"—not reckoning their sins against
them, or even mentioning them to them.   This was
what the Cross enabled God to do in relation to
Forgiveness.   It did not enable Him to forgive men,—
which in His heart He had already done,—but to come
to them *proclaiming* His free and full forgiveness.   His
righteousness had been adequately set forth in what
Christ did and suffered in our name.   In Him men
have been made at one with God.   It is only now for
them individually to *respond* to this Divine seeking love,
to "*receive* the Grace of God, not in vain," to draw nigh

to Him who so graciously draws nigh to them, to enter
into the Reconciliation thus opened up. This was the
Gospel of Reconciliation or At-one-ment, the Christian
Gospel, the "message" from God to men which Paul
said the Apostles went forth as ambassadors from God
to proclaim, beseeching men to be reconciled to God.
All that was wanted was their response.

Men were certainly called on to repent; but to put
repentance or anything else between the sinner and
God is to obscure the Gospel of the Cross; it is to go
back to Old Testament times, to "Law" away from
"Grace." But is not this dangerous? Are we not going
against Righteousness in preaching such a Gospel?
Are we not in danger of fostering Antinomianism? So
Paul's enemies objected to him. But, "nay," said Paul,
"in this way we establish the law"; it is only in those
who are freed from the Law, brought under "Grace,"
delivered from self and inspired by the Spirit of God,
that "the requirement of the Law" can be fulfilled.
The one thing that can most effectually lead men to
repentance, issuing in the new life of the Spirit, and so
in real salvation, is experience of the pardoning love of
God in Christ. Turning to God in acceptance of His
Grace is the essential thing in repentance.

Let some things, however, be here observed:

1. That the Forgiveness and acceptance in Christ
which goes forth through the Cross does not imply the
negation of all the consequences of sin in him who
accepts it. Law works steadily on as well as Love.

But it implies the removal of the worst consequence of sin—separation from God, and the bringing of His Love into our lives so that a new power begins to operate. This new Power, Law will also serve, to the annulling of much that would otherwise have ensued, and to the making of our whole experience, even such consequences of sin as remain, work for our highest good.

2. That men never really make Forgiveness their own unless they do really come to *God*. And God is *Love*: that very Love that is seeking them. To come to God is to come to Holy Love. Otherwise God is but a *name* to us,—three letters forming a word,—and, however confident we may be that we are forgiven and "saved," because we "believe" this or that, we are still ignorant of God. For, says the Apostle, "He that loveth not, knoweth not God; for God *is* Love." All that Christ said about the spirit of the forgiven person in relation to his fellow-men and about the need of forgiving if we would be forgiven, remains wholly true. But this love is not the *condition* of Forgiveness, but its result, as Jesus taught in the house of Simon the Pharisee: "to whom little is forgiven, the same loveth little," implying that to whom much is forgiven the same loves much, as in the case of the woman before them. Now, what will bring men to this love if it be not that manifestation and proclamation of the freely forgiving love of God in harmony with His righteousness that comes to us through the Cross of Christ? Love kindles answering love; Holy Love quickens like Holy

Love.   It is in this way that the Love that God *is* gets into our hearts and becomes the principle of our lives. It is thus that the Gospel of Reconciliation in Christ becomes the really saving power.   It is thus that, as Paul said, the Law as requiring righteousness is established.

3. The real evil from which we need to be saved is *self*—mere self-dependence, self-love, and self-serving. It is *self,* cherished in its separateness, that is the great enemy of God in man.   We are excluded from the Eternal Kingdom, not merely because "guilt" rests on us, but because we are *sinful*—because *self* is the life-principle instead of God.   God must take the place of self in our hearts if we are to be truly *saved.*   The Gospel is designed to effect this.   But if our forgiveness and acceptance be made dependent on anything what-ever in ourselves,—repentance, or faith, or anything else, —the very purpose of the Gospel is defeated; *self* is still the ground of our confidence; self still lives and, whatever we may believe, we are *not* truly saved. "Believing" is not the *condition* of forgiveness, but is simply the means of apprehending it; and, while re-pentance, in the sense of turning to God, is, of course, always implied, it is not because of our repentance that we are forgiven.   Experience of the Divine Love will work in us a continual ever deepening repentance.

4. It is *in Christ* that God comes to us in His reconciling Love; it is in Christ that we meet with God.   The Gospel is that of God's free forgiveness,

but it is thus that it comes to us. It was in Christ that God came to men in "the days of His flesh," and it is in Christ in His Cross and risen life that God comes to us now. As Paul says, God was *in Christ* reconciling the world to Himself, and "the free gift" is "unto all them that believe," or "who are of the faith of Christ." Therefore Christ also called for faith in, and the reception of Himself. All is centred in Christ and comes through Him. It is in accepting Christ as that which He has been "made unto us of God"—righteousness (acceptance, justifying righteousness, a right relationship to God), and "Sanctification" (Holiness), and Redemption (deliverance from death and from all real evils)—that we enter into the Gospel Reconciliation.

But this is no *condition* laid down of acceptance. Christ is the channel through which the Grace of God comes to us, and He is "freely offered unto us in the Gospel." God does not say, "*If* ye accept Christ I will forgive you," but "*In* accepting Christ, ye enter into My reconciliation, and so into the state of salvation." We show that we *do* enter into the Reconciliation by this acceptance of Him in whom God appears reconciling the world to Himself. Entering into God's Reconciliation must *mean* something to us; otherwise it would be a mere empty phrase. And this is what it means, the acceptance of Christ as our Saviour and Lord. But the whole provisions of the Gospel are in Christ absolutely and unconditionally free. It is with the word of Forgiveness that Christ comes to us.   Like rebels in a distant land, to whom their Sovereign sends His Son as His representative with a message of peace, or proclamation of an amnesty ; or children to whom a father sends an elder brother,—we show that we become reconciled, loyal subjects of our Sovereign, or obedient children of our Father by receiving His Son as He sends Him to us.

5. While the Gospel comes proclaiming the free Divine Forgiveness and acceptance in Christ of all who will receive it, it is not *final salvation* that is thus secured, but *present acceptance with God*, in order that we may become truly His children, and, sharing in the one Divine and Eternal life, be finally saved. Both Christ and Paul always taught that *all* should be ultimately judged according to their works and character.   If we are accepted *in* Christ, the Righteous one, it is in order that " Christ may be formed in us."   By His Spirit in us He is able to conform us to Himself and "to present us to His Father without reproach, if we continue in the faith of the Gospel."   There is thus no opening for Antinomianism in the Gospel.

Has this rich, free, unconditional Gospel of God's Love been widely and faithfully preached in the world?   Has the unrestricted "message of reconciliation" in which God is "beseeching" or "entreating" sinful men to be reconciled to Himself, "not imputing their trespasses unto them," with no "ifs," but just the one word "Come," been proclaimed as Paul went forth proclaim-

ing it? Have men in their indifference and sin been
made to feel that the God whom they ignore and
oppose is a God who loves and forgives them like this,
and who is pleading with them to be friends? Has
not the Gospel of Reconciliation been often so hedged
round with restrictions, supposed safeguards, conditions,
and theological explanations, that its power has been
largely lost? And is not this the reason of the
comparative failure of the Church to present a more
Christ-like appearance and to bring the world to
God?

Here and there throughout the Christian centuries
there have been those who have apprehended and
preached with effect this Gospel. To its *practical*
preaching all true spiritual *revivals* have been due.
In some of the more recent books on the Cross we
observe a movement towards it. But too often the
old spirit of legalism and the fear of Antinomianism
has kept back the full Gospel proclamation, and some
of our "new theologies" seem to have got away from
it altogether. Men have had a zeal for righteousness
without knowledge. They have failed to see how
really coming to *God*, responding to His advance as
He comes to us in Christ, ensures all they have been
anxious for in the interest of morality. If we would
only believe it, God is "wiser than men," although His
Wisdom should be accounted "foolishness." It is
"Grace, free Grace," that saves the soul. "All is of
God," says Paul, "lest any man should boast." All

must be of God, if He is really to live in us, not constraining, but winning our wills. Christ's first word to the suffering man, "Son, thy sins are forgiven thee," still carries in it the Divine healing power. "He loves much who has much forgiven." It is the forgiveness that kindles the love, not the love that brings the Forgiveness. We repeat this ; for it is just here that we have the real difference between evangelical and non-evangelical.

Thomas Erskine states well the philosophy of it. "The great cause of the disorder and misery which distract the human mind is *aversion* or *indifference to God.* The love of God, the key-stone of the arch, is fallen from its place, and all has in consequence gone to wreck. . . . The only cure for this dreadful and wide-spreading disorder must therefore be something which will replace the key-stone in the arch—something which will re-kindle love towards God by taking away fear and imposing confidence.

"Now, the manifestation of the character of God contained in the gift of Christ is exactly fitted for this purpose. It is not a mere deliverance from penalties. Indeed, the penalties are not cancelled. . . . The forgiveness of the Gospel meets the penalties of the law, not by cancelling them, but by associating them with the purpose of a loving Father to deliver from sin, instead of a purpose of mere retribution. . . . Access into the presence of God is thrown open ; all are invited and urged to come in. He hath loved us and given *Himself* for us. The medicinal virtue of the Gospel—the virtue which heals the disease of the soul, which destroys enmity and enkindles holy love, which does away with the cowardly fear of punishment, and at the same time implants and strengthens the holy fear of sinning,—the medicinal virtue which effects this, lies in the manifestation of that love of God which passes knowledge, that holy love with which God so loved the world as to give His only-begotten Son for it. Love is the great principle developed in the Gospel, which reveals the union of an infinite abhorrence towards sin and an infinite love towards the sinner. This mysterious history is the mighty instrument with which the Spirit of God breaks the power of sin in the heart and establishes holy love and filial confidence."

Since the great foe to man's true life is his self-will and self-dependence, "nothing but a true sense of the absolute unconditional gratuitousness of the Gospel can write the law of God on the heart of man. And yet this doctrine of gratuitousness is opposed as if it were antinomian. The true reason of the opposition is that it opposes the pride of man. Man *therefore* opposes it. There is something very striking in the perverse ingenuity with which man endeavours to dilute the medicinal virtue of the Gospel. He *must* have *self* to lean on, and so when he is obliged to surrender his own works he betakes himself to *his own faith* as his prop. But this is still *self*: and in whatever form it appears, as long as it is the ground of hope it must command the will. . . . *Self*, in fact, is the great antinomian, because it is the great Antichrist: where self acts and tries to establish a claim to the forgiveness of sins, either by faith or works, it incapacitates us for spiritual obedience, by cutting us off from the true source of spiritual life" (*The Unconditional Freeness of the Gospel*, pp. 65, 66).

What the Gospel seeks to effect is the possession of the soul by *God*. It is not a doctrine *about* God that we are invited to believe and receive, but *God Himself* as He comes to us in Christ and His Cross, manifesting a Presence that is always with us, and that seeks to dwell within us as the inspiration of our life. "The living personality of God must," still further to quote from Erskine's now little read book,[1] "if I may use the expression, animate and fill out our systems of Christian doctrine — otherwise they only tend to add a fatal security to the sleep of the soul. They may be subjects of talk to us, as the gods of silver furnished talk to Belshazzar and his lords, until some Providence surprises us, as the handwriting on the wall surprised them, and makes us feel and know what it is to be in the presence of the real God whom we have not

---

[1] Mr. Erskine towards the end of his life was induced to consent to a republication of this Book, having convinced himself that it was in substantial harmony with his later views. A new edition was accordingly published, with a few changes "either dictated by himself or cordially approved of by him" (Edinburgh : David Douglas, 1879).

13

glorified. I feel persuaded that no idea of a power external to us, however mighty, can ever produce the sentiment of creaturely dependence in the heart: there must be the sense of God within us as the root and basis of our being—as the continual supplier of strength for thought and action—as the fountain from which our current runs, or else dries up" (pp. 20, 21). In Paul's doctrine of the Indwelling of God in the Holy Spirit we see how truly the reception of his gospel led to this sense of the indwelling, inspiration, and sanctification of the soul by God.

It cannot be doubted, and it needs to be emphasised, that one of the greatest evils in Christian history from which both the Church and the world have suffered, has been the mere belief in doctrines *about* God, instead of receiving the reconciling God Himself. Because of this, many, while professing to believe in God, have been living in a kind of "practical Atheism." When doctrines are separated from God and His omnipotence —"when they become mere syllogisms or emblazonments, they can take their place under the dark shadow of the Atheism of the heart as well as the syllogisms of any other science."

As we have already seen, it is not Forgiveness merely that the Gospel of Reconciliation brings to men, but what Paul terms "Justification," that is, Acceptance with God in Christ as His children and heirs. This is just entering into our right relation to God and man. In the Gospel, God Himself comes, or rather we should

say, unveils His face to us—for He is always near—
in all the greatness of His love, makes Himself known
within the soul as the Source of our true life and
salvation. We are, Paul teaches, united to Christ, in
Him we are made at one with God. God as He is in
Christ is *in* the man who accepts Christ, and Christ
Himself is in him a real *spiritual*, helping, saving,
and perfecting Power in relation to God and to that
true life and eternal destiny which have been realised
by Christ in our name, and which, through that Spirit
which is at once that of God and of Christ, can be
realised in us all. The human soul is much greater
than most people allow themselves to discover. It is
not only in the image of God, but His Dwelling-place
and Temple. The soul can realise its relation to God
and at the same time to Christ, and can recognise the
presence of Both within itself in the one Holy Spirit,
which at once calls the soul upward and enables it to
ascend.

The Reconciliation is *complete on God's part*. It is
not primarily the reconciliation of man to God, but
God's reconciliation of Himself in His Righteousness
with man in Christ and His Cross—by means of which
He goes forth "reconciling the world unto Himself."
It is the reconciliation of an absolutely righteous God
with a sinful world, because the Divine Righteousness
in its relation to sin has been adequately set forth.
"By whom," says Paul, "we have *received* the reconcilia-

tion." It is as if a Friend whom we have injured comes to us and says, " I forgive you.   Come and be friends." There is nothing whatever lacking on God's side with respect to even the greatest sinner in the world, and there is nothing which he is asked to do but simply *to receive* that which God sends him in Christ, which is really to receive *God Himself* as He thus comes to him for his salvation.

The old Calvinistic Puritans, such as Dr. John Owen, saw clearly that the reconciliation was complete on God's side, and they believed that it must also be complete on man's side.   But they could not help seeing that it was not actually universal on the human side.   Therefore they concluded and argued earnestly that the whole was confined to the *elect*.   But this was a strange conclusion.   Surely a person may be reconciled to his enemy and send him a message of reconciliation which he declines or fails to accept.   To his message of Reconciliation St. Paul adds the warning, " See that ye receive not the grace of God *in vain*." It is always possible to do this.   When it is said that on him who believes not on Christ " the Wrath of God abides," what is meant by " wrath " is not a feeling like human anger or active resentment, but that aspect of the Divine Being by which sin is inevitably punished. God's reconciliation of the world to Himself in Christ means that men may thereby come under the operation of His " Grace " instead of being under the operation of His sin-punishing " wrath."   But if a man refuses to enter into this reconciliation with God, he remains where he stood, under the operation of that "wrath" or judgment-element which belongs essentially to the Righteousness and Love of God, and which makes sin its own punishment.

The universality and unconditionedness of the Gospel is necessary for that *Assurance* of Forgiveness and Acceptance with God which is so essential for the full life of Sonship toward Him. How else can the in-dividual sinner rightly attain to it? For want of perceiving these features of the Gospel many never do attain to it—which is a great loss to themselves and to the world. Do we say that God forgives us if we repent? But how can we be sure that our repent-ance is adequate? Have we done "the works meet for Repentance"? Have we forgiven our brother from the heart? Have we made full restitution to all those whom we have wronged? Is not that impossible? Are there not some to whom, alas! restitution or reparation cannot now be made on our part, however willing we may be to make it? Is it said that Forgive-ness and acceptance are assured to all who believe in Christ? That is true if we take "believing in Christ" as being equivalent to "receiving Christ"—simply, the means of appropriating what God sends us in Christ. But if we make "faith" a *condition*, how can we be sure that we have complied with the condition? If we regard "believing in Christ" in such a light, must we not ask more seriously than is often done, what is meant by it? and whether we have really complied with the requirement? In all this we are away from the Gospel of Reconciliation, back to legalism and separateness and dependence on ourselves: *Self* is in some measure keeping out God.

But "Assurance" is very necessary if we would experience the full power and blessedness of the Gospel Salvation and have God's Love to live in us as it seeks to do. For want of it many are "weak," and our Christianity a much poorer thing than it is meant to be. We have referred to the conviction which the Puritan Calvinists had of their Divine Acceptance on the ground of the completeness of the Divine Reconciliation for the elect. Calvinism made strong and brave (if sometimes stern and narrow) men and women, because it gave them confidence in their acceptance by God. The want of a like confidence is one of the causes of the weaker Christian life of to-day. Our present-day Christianity has other desirable features, but it lacks the old Puritan backbone. But Calvinism had another and darker side to it. It was not every earnest soul who could attain to confidence in his election by God. Many humble, sincere souls could find no sure grounds for that belief in their own case, and therefore their lives were often lives of misery—a constant alternation of believing and doubting, hoping and fearing, trusting and despairing. Some were driven insane by anxiety and uncertainty, and others drowned in a deep gulf of

despair.   But Calvinism was a strange misreading of
the Gospel of the Grace of God.   While there are
various forms of "election" in the Divine economy,
the Augustinian and Calvinistic doctrine of the election
of individuals to eternal salvation was founded on a
gross misunderstanding of the Apostolic teaching.   Calvinists were quite right in believing that they belonged to
the election of God ; where they erred was in supposing
that others were excluded from it.   Paul's doctrine of
election to salvation was the very *opposite* of the restricted Election of Calvinism.   It was the *extension*
of God's election of Israel as His people to the Gentiles,
to the whole wide world, *to all who chose to come into it*
by responding to His Grace in Christ.   What Paul
proclaimed on the basis of the Cross was that God's
election, or choice of a people, was now open to all
men, that it was no longer confined to Israel; that
the eternal purpose, long hidden, had now been
revealed "that the Gentiles are fellow-heirs and fellow-
members of the body, and fellow-partakers of the
promise in Christ Jesus through the Gospel" (Eph. iii.
1–7).   It was *this* that made him so obnoxious, not
only to the bigoted Jews, but also to the judaising
Christians.   This understanding of "Election" as the
extension of the Kingdom of God to all mankind shows
clearly the grounds of confidence for all who will
accept the Divine invitation.   All are invited to enter
it.   The more we think of it, the more clearly will it
appear that there can be no other sure ground of

assurance before God for any one but the proclamation of a *universal and unconditioned Gospel*—the going forth from God to the whole sinful world of a Divine Grace and Love which only needs to be *received* by men—the opening of a world-wide Reconciliation which only waits to be entered on our part. Only thus can I be certain that it is all for *me*.

It may be asked, *How does this Forgiveness come to us?* In one aspect, it does not *come* to us at all. It is always there for us in God who is always with us. When we come to God we come to His Forgiveness. A separate act of Forgiveness is not necessary for each individual. It is a universal Forgiveness which we make our own, "receive" or appropriate for ourselves. In another aspect, it may be said to *come* to us in the same sense as that in which Light comes into a darkened room when the shutters are opened. The Light was always there, and always the same thing. But it was excluded from that room, and now it has entered it. There is now a difference in our relation to it, and a corresponding difference in its relation to us in that room. But there is no change in the Light. The only difference is that we have opened the shutters and let it enter. When the Divine Forgiveness enters the soul it is so real and so truly of God that, just as the physical light entering the room makes itself manifest as light, so God's forgiving Love makes itself felt as such within the soul: "the Love of God is shed abroad" through the Holy Spirit within us, bestowing a "peace with God through the Lord Jesus Christ" which no efforts of man can impart. We have then the *proof* of that which we have believed.

Of course, *in its completeness*, Reconciliation with God —At-one-ment with Him—means unison with God in every aspect of His being and relation to us, and this is not all at once made actual in our experience. It is something to be continually striven after, and may mean much, sometimes painful, surrender of our own will and desires. It is something that we may never feel we have wholly and permanently reached. Our entrance into the Divine Reconciliation does not imply that we shall never sin more, or that we may not need a constant prayer for the forgiveness of sins and shortcomings of the past, or of which we are conscious in the present. On the contrary, the more clearly we see what is sin and what reconciliation with God in its completeness means, the more deeply will we realise the need of asking forgiveness, and the more earnestly will we strive after complete harmony with God. And there are no limits set to our possible attainment, save those that exist within ourselves. But when we respond to His Grace in Christ, we know that we are accepted by God in His forgiving Love; we have "come to *God*"; we are at one with Him in *spirit* and *principle*; and, in the endeavour after a complete acceptance of His providence, a complete surrender of our whole being to His will and service, and a growing likeness to His character, the At-one-ment is becoming ever more and more complete in our experience.

Finally, we remark that it is the unrestricted preaching of such a Gospel that is most likely to win men to God and the new life. When the appeal is made in the name of "the law" it is apt to fall powerless, although a sense of the reality and evil of sin is necessary. Men already know what they ought to do; what is needed is something that will move them and help them to do it. When conditions are laid down—what they must do if they would find Divine acceptance—their hearts are chilled—these are the very things they feel themselves unable to do. In the Life of Dr. Dale we find him remarking in a letter to Dr. Wace, that "Moody in his last visit to Birmingham insisted much on the necessity for repentance, and with far less effect than on his former visit. In 1875 he preached in a manner which produced the sort of effect produced by Luther, and provoked the same kind of criticism. He exulted in the free grace of God. The grace was to lead men to repentance—to a complete change of life. His joy was contagious. Men leapt out of darkness into light and lived a Christian life afterwards. The "do penance" preaching has had no such results. I wrote him about it a few weeks ago. He said in reply that it had set him a-thinking, and he wanted to talk it over with me."

What is wanted is something that will lead to real repentance—the open door, the Father's outstretched

Hand, the kindly appeal to come home for all is forgiven and will be forgotten. This is what is provided by the Gospel rightly understood. It is the drawing nigh of the Holy God and Father to sinful men with the word of Forgiveness on His lips, spoken forth with fulness through that Cross on which He gave up His Son to die for our salvation, in whom we have been made at-one with Himself representatively and can be so actually, if we only will. Away from God, serving other gods, or living as if self were a god, thus, not only injuring ourselves but deepening the misery of a world without God, we are really in the position of " enemies " to God. We are opposing His loving purpose in ourselves and in His world. What is more likely to melt down the opposition of an enemy than to " heap coals of fire "—the fire of Divine Love—" on his head "? This, God comes doing in Christ, if we would only open our eyes to see it. He comes, we say once more, to every sinner, to His greatest enemy, saying, " You wrong yourself and you wrong Me, your Creator ; but I forgive you ; I am reconciled ; I long to have you as My child ; Come ! be reconciled to Me, for your own sake, for My sake, and for the sake of My world." This leads us to speak of the Gospel in its *Social* application.

XII

THE SOCIAL ASPECT OF THE GOSPEL

CHAPTER XII

THE SOCIAL ASPECT OF THE GOSPEL

IT would be a grave omission if we failed to consider the Gospel of Reconciliation in its *social* bearings. The desire and cry of to-day is for a Social Gospel, a Gospel which shall not merely address itself to the individual, but shall bring such influences to bear on Society as shall change its order, so far at least as to make life in its fulness more open to men and women as a whole,—a Gospel that shall perfect the collective life. This is greatly to be desired ; and this the Gospel of Christ is designed to do. It is certainly, as we are often reminded, a *spiritual* Gospel, one which must make its appeal to the individual as a spiritual being, not in view of his material interests ; but this by no means limits its purpose or circumscribes its influence. Its social bearing makes itself manifest from many points of view.

1. The Reconciliation to be effected through Christ is unlimited in its scope. " It was," we read, " the good pleasure of the Father that in Him should all the fulness dwell ; and through Him to reconcile *all things* unto Himself—whether things upon the earth or

things in the heavens." It begins with the individual soul, but it does not end there. Paul teaches that the entire creation shall share in the redemption in Christ. As long as there is anything on the earth out of harmony with the mind and will and Love of God, the Reconciliation on the created side is not complete.

2. It is the reconciliation of God to *man*: it is as a Gospel, not to the individual merely, but to the *race*, to "the World," that it comes to us. Only because it is such can the individual find a Gospel for himself in it. The idea that any one can appropriate that Gospel selfishly, or on any other ground than the fact that he is a human being, is condemned by the very statement of the fact of the Gospel.

3. Reconciliation with *God* means, as we have seen, coming into oneness of spirit with the Love that God is. That is a universal Love in which there is "no respect of persons," the love of a Father to whom all His children are equally dear, whether regarded in their individual or in their collective life. To think that we can be reconciled to God without being brought into oneness with that universal Love which God *is*, is wilfully and inexcusably to deceive ourselves.

4. Again, it is impossible to be reconciled to God without being in the same act reconciled to *man*. God is our Father, but each man is our brother; and the child who thinks that he can be at one with such a

Father as God is without being at the same time at
one with his brothers and sisters in the world, quite
misunderstands that Father's character. Nay more,
it is in man that God is made most manifest to us.
In Society, men should be found living together as
the one great family of God in this world. Therefore
Jesus said that if a man would bring an acceptable
offering to God he must first be "reconciled to his
brother"; and the Apostle asks: "If a man love
not his brother whom he has seen, how can he
love God whom he has not seen?" and he adds,
"This command have we of Him, that he who loves
God, love his brother also." It is a real and loving
Family that the great All-Father seeks to behold on
the earth.

4. We have seen that Humanity is ideally *an
organism* of which Christ is the Head. In every
organism each member has its own place to occupy,
its own function to fulfil, according to what it is fitted
to do. So in the great human organism there is for
each member a place to occupy, a function to fulfil
in obedience to the Head. This implies opportunity
for each to take his proper place and to do his appointed
work in loving union with all the other members of
the social Body.

5. Christ's great mission, for the accomplishment of
which He laid down His life, was the establishment of
the Kingdom of God. That means the reign of God,
the ascendency of His will, the rule of all that is pure

14

and true, just and loving among men in every sphere
and aspect of life. It is impossible that the idea of
the Kingdom can be realised by men and women as
separate individuals merely, thinking that they can
love God in their spirits, while ignoring or indifferent
to the condition of their fellows in their individual or
in their collective life.

6. A *spiritual* Gospel is one which addresses itself
to that spirit in man which is the centre of his personality. If a man's *spirit* be made one of holy love, or
the abode of God in His love, it will inevitably show
itself as a spirit of Love in his conduct in relation to
the whole of life and to all human beings. To say
that a man is converted to *God* whose spirit is not
made loving, or who shows no proof of Love in his
life, is a contradiction in terms. It is the want of this
Love in the practical everyday life that is the only
real argument against Christianity, and it is this, more
than anything else, that keeps the world from being
converted to God. If I am starving, for all that my
Christian brother cares, how can I believe in the *Love*
he tells me of?

To seek the removal of social evils and the perfecting
of the social and collective life is, therefore, essential
if we are to stand in a right relation to the universal
God and Father. But how is this social perfecting
to be reached, except through the response of the
individual members of society to that Divine Love

which seeks to make them at one with itself and with each other ?   The Christian conception of a perfected Society is that of a great organism, each member obeying the Head, and the whole acting harmoniously as animated by the Spirit of Love, in mutual regard and common service.   There can be no power working on Society from without so as to reform and perfect it, save the Divine power of Holy Love operating through the individuals that compose Society, and only as Society as a whole becomes permeated by that Spirit can its perfecting be reached.   What stands in the way is the natural *self-love* that usurps the place of the Divine Love in man.   Until this be changed there can be no permanent social well-being.   Of course, everything that tends to remove injustices and evils and to bring about more just and loving relations amongst men, commands the interest and support of all who belong to Christ.   But it does not follow that any and every scheme which men may deem good must receive the adherence of Christians.   The love that God is is a wise and righteous love which seeks the welfare, not of any particular class as such, but of man as man, which ignores all class distinctions, and has no respect of persons.   If, however, there be any class of men which is placed at a disadvantage in relation to the life which God means all men to live, whether physically, intellectually, or morally and spiritually, it must be the endeavour of those more favourably situated to free that class from its disadvantages and to place all men, as far as may be, on an equal footing of opportunity in relation, not to mere material gain, but to true life. Especially, if there be those who have *no* opportunity at all to live as God means them to live, it seems a bounden duty for Christians to see that it is in some way provided for them—unless we can be *certain* that God never meant them to be here at all. And if some classes have more influence in the making of Society than others, to them the appeal must be made in the name of Christ and of God. But the Christian man knows that there can be no ultimate perfecting of Society, apart from the perfecting in Love of the individual members of Society. No one has shown greater earnestness in the cause of social reform than Count Tolstoy, yet in his Manifesto of *The one thing needful* he says: "Man attains this aim—his own and other men's welfare—only through the inner alteration of himself, by elucidating and strengthening in himself, a rational religious consciousness, and then ordering his own life conformably to this understanding of life. As only burning material can ignite other material, so only the true faith and life of one man, being communicated to other men, can spread and confirm religious truth. And it is only the spreading and confirmation of religious truth which improves the position of men. And therefore the means of deliverance from all those evils from which men suffer lies—however strange it may seem—only in one thing, the inner work of each man upon himself" (with, of course, its influence on other men). This is most true, and it is just the design of the Gospel to lead men to the experience and practice of this true personal life. It is simply the false life instead of the true, the natural self-love, self-seeking, self-pleasing, that keeps alive the evils under which men suffer ; and if these evils are to be removed their cause must be removed, this irreligious self-love must be changed into the real love of God and man. If such love were active in every heart and wisely directed, Society would infallibly become what we in our best moments desire to see and what God means and seeks it to be. Oneness with God means feeling with Him and working with Him to the end that the men and women whom He loves as His children shall become united as His family on the earth. How else can we be true to His Fatherhood, or be really at one with God?

But many are losing faith in the power of the Gospel appeal to the individual. They point to long existing evils, and remind us of how little effect all these appeals seem to have had. They say they are weary of hearing them, and wish to see some more direct action on the existing social order. It cannot be denied that too little attention has been given to the practical working out of the Christian spirit in social life. Mere individualism has too largely prevailed in the name of religion. It was not so in the early days of the Christian Church. Under the pristine influences of the love of God in Christ, a real, practical love to man was quickened and made itself manifest in many ways, to the changing of much that had ruled in social relations. But it must be remembered that Society cannot be changed in a day or in a century, and that, although the spirit of real love to man has filled many individual hearts, it has been often impossible to give complete practical expression to it. If to-day the feeling for social redemption has grown strong, it is due, we believe, to the cumulative influences of Christian feeling which have passed on from age to age and from heart to heart, gathering strength as they have proceeded, till now they are demanding adequate practical expression. It is certainly the duty of all who seek to live in reconciliation with God to promote every wise and just endeavour to bring all the machinery of Society into harmony with the Divine will for man, and so be co-workers with God in His purpose to "reconcile *all things* to Himself." But what many Christians are waiting for to-day is to see some well-considered and feasible plan for the perfecting of social relations. They love their fellows and long to help them, but the way is not yet manifest by which they can effectually help, except by holding forth and seeking themselves to be true to the Christian ideal for the individual. And, after all, this is perhaps the only way by which the social ideal can be reached— by each man and woman, of whatever class, endeavouring in the circumstances in which he or she is placed, and by every available legitimate means, to be thoroughly loyal to the Christian ideal, which is, in other words, obedience to Christ the Head.

We are sometimes told, indeed, that the ideal of the Christian life is impracticable or unrealisable in the arrangements of modern Society. One who writes with intelligence in a daily newspaper says, " Men grow tired of being presented with ideals which cannot by any ingenuity of personal effort be woven into the fabric of daily life. A certain sense of need for consistency compels many men to cease trying what they find impossible, *e.g.*, to translate the dynamic force of religious feeling into the working of the social mechanism of which they are themselves part." We know that this is true, and can sympathise with it. What such men long to see is the social system altered so as to make the Christian life of love possible. But is there not a fallacy—or more than one fallacy—underlying this ? Is it not *the Christian spirit in the individual* that is to bring about those changes, instead of waiting to see them brought about for it ? What else can ever bring them ? The Cross of Christ teaches that the higher life of Love is *never* easy for man rooted in nature-life. It means self-denial, the death of the lower *self* in its initiative and at every step. To make it easy would be to make it something else, until the Spirit of Love becomes universal and the higher nature totally supplants the lower. It meant for Christ Himself *the Cross* in the society which surrounded Him. That Cross is the symbol of Christianity; but if Christ's followers are to shirk the Cross when it comes to them, how can the world or they themselves be saved? It is this shrinking on our part from the Cross in which we glory as we see it borne by Christ, that keeps the world back. Men would gladly be saved through the Cross of Christ, but they refuse it in their own life. They want their life made *easy*. It is for this reason that our Christianity is so uninfluential.

If to act out the Christian law of Love would mean discomfort, or it may be pecuniary loss to some of us, we must take up the Cross that comes to us. We must be willing to be "crucified with Christ," if we would "live together with Him" in real oneness with God and man and with our own higher selves.

It will not do to throw the blame on circumstances or on the machinery of Society. At the same time, much of the social machinery needs to be altered; but we ask again, how is the change to be brought about except by the action of those who are brought into real reconciliation with God and inspired by His Spirit of wise and Holy Love? Apart from such inspiration and action, the case of Society seems hopeless. Only *force* remains, and we all know that "force is no remedy."

The Gospel is here for the very purpose of inspiring men with this spirit. Yet it is all too plainly manifest that Love does *not* rule in the life of even Christian nations. Has the Gospel in this aspect failed then?

or have *we* failed to grasp and preach and illustrate it in all the breadth of its Divine application? One of the two alternatives must be true. What is needed is that God's Gospel of At-one-ment be faithfully and earnestly preached in both its individual and social aspects. Men must be made to feel that over all there is *God*, the Common Father of us all; that the first great thing in order to any real good is to be right with God, one with His will, inspired by His Love, and that it is *this* that God in the Gospel of His forgiving Love pleads with us to become. They must be fearlessly told that they never do come to God unless they come to *Love*; that it is impossible to be reconciled to God unless they are at the same time reconciled to man; that the Love with which we are called on to be at one is a Love that goes out impartially to all human beings (and to all God's creatures) in every aspect of individual and social life; that it not only acts with strict justice towards all, but seeks to "do good to all men as we have opportunity," and will *make* opportunities for service to others. The Gospel comes to make us co-workers with God in making ourselves and the world what God in His love seeks them to be.

We are not here laying down *conditions* of Reconciliation, but simply stating what the God who seeks us to be at one with Himself *is*, what reconciliation with *God* really means when it is thought out. All this may not be clearly defined to the soul that responds to God's gracious call in the Gospel. But it is all implicit in a real response to it, and it will show itself explicitly as the light of the knowledge of God shines upon the heart and the knowledge of duty visits the conscience. Without a continuous and growing response to God as He increasingly makes Himself and His will known to us, we are amongst those "who draw back." The hindrances to such a manifestation in the life are great—the temptations that have to be fought against and mastered, the crosses that we may have to bear if we are to follow Christ in His oneness with God, the sacrifices that we may have to make if we are to show His Spirit. But without sacrifice, not on Christ's part only, but on the part of His representatives and followers, the world can never be brought into oneness with God. Yet what real sacrifices do many of us make? Is it not rather some form of personal gain that not a few of us look for?

It is the *Christian Church* that needs first of all revival by the fuller reception of the Spirit of its Master. The Church has come too greatly to exist for itself, and to seek the support of the world which it is here to convert. It has been afraid of losing status, and has failed to preach the Cross as Christ preached it in both word and deed, and to utter in His name the warnings which He gave against "riches" and engrossment with "the cares of this life"; and now it is beginning to find that "the common people," who "heard Christ gladly," are losing faith in it and in its preaching

as a means of help and salvation from conditions which
they are convinced are not according to the mind and
will of God.   We should ask ourselves seriously, what is
the good of our Churches and Colleges and ecclesiastical
machinery, even of our Gospel preaching, if the God
of Love is not made manifest to men, as dwelling, not
in a distant heaven, but in the hearts of His children,
as living and acting through them in this present everyday world?   Surely, if this be not the case, "the salt
has lost its savour," the lamp which Jesus said should
enlighten the world and by "good deeds glorify the
Father" has ceased to shine.   God can only be seen
as His children manifest Him, and through men only
can He be the Helper and Saviour of men.   Jesus gave
His *life* for the salvation of the world.   He did it,
not that men should find lives of ease or of temporal
gain through His sacrifice, but that "we should
follow in His steps," and, if necessary, with Paul,
"fill up in our own persons whatever is lacking in
Christ's afflictions on behalf of His body the Church,"
and for the accomplishment of His purpose in
the world.   Not without sacrifice can the world be
saved.

If the Gospel has been preached in a manner too
individualistic, and if there are those who say they love
God yet give no evidence of love to their fellow-men
except as "spiritual beings"; if men have been led to
believe that religion can be a purely individualistic
enjoyment,—the Gospel is not to be blamed for this.

The Christian Gospel of Reconciliation is that of God *with the whole world*; it is the Gospel of His love for man as man. And if that Gospel fails to inspire our hearts with love for God and man, then —whatever change and amelioration may be possible—there is no other hope for the world's real salvation.

We have already said that if Christ had been received when He first came, even the nation would have been saved from the awful Judgment that fell upon it through the resort of its Leaders to the arm of flesh against the Roman power. That lesson ought not to be forgotten at the present time. We know how Christ mourned over the beloved city: "O Jerusalem, Jerusalem, how often would I have gathered thy children as a hen gathers her chickens under her wings, but ye would not! Now the things that belong to thy peace are hid from thine eyes, and thy house is left to thee desolate." He loved His people, and longed to save them from the disaster which He foresaw should be their fate if God's gracious visitation in Himself was rejected. They laughed at His warnings. But the doom fell—a doom from which that nation has not yet recovered. Other nations have in like manner suffered in more recent times because the Spirit of Christ, the Spirit of real practical Love, has not ruled in them. To-day, Christ's spiritual Gospel is able to save the world even socially; but if God as He comes to us in His Son be rejected, the old error will be repeated with the old consequences in a new form. The word, through the prophet, comes to us to-day as the call of God : " Look unto *Me* and be saved, all ye ends of the earth ; for beside *Me* there is *no* Saviour."

XIII

THE FINAL QUESTION

CHAPTER XIII

THE FINAL QUESTION

WE trust that from what has been said the relation of the Cross to the Gospel of Reconciliation and Forgiveness will be apparent. But we believe so strongly in the reality of the Divine Forgiveness, and see so many examples of its saving power, that we are anxious that any possible obstacle to its experience may be removed. It has been for the sake of the Gospel, that it may continue to come to us in all its power and freed from elements which hinder or pervert its influence with many, that we have sought to re-state the doctrine of the Cross. We are more anxious that the Gospel should be believed in than to establish any particular theory. If the Cross be regarded so that men see it to be the means by which God comes to them in His reconciling Love, that is the chief concern. The Divine meaning and purpose of the Cross is to bring us to God, so that His Love may displace self-love in the heart and bring God Himself in His Holy Spirit to live in us and act through us. Whatever has that effect is truest for *us*. In preaching the Gospel a detailed theory of the Cross is not necessary. It is sufficient if it be shown to be that great sacrifice in

15

which both the righteousness and the love of God were supremely manifested—the completion of Christ's great life-work of the at-one-ment of God and man, and the inspiration to our own true life in the Spirit of Christ.

We can still use the old phraseology, although in clearer light and with deepened meaning. When the first Christians said that Jesus "died for our sins" or "bore our sins," they spoke in the language of sacrifice, and meant that Jesus died in order that God's Forgiveness might be theirs. They saw God's love in His gift of His Son as a sacrifice for their sins. *We* can see now, that while Jesus truly died on account of our sins, and bore our sins, no sacrifice was required in order to forgiveness, but that God's giving up His Son to die for us was the supreme proof of His forgiving love. When Paul said that it was to demonstrate God's righteousness in view of His passing over sin that Christ died, he had primarily in view the doom of sin under "the Law." *We* can see that there was no externally given Law that had any such claim on God as required to be met by the death of His Son. But we can also see that God's righteousness in relation to sin was demonstrated, both by Christ's representative death to sin, and by His being given up to suffer the worst consequences of sin, as these come on man through the Divine punitive righteousness which makes sin its own punishment till it shows itself destructive of the true humanity. And we can believe that such a manifestation of the evil of sin and of God's righteous judgment on it was necessary in order that, while He

was forgiving sin, His righteousness should be manifested and men saved from the sin which has such
consequences. It was thus that Christ "died for our
sins," and that God was in Christ reconciling the world
to Himself, that, His righteousness being thus once for
all set forth, the Forgiveness already in His heart might
go forth to the world so as to save it. The Cross was
thus at the same time the supreme manifestation of the
Love of God and of His own suffering through sin.
It was through His Cross that Christ's Gospel of the
Heavenly Father's love received its complete and final
expression.

It is with the *Gospel* that the Church, as carrying on
the "ministry of Reconciliation," should be *primarily*
concerned ; and only with other matters as these bear
directly on the Gospel and its work individually and
socially. Although deeper questions lie behind it, the
Gospel is in itself a very simple thing, and it has proved
its reality in the experience of men. It is something
that stands out clearly, so that it can be seen and
believed by all on the ground of its proved efficacy as
God's remedy for sin and the means by which His
purpose in man's life can be realised. Nothing can
shake that which has so entered as a power of God
into human experience. But we do not breathe the
same intellectual atmosphere as even our fathers did.
Our most pressing duty at the present time is to remove
all that may tend to obscure the truth of the Gospel,
and to present it so that it shall appeal to the intelligence of to-day. If it be widely and heartily believed

at home, it will not only do its own work amongst ourselves, but it will be speedily sent abroad for the salvation of the world. When we have more real belief ourselves, the Mission field will find a more complete and a more spontaneous support.

But at a time when everything is questioned, there are doubtless those who are not only unable to believe any particular doctrine of the Cross, but who will ask themselves—and, indeed, it is a question we should all ask—*How can we be sure that there is a Gospel at all?* How can we know that God is that God of pardoning and saving love which the Gospel of Christ declares Him to be? To say that Jesus declared it will not be deemed sufficient: it will be asked—"How did Jesus know?"

1. Let us say then, in the first place, that it is an error to which Scripture gives no support to suppose that the Divine Forgiveness is *grounded* on the Cross. The Divine Forgiveness goes forth to men, not because of the Cross; on the contrary, the Cross came to Christ *because God was forgiving men.* Instead of Forgiveness being grounded on the Cross, the Cross is grounded on the forgiving love of God.

Christ, we have seen, came preaching "the Gospel of God." The Gospel that goes forth through His Cross is not a *different* Gospel, but is that same Gospel, with its full Divine attestation and in the completeness of its power. The idea that the Gospel that Paul preached was an entirely new Gospel, different from that which Jesus preached, has misled many. Jesus preached "the Gospel of the Kingdom of God," and so did Paul. To both Jesus and Paul it was a *spiritual* Kingdom. To Paul it came in power through the Cross, as Jesus believed and said it should do. It was, Paul said, "righteousness and peace and joy in the Holy Spirit," made ours through faith in Christ. Both Jesus and Paul sought to make men members of God's Kingdom, both called them to sonship. Jesus sought faith in Himself as He presented Himself to men : it was "their faith that saved them." Paul also preached "salvation" through faith in Christ as Christ had been finally presented to men. In Christ's earthly lifetime, faith in Him made men partakers in the healing power of God that manifested itself in Him, and, according to Paul's teaching, it was also faith in Christ that made men partakers in God's saving Grace. Both preached salvation through faith in the Son of God ; only, Paul asked for faith in the completed manifestation of God in Christ. And, we repeat, that the result, in the case of both,—although, of necessity, because of the completed Gospel, more widely in Paul's case,—was to make men the true sons of God and members of His spiritual and eternal Kingdom.

2. We need to remember *what* the Divine Forgiveness is. We have already said it is not the annulling of all the consequences of sin, but our restoration to the consciousness of the forgiving love of God, whereby new saving influences are set a-working within the soul. It is sometimes said that there is no forgiveness in Nature ; but even in Nature there is certainly

restorative action : and when we come to *God* we have
come to that which is much higher than Nature, to One
whose Spirit can work in us mightily to our entire
spiritual recovery and upbuilding in our true life before
Him.   The Forgiveness is *here,* in God Himself, in a
Divine forgiving Love that goes forth to all the world.
We do not have to *wait* till it comes to us, but only
to receive God into our hearts as He has come to us
in Christ.

3. To find an answer to the question, How does
there come to be a Gospel of Forgiveness at all? or
How are we warranted in our belief in it? we must
bear in mind *how we know anything* about God's
character at all.   Man's knowledge of God has been
of a very slow and gradual growth.   We only know
what God is by means of His self-revelation in Nature
and man ; in the moral order ; in the experience of
those who have believed in Him, looked to Him, trusted
in Him, and sought to live truly before Him ; above all
in life wholly devoted to Him.   The supreme record of
such revelation we have in the Bible, especially in the
writings of the Prophets and Psalmists of Israel, culminating in Christ and His Apostles.   The view of
those early prophets was no doubt limited, but experience showed it to be true as far as it went.   Their
ideas were germinal ones, capable of an indefinite ex-
pansion, as they themselves were confident should yet
be made manifest.

The conviction of the reality of the Gospel came to
men in the first Christian age—came, so far as human

channels were concerned, to Christ Himself—mainly in connection with the teaching of those Hebrew prophets, and specially, as arising out of their confidence in that fuller manifestation of God in His Grace which should be given by the coming of the Messiah : " A Redeemer shall come to Zion, and to them that turn from transgression in Jacob, saith the Lord " (Isa. lix. 20). A Day of Divine acceptance was to dawn upon them (Isa. lxi. 1, etc.). " Behold the days come, saith the Lord, that I will make a new Covenant with the house of Israel . . . for I will forgive their iniquity, and their sin will I remember no more " (Jer. xxxi. 31–37). " I will sprinkle clean water upon you, and ye shall be clean . . . I do this, not for your sakes, O house of Israel, but for Mine own holy name. . . . Then shall ye remember your evil ways, and your doings that were not good, and ye shall loathe yourselves in your own sight for your doings that were not good " (Ezek. xxxvi. 25–33, etc. etc.). Such were some of the prophetic assurances which led to the expectation of the coming of God in His grace to the nation.

Jesus was confident that God was thus actually near His people, if they would only open their hearts to Him. " This day," He said, " is the Scripture fulfilled in your ears." If we ask how He came to have this confidence, the true answer is, we believe, that it was implied in that very conception of God as the Heavenly Father which He entertained as His deepest conviction—which, indeed, God *must be* as the sole Source of our being. This was what made Him the true Christ. He felt

Himself called to proclaim the Gospel of the nearness
of God in His Fatherly love, inspired, even constrained
to it.   And He felt Himself endowed and fitted for His
mission.   He had such a knowledge of God, such indwelling of and union with the Divine, such a confidence in the Divine love and in the nearness and
gracious relationship of God to men, such experience
of Sonship in His own Soul, that He went forth preaching with confidence, telling the people to wait no longer
for signs and visitations from heaven, but to turn to the
God who was near them *now* in His Forgiving Love,
and who had sent Him to declare this to them : " The
time is fulfilled," He cried, " the acceptable year of the
Lord has come; turn to God and believe the glad
tidings which I bring you."   He bade them look no
longer for the setting up of an outward Kingdom : let
them turn inwards, in true purpose of heart, and they
would find God; ";for, lo! the Kingdom of God is
within you."

Although few of them rose to the full conception of
the spirituality of the Kingdom, the first Christians
believed that Jesus was the true Christ, and they therefore believed in His " Gospel of God."   For a moment
the Cross staggered them ; but they came to see it, in
various ways, as the supreme attestation of Christ's
Gospel.   Paul, in particular, interpreted the Kingdom
of God spiritually, and regarded the Cross as that
which brought the Divine Forgiveness to men con-
sistently with the Divine Righteousness, and, therefore,
savingly.

Is this belief in the Messianic forgiveness as proclaimed by Christ a valid foundation for *our* belief in the Divine Forgiveness? Rightly understood, it is. As we have said, we only know God through His gradual revelation, chiefly in man, in history, and in human experience. His *graciousness* was thus made known to Israel, proclaimed by the prophets, and realised in some measure by the nation. The days were to come when it should be revealed in all its fulness. This was done in that human life of Christ which culminated in His acceptance of the Cross for man's salvation. If we believe in God at all, we must believe that He is most truly manifested in a human life of which He is the inspiration, a life devoted to the Highest and Best, wholly responsive to the Spirit of God within. If there be any Divine revelation at all, or any knowledge of God possible, it is here that we shall find them most fully given us. In Christ, in His perfect oneness with the Highest and Best—with God in His Holy Spirit—we have truly "God manifest in the flesh." How could we have Him more truly manifest? The Eternal *Word* which went forth creating is here speaking itself forth in a human form, the highest form in which God can manifest Himself in this human world. God the Creator is thus incarnating Himself, and, in and through that sacrifice which is the expression of the very life of God, is working towards the redemption and perfecting of His creation. His work in Christ is in line with, and is the consummation of, all His previous working in the world. What we behold in Christ is the expression in human form of the otherwise invisible Divinity within and above us all, and which has been striving to find expression *everywhere* in man. Nowhere can we look for a higher or truer knowledge of God: for there is nothing higher than a perfect Righteousness, Truth, and Love. In no way can the ethical character of God be known save as it becomes expressed in a human life obedient to the Highest and Holiest that moves within, and one with the guiding and overruling Divine Will or moral order. It is often said disparagingly that man makes his God in his own image. He cannot do anything else; and if he does not confine himself to his own individuality, but looks to the highest manifestations in humanity, he is in the right way for finding the knowledge of God. For man is the highest work of God on earth, and man in his truth, *i.e.*, in his unity with the Highest, Holiest, and Best that inspires him, is the truest representative and revelation of God to man. Now,

1. Christ's whole life was the expression of the Holy and loving Spirit of God, the proof of His goodwill toward men and of His gracious purpose for them. "He went about doing good, healing all that were oppressed of the Devil," and left a legacy of the highest truth for our guidance and uplifting.

2. His acceptance of the Cross for our sakes was the crowning proof of the Divine Love that moved in Him towards mankind. The very fact that God thus gave up His Son—moved Him to accept and surrendered Him to endure the suffering and death of the Cross

for our salvation—*in whatever way we may explain the Cross*—was surely the clearest evidence of the going forth to men of a Divine forgiving Love. As we have seen, God Himself was not merely outside, but truly suffering with and in His Son. The simple fact of the Cross endured for our salvation is, therefore, the highest and the abiding proof of the forgiving love of God. We do not need to know what precisely was in the mind of God or of Christ as to the necessity for that Cross, in order to believe in the Gospel that goes forth supremely through it. We *know* that, moved by the Divine love, Christ accepted that Cross for our sakes. That should be sufficient for our confident belief in the Gospel of Divine Forgiveness. And, while Paul gave that fuller explanation of the Cross in its relation to Forgiveness (as it appeared to him) which we have had before us, with him also the deepest ground of confidence in the Grace that came to men in Christ was the love of God for sinful men which the Cross manifested. "God," he says, "commendeth His own love towards us, in that, while we were yet sinners, Christ died for us" (Rom. v. 8). "He that spared not His own Son, but delivered Him up for us all, how shall He not also with Him freely give us all things?" (Rom. viii. 32.) "Herein," says John also, "was the love of God manifested in our case, that God sent His only-begotten Son into the world that we might live through Him. Herein is Love, not that we loved God, but that He loved us and sent His Son to be the propitiation for our sins" (1 Ep. iv. 9, 10). All that was done in Christ was due to the love of God, and was the manifestation of that love.

3. That conviction of the consistency of Forgiveness with Righteousness, which must be felt if the guilty conscience is to rest with confidence in the Divine Forgiveness, may also be ours if we remember that it is the Forgiveness of *God* that thus comes to us. We may be sure that God can never be inconsistent with Himself. Even though we do not see *how* it is consistent with Righteousness, we may be sure that it is so, just because it is God's act. We have further evidence of such consistency in the fact that God's forgiving love becomes the means of saving men from sin to Righteousness—the most potent means of doing so.

But, while confidence in God's forgiving love does not *depend* on any theory of the Cross,—and, as a sure matter of fact, it has been enjoyed by many holding quite different theories of it,—if we see how truly Christ was the Head and Representative of our Humanity, we shall be able with Paul to see both the love and the righteousness of God manifested in that voluntary acceptance of the Cross by Christ, in obedience to the will of God and for our salvation, to which the Gospel history bears witness, as we have endeavoured to set it forth. This is the distinctively Christian ground of confidence.

And if we realise what *sin* is before God, how constantly we need the Divine forgiveness, how our higher life requires it as its very atmosphere, how truly sin has its seat in the self-love and self-will of our hearts, and is the fruitful source of individual unhappiness and of social misery, we shall feel how entirely opposed it is to both the righteousness and the love of God, and how necessary it was, if the world was to be awakened to a higher life, if it was to be really reconciled to God and saved from its sinfulness, that such a manifestation of both the Divine Righteousness and Love should be given as was actually made in the Cross of Christ.

Deeper consideration will, we think, show how unable we are to do without the old Pauline Gospel, how truly we need Christ to be "made of God unto us, Wisdom, even Righteousness and Sanctification and Redemption." It will be felt that, without being like the Pharisee of old, whom our Lord pictured praying in the Temple, we cannot claim such a righteousness of our own, or of "the law," as shall make us worthy of "the glory of God"—how truly it is only in Christ that man stands righteous before Him in that complete righteousness of the spirit which alone is true righteousness. Knowing the necessity for that Righteousness in which we are accepted becoming actual, in our experience,—that "without Holiness no man shall see the Lord,"—and being sensible of the evil of our own hearts, we shall despair of our ability to work out that Holiness by our own unaided efforts, we will feel the need of our being *possessed* by a Holier Spirit made our own, so that Christ must also become "Sanctification" unto us. And, finally, although we may not look on physical Death as the wages of sin, we will see it claiming all mankind, and we shall look in vain for any clear evidence of " Redemption " from it, save in the case of Him who is the Christian's living Lord and Head, and who by His Spirit becoming ours is able, according to the analogy of all life, to make us sharers in that Eternal life in God which is *His* life.

But, we repeat, the Gospel of Reconciliation has its Source in that Love of the Eternal Father which lived and moved and manifested itself in the life and death of Jesus Christ as the Son of God in human form. Had not God " so loved the world," and had He not been forgiving men, that Cross would never have been heard of. Jesus might, indeed, have been put to death by His enemies, but that voluntary laying down of His life by the will of the Father for the express purpose of men's spiritual salvation would have been awanting. It is this, in its relation to both God and man, which, while it illuminates and explains all the martydoms of human history, lifts the sacrifice of Christ above them all, and gives it that unique position and Divine power which it has manifested in the past, and which it shall continue to manifest till time shall be no more. And even then shall be sung " the Song of Moses and of the Lamb."

INDEX

Printed by
MORRISON & GIBB LIMITED,
Edinburgh

Charles Scribner's Sons'

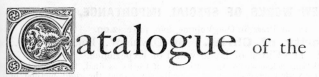 **Catalogue** of the

Publications

of

T. & T. Clark, Edinburgh.

The London SPECTATOR says: 'We may highly commend anything, periodical or other, that comes out from the publishing house of T. & T. CLARK, EDINBURGH.'

MESSRS. CHARLES SCRIBNER'S SONS, SOLE AGENTS IN THE UNITED STATES for the above well-known house, invite the attention of the Trade and the Public to the subjoined List of valuable Books, embracing the widest range of sound and useful Theological and Philosophical Thought and Discussion.

Charles Scribner's Sons,

153, 155, & 157 FIFTH AVENUE, NEW YORK CITY.

LATEST ISSUES.

NEW WORKS OF SPECIAL IMPORTANCE.

In the Press, in One Volume, 8vo, price $2.00.

The Authority of Christ. By DAVID W. FORREST, D.D., Author of 'The Christ of History and of Experience.'

While all Christians acknowledge the authority of Christ as final, there is a wide diversity of opinion with reference to what it really covers and the right method of construing it. The purpose of this book is to inquire as to the sphere in which Christ's authority operates, and as to its character within that sphere.

In the Press, in Two Volumes, post 8vo, price $3.50.

The Knowledge of God. The Gifford Lectures. By Professor H. M. GWATKIN, D.D., Cambridge.

James: The Brother of Our Lord. By Principal W. PATRICK, D.D., Winnipeg. Post 8vo. Nett $3.00

This volume treats the life of James the Lord's brother with the fulness and thoroughness which its importance demands, and thus makes a contribution to the settlement of some of the most difficult problems belonging to the history of the primitive Church.

The New Reformation: Recent Evangelical Movements in the Roman Catholic Church. By Rev. JOHN A. BAIN. Post 8vo.
Nett $1.50

The intensely interesting and important religious movements in Roman Catholic countries at the present time are here described.

Primitive Christian Education. By G. HODGSON, B.A. (T.C.D.), Lecturer on the History of Education, University College, Bristol. Square crown 8vo. Nett $1.50

A work greatly needed by all interested in education; discussing the attitude of the early Christian Church to education.

A Grammar of New Testament Greek. By JAMES HOPE MOULTON, D.Litt. Vol. I. THE PROLEGOMENA. Demy 8vo.
Nett $3.50

No other grammar gives an adequate record of those wonderful discoveries of Greek papyri, which within the last few years have altered the entire basis of the study of New Testament Greek.

The Religion and Philosophy of India. The Upanishads. By Professor P. DEUSSEN, University of Kiel. Translated by Professor A. S. GEDEN, M.A. Demy 8vo. Nett $3.50

The Growth of Christian Faith. By Rev. GEORGE FERRIES, D.D., Cluny. Demy 8vo. Nett $2.50

The Gift of Tongues, and other Essays. By DAWSON WALKER, D.D., Durham University. Post 8vo. Nett $1.50

The Christian Doctrine of the Lord's Supper. By Rev. ROBERT M. ADAMSON, M.A., Ardrossan. Square crown 8vo.
Nett $1.50

'A scholarly, large minded and trustworthy statement of a great religious and Christian theme.'—*Christian World*.

The Religious Doubts of Common Men: The Duty of the Christian Churches to their Members. By a LAYMAN.

THE SCHOLAR AS PREACHER.

These volumes are carefully chosen. They are chosen because their authors
*are scholars as well as preachers, for the suggestiveness of their thought, and
because they are saturated with the most promising ideas of the present day.*

The Eye for Spiritual Things. By H. M. GWATKIN,
D.D., Cambridge. Post 8vo. Nett **$1.50**

Faith and Knowledge. By the Rev. W. R. INGE, D.D.,
Hertford College, Oxford. Second Ed. Post 8vo. Nett **$1.50**

'The volume is one which is likely to be especially helpful to preachers, as
giving them fresh materials for thought.'—*Guardian.*

'The thought is always lucid and well arranged, and the pages hold the interest with ease. The book is a contribution of value to the storehouse of faith.'
—*Watchman.*

Christus in Ecclesia. By the Rev. HASTINGS RASHDALL,
D.C.L., New College, Oxford. Now ready, post 8vo. Nett **$1.50**

'A book which should prove very useful to the inquiring student.'—*Oxford
Review.*

Bread and Salt from the Word of God. In Sixteen
Sermons. By Professor THEODOR ZAHN, University of
Erlangen. Post 8vo. Nett **$1.50**

'We fear that Dr. Zahn's reputation as a scholar is not as widespread in England as it
should be, although the University of Cambridge has conferred upon him an honorary degree.
This is due, no doubt, to our insular backwardness in the acquiring of other languages. . . .
The chief reason why we desire to bring the sermons within the reach of English readers,
is rather that they may see for themselves how exact and profound learning is compatible
with a spirit of childlike reverence and humility, a directness of speech in rebuke of
prevalent ungodliness, an ardour of devotion to Christ as the One Master, and to the leading
of the Holy Spirit, which are thoroughly in accord with the teaching of the Apostles, and of
the Primitive Church.'—From the TRANSLATOR'S Preface.*

BY THE REV. ALFRED PLUMMER, D.D.

'To see what can be done in the way of making the history of the Church attractive reading, to
see what can be done in the way of making the reading of Church History thoroughly profitable,
read these books.'—EXPOSITORY TIMES.

English Church History. From the Death of King Henry VII.
to the Death of Archbishop Parker. Four Lectures by the Rev.
ALFRED PLUMMER, D.D. Crown 8vo. Just Published. Nett **$1.00**

English Church History. From the Death of Archbishop
Parker to the Death of King Charles I. Four Lectures. By the
Rev. ALFRED PLUMMER, D.D., late Master of University College,
Durham. Crown 8vo. Nett **$1.00**

'The treatment is succinct, dispassionate, and fair, the style is clear and strong; and
this volume will form a useful introduction to the study of the period.'—*London
Quarterly Review.*

The Life Everlasting: Studies in the Subject of the Future.
By DAVID PURVES, D.D., Belfast. Crown 8vo. Nett **$1.50**

Prof. MARCUS DODS writes: 'I have read Dr. Purves' "The Life Everlasting" with
great satisfaction, and mean to read it a second time. I think he shows great capacity
for dealing with doctrinal points. At the present time there is considerable interest—
as indeed there always is—in immortality, and I know of no treatment of the subject at
once so full and so compact, so well informed and so temperate, sane and convincing.'

The Creation of Matter; or, Material Elements, Evolution, and
Creation. By Rev. W. PROFEIT, M.A. Second Edition. Crown
8vo. Nett **$1.00**

'A storehouse of information, takes cognisance of the most recent discoveries.
Packed with thought, but there is no obscurity. A timely and able volume.'—*Methodist
Recorder.*

Now ready, in One Volume, demy 8vo, price **$3.00** nett,

Bible Studies. Contributions, chiefly from Papyri and Inscriptions, to the History of the Language, Literature, and Religion of Hellenistic Judaism and Primitive Christianity. By Dr. G. Adolf Deissmann, Professor of Theology in the University of Heidelberg. *Authorised Translation* (incorporating Dr. Deissmann's most recent changes and additions) by Rev. Alex. Grieve, M.A., Ph.D.

Note.—In addition to the supplementary matter specially contributed by the Author, the translation shows considerable alterations in other respects. Not only has the later volume, 'Neue Bibelstudien,' found a place in this edition, but the order of the Articles has, at the Author's request, been completely changed. The Indexes have been combined, and an Index of Scripture Texts has been added. The English translation is therefore virtually a new work.

'In every respect a notable book.' . . . As to its value there can be no hesitation about the verdict. . . . Words, syntax, and ideas can all be tested over again by a completely new apparatus of study, the lexicon of the New Testament can be enriched, the grammar re-written, and the theology re-vivified and humanised.'—Dr. J. Rendel Harris in the *Examiner*.

In One large Volume 8vo, price **$4.00** nett,

Justification and Reconciliation. By Albrecht Ritschl. Edited by H. R. Mackintosh, D.Phil., and A. B. Macaulay, M.A.

'Dr. Mackintosh and his coadjutors have earned the gratitude of all theological students in this country. . . . The present translation meets one of the most urgent wants of the hour. Now the great systematic work of Ritschl is open to all.'—Prof. J. Denney, D.D.

Sixth Edition, Revised throughout, in post 8vo.

The Miracles of Unbelief. By Rev. Frank Ballard, M.A., B.Sc., London. Nett **$1.00**

'Written by an expert in science as well as theology, a fair-minded man who faces religious difficulties, not ignores them, and one who knows how to reason out his case like an accomplished advocate, without pressing it like an unscrupulous one. Mr. Ballard has rendered valuable service to the cause of Christian truth, and given us an excellent and useful book, deserving a large circulation.'—Professor W. T. Davison, in the *Methodist Recorder*.

'It is a perfect mine of quotation for men with little time for study, who are called, as modern ministers are, to be not only visitors and workers but also preachers and teachers.'—*Guardian*.

The Relation of the Apostolic Teaching to the Teaching of Christ. By Rev. Robert J. Drummond, D.D. Edinburgh. Second Edition. 8vo. Nett **$3.50**

'No book of its size has taken such a hold of us for many a day. . . . It is a strong book, the book of a scholar and thinker, fearless, yet reverent, new and yet built on a solid foundation of faith and experience.'—*Expository Times*.

Christian Character. By Professor T. B. Kilpatrick, D.D. Crown 8vo. Nett **$1.00**

Contents :—Part I. The Importance of Character—The Sources of Christian Character—Its Culture : Physical and Mental Powers ; Moral Powers. Part II. Character and Conduct—The Family—The Work of Life—Social Relations—The State—The Church—Concluding Remarks.

'Throughout the exposition is clear and intelligible, and the book is written in an interesting and attractive style. It forms a valuable contribution to the study of Christian Ethics, and should be in the hands of all who have to do with the moulding of character and the guidance of conduct.'—*Methodist Times*.

2

The Christ of History and of Experience. By
DAVID W. FORREST, D.D. 8vo.　　　　　　　Nett $2.00

'The subject has been opened up most admirably in the series of topics which form the subject of the nine chapters. . . . The volume as a whole deserves most serious attention. . . . Many of its discussions, like that of miracles, and the relation of Messiahship and Sonship, are admirable.'—*Biblical World* (Chicago).

The Historical New Testament: Being the Literature of the
New Testament arranged in the order of its Literary Growth and according to the Dates of the Documents. A new Translation, Edited, with Prolegomena, Historical Tables, Critical Notes, and an Appendix, by JAMES MOFFATT, B.D. Second Edition, in One large 8vo Vol.　　　　　　　　　　　　　　　Nett $4.50

In the preparation of the Translation the Author has had the valuable assistance of Professor DENNEY, Dr. H. A. A. KENNEDY, Professor MARCUS DODS, Rev. Canon GREGORY SMITH, Professor WALTER LOCK, and the Rev. LL. M. J. BEBB.

'The most important book on the credentials of Christianity that has appeared in this country for a long time. It is a work of extraordinary learning, labour, and ability.'—*British Weekly*.

The Pauline Epistles. Introductory and Expository Studies.
By R. D. SHAW, D.D., Edinburgh. Second Ed. 8vo. Nett $3.50

'A careful and very valuable study of the writings of the great apostle.'—*Interior*.

'Of all the Introductions to St. Paul's Epistles I have read, this is the best.'—*Methodist Times*.

'A thoroughly good and useful book.'—*Guardian*.

'This book is as genuine a surprise as we have had for many a day. Clearly Dr. Shaw is one of the youngest men of whom the Scottish Churches are so proud—steeped in the literature of the subject he has chosen to write upon, and strong enough to handle it with refreshing candour, and yet concerned always and most entirely to reveal the treasures of wisdom and knowledge which the Pauline Epistles contain.'—*Expository Times*.

Hebrew Ideals from the Story of the Patriarchs. By
the Rev. JAMES STRACHAN, M.A., London.

PART I. GEN. 12 TO 25. Price $.60.　PART II. GEN. 25 TO 50. Price $.60.

　　. *The Two Parts can now be had bound in One Volume.* Nett $1.00.

'This volume is exactly the thing we wanted. It is one of the freshest and most illuminative books on Genesis we have seen. As a mirror of manners and ideals to make life worthy, it is altogether unique. . . . The book is written in delightful English, piquant and crisp, and the surprises of its style make it easy reading.'—*Critical Review*.

A Primer on Teaching. With Special Reference to Sunday
School Work. By JOHN ADAMS, M.A., B.Sc., Professor of Education in the University of London.　　　　　　　Nett 20 cents

CONTENTS:—Child Nature—Ideas—Attention and Interest—Class Management—Use of Language—Method in Teaching—The Socratic Method—Questions and Answers—Illustrations.

'Extremely readable and suggestive, clear as the light.'—*Sunday School Chronicle*.

A Dissertation on the Gospel Commentary of S.
Ephraem the Syrian. With a Scriptural Index to his Works. By J. HAMLYN HILL, D.D. 8vo.　　　　Nett $2.25

The BISHOP of GLOUCESTER and BRISTOL writes: '. . . It is a monument of patient research and intelligent industry, which deserves very hearty recognition.'

The Oldest Code of Laws in the World. The Code of Laws
promulgated by HAMMURABI, King of Babylon, B.C. 2285–2242. Translated by C. H. W. JOHNS, M.A., Lecturer on Assyriology, Queens' College, Cambridge. Crown 8vo.　　　　Nett 75 cents

'A little book but one of great value.'—*Interior*.

Comparative Religion: Its Genesis and Growth. By the Rev. LOUIS H. JORDAN, B.D., late Special Lecturer on Comparative Religion at the University of Chicago. With Introduction by the Rev. Principal FAIRBAIRN, D.D., Oxford. 8vo. Nett $3.50

*** The Volume contains an exceptionally full and carefully prepared Index ; and also several Coloured Charts giving a Comparative View of the present numerical strength, and of the Territorial Distribution, of the Principal Religions.

'A most excellent and painstaking monograph. Clear in argument, full in information.'—Principal A. M. FAIRBAIRN, D.D.

'Comparative Religion is with us now. Of that there is no longer any doubt. This handsome volume is itself the unmistakable evidence. . . . Mr. Jordan has that spark of life which responds to our more popular conception of genius. His enthusiasm carries him from page to page, down through many notes, and even to the end of model Indexes.'—*Expository Times.*

By Nile and Euphrates. A Record of Discovery and Adventure. By H. VALENTINE GEERE. Nett $3.50

'Mr. Geere, a member of the staff of the Babylon expedition sent out by the University of Pennsylvania, gives many interesting pictures of life and work while in the pursuit of archæological finds, describes the people and country of the Euphrates and Tigris, and sketches some of the out-of-the-way places in that unfrequented region.'—*Bulletin of the American Geographical Society.*

'Mr. Geere's volume makes fascinating reading.'—*Pall Mall Gazette.*

The Religions of Ancient Egypt and Babylonia. The Gifford Lectures on the Ancient Egyptian and Babylonian Conception of the Divine. By A. H. SAYCE, M.A., LL.D., Professor of Assyriology, University of Oxford. 8vo. Nett $3.50

'Those who are interested in comparative religion will find this latest work of a distinguished Orientalist most valuable. Sympathetic appreciation and discriminating criticism are in these lectures felicitously joined.'—*New York Outlook.*

'Extremely interesting. . . . One can have no guide in these complex subjects more learned or more considerate to his readers' difficulties than Professor Sayce. He always writes from the amplest knowledge, and he always writes clearly.'—*Spectator.*

The Fatherhood of God in Christian Truth and Life. By the Rev. J. SCOTT LIDGETT, M.A. 8vo. Nett $3.00

This book is an attempt to establish the Fatherhood of God as the determining fact of Christian life and the determining principle of Christian Theology. Among the subjects dealt with are: The New Testament Doctrine of the Fatherhood of God. Place in New Testament Theology. The Relation of the Old Testament Doctrine to the Fatherhood of God. The Doctrine in Church History. Validity and Content. Manifestation.

'The work of a devout and vigorous Christian thinker. It is well planned and arranged, and clear in style and diction, more constructive than critical, more expository than controversial in its method.'—*Interior.*

The Times of Christ. By LEWIS A. MUIRHEAD, D.D. With Map. New and Revised Edition. Crown 8vo. Nett 60 cents

'One of the very best of the handbooks for Bible classes—and that is saying a great deal. There is evidence on almost every page of exact and ample scholarship. Yet Dr. Muirhead is never dry ; his chapters are always luminous and readable. This is certain to prove a most useful text-book.'—*Sunday School Chronicle.*

The Sacraments in the New Testament. By Rev. J. C. LAMBERT, D.D. 8vo. Nett $3.50

'A real contribution. It is the book to which one can turn for a fresh, careful, truthful, lucid interpretation of the Sacraments.'—*Biblical World* (Chicago).

'Will, without doubt, come to be regarded as a classic work upon the Sacraments.'—*Methodist Times.*

Outlines of the Life of Christ. By W. SANDAY, D.D., LL.D., Litt.D., Lady Margaret Professor and Canon of Christ Church, Oxford. Post 8vo. Nett $1.25

Although this book is, in the main, a reprint of Dr. Sanday's well-known article, 'Jesus Christ,' in Dr. Hastings' Bible Dictionary, the Author has worked carefully over the material, and has broken up the text into Chapters and Sections. An important new Map of Palestine is added.

'The most unconventional and illuminating of all extant works of the kind. We recommend this issue to our readers as the best modern work on the life of our Lord.'—*Methodist Times.*

The Spirit and the Incarnation. In the Light of Scripture, Science, and Practical Need. By the Rev. W. L. WALKER. Second Edition, Revised and Re-set. Demy 8vo. Nett $3.00

In a leading article, headed '**A GREAT BOOK**,' in the *British Weekly*, Professor MARCUS DODS writes : 'It may be questioned whether in recent years there has appeared, at home or abroad, any theological work more deserving of careful study. He who intelligently reads it once will inevitably read it again and again.'

The Cross and the Kingdom, as Viewed by Christ Himself and in the Light of Evolution. By the Rev. W. L. WALKER, Author of 'The Spirit and the Incarnation.' 8vo. Nett $3.00

This book is intended as a defence and restatement of the Evangelical doctrine of the Cross based on the teaching of Christ in the first three Gospels, and on His work as the Founder of the Kingdom of God.

'We desire to speak with admiration of the good work done in this book. It is worthy to stand beside his former treatise. Taking both together, they form a magnificent contribution to the theological literature of the age.'—Professor IVERACH in the *Expository Times.*

The Ritschlian Theology. Critical and Constructive : An Exposition and an Estimate. By the Rev. A. E. GARVIE, M.A. (Oxon.). 8vo. Nett $3.00

'Mr. Garvie's grasp of the subject is unsurpassed. . . . Nothing could be clearer or, indeed, more fascinating in theological writing than this.'—*Expository Times.*

'Ritschlian literature is permanently enriched by this publication.'—*British Weekly.*

'The weightiest, warmest, and fairest work in English on its subject.'—Dr. P. T. FORSYTH in the *Speaker.*

The Trial of Jesus Christ : A Legal Monograph. With Two Illustrations. By A. TAYLOR INNES, Advocate. Post 8vo.
Nett $1.00

This twofold transaction, the most famous occasion on which two great systems of law, the Hebrew and the Roman, crossed each other, is described as thus presenting ' probably the most interesting isolated problem in historical jurisprudence.'

'Mr. Innes gives what to most of his readers will be wholly new light and fresh thoughts . . . This volume is a striking example of the value of the critical examination of historical problems by an accomplished lawyer.'—*Times.*

The Theology of the Epistle to the Hebrews. With a Critical Introduction. By Rev. GEORGE MILLIGAN, B.D. In post 8vo. Nett $2.00

' Any book with the name of Milligan upon it is sure of a ready welcome. . . . We can unreservedly recommend this volume as a sensible as well as a fertilising study of the outward features, but especially the inner thought, of this great Epistle.'—*Expository Times.*

The Christian Salvation. Lectures on the Work of Christ : Its Appropriation and its Issues. By Prof. J. S. CANDLISH, D.D. Demy 8vo. Nett $2.25

'They deal with five great subjects : the Work of Christ, the Doctrine of the Church, the New Life, the Sacraments, and Eschatology. In each case we have a treatise on the subject, lucid, connected, and fairly complete.'—*Expository Times,*

The World's Epoch=Makers.

EDITED BY OLIPHANT SMEATON, M.A.

NEW SERIES. IN NEAT CROWN 8VO VOLUMES. PRICE $1.25 EACH.

'An excellent series of biographical studies.'—*Athenæum.*

'We advise our readers to keep a watch on this most able series. It promises to be a distinct success. The volumes before us are the most satisfactory books of the sort we have ever read.'—*Methodist Times.*

The following Volumes have now been issued :—

Buddha and Buddhism. By ARTHUR LILLIE.

Luther and the German Reformation. By Principal T. M. LINDSAY, D.D.

Wesley and Methodism. By F. J. SNELL, M.A.

Cranmer and the English Reformation. By A. D. INNES, M.A.

William Herschel and his Work. By JAMES SIME, M.A.

Francis and Dominic. By Professor J. HERKLESS, D.D.

Savonarola. By G. M'HARDY, D.D.

Anselm and his Work. By Rev. A. C. WELCH, B.D.

Origen and Greek Patristic Theology. By Rev. W. FAIRWEATHER, M.A.

Muhammad and his Power. By P. DE LACY JOHNSTONE, M.A. (Oxon.).

The Medici and the Italian Renaissance. By OLIPHANT SMEATON, M.A., Edinburgh.

Plato. By Professor D. G. RITCHIE, M.A., LL.D., University of St. Andrews.

Pascal and the Port Royalists. By Professor W. CLARK, LL.D., D.C.L., Trinity College, Toronto.

Euclid. By Emeritus Professor THOMAS SMITH, D.D., LL.D.

Hegel and Hegelianism. By Professor R. MACKINTOSH, D.D., Lancashire Independent College, Manchester.

Hume and his Influence on Philosophy and Theology. By Professor J. ORR, D.D., Glasgow.

Rousseau and Naturalism in Life and Thought. By Professor W. H. HUDSON, M.A.

Descartes, Spinoza, and the New Philosophy. By Principal J. IVERACH, D.D., Aberdeen.

Socrates. By Rev. J. T. FORBES, M.A., Glasgow.

The following have also been arranged for :—

Marcus Aurelius and the Later Stoics. By F. W. BUSSELL, D.D., Vice-Principal of Brasenose College, Oxford. [*In the Press.*

Augustine and Latin Patristic Theology. By Professor B. B. WARFIELD, D.D., Princeton.

Scotus Erigena and his Epoch. By Professor R. LATTA, Ph.D., D.Sc., University of Aberdeen.

Wyclif and the Lollards. By Rev. J. C. CARRICK, B.D.

The Two Bacons and Experimental Science. By Rev. W. J. COUPER, M.A.

Lessing and the New Humanism. By Rev. A. P. DAVIDSON, M.A.

Kant and his Philosophical Revolution. By Professor R. M. WENLEY, D.Sc., Ph.D., University of Michigan.

Schleiermacher and the Rejuvenescence of Theology. By Professor A. MARTIN, D.D., New College, Edinburgh.

Newman and his Influence. By C. SAROLEA, Ph.D., Litt. Doc., University of Edinburgh.

The Note-Line in the Hebrew Scriptures. Commonly
called Pāsēq or Pĕsîq. By James Kennedy, D.D., New College,
Edinburgh.   Post 8vo.   Nett $1.75

*This treatise is the result of a special inquiry, subsidiary to more extensive research into the
Hebrew text of the Old Testament. Careful examination led to the conclusion that the line must
have been purposely placed beside remarkable readings in the Hebrew Bible. A survey has been
made of the entire Scriptures, and the conclusions are now placed before students of the Old
Testament as a contribution towards a better understanding of certain phenomena presented in
the Massoretic texts.*

'Dr. Kennedy, with a delightful avoidance of pedantry, has given an example of the
patient, careful, unobtrusive work of which so much must be done before the text of the
Old Testament can be satisfactorily restored. If, as seems probable, the "Note-line"
does frequently indicate error, it will be a valuable guide to the textual critic.'—*Church
Quarterly Review.*

The Gospel according to St. John : An Inquiry into its
Genesis and Historical Value.   By Professor H. H. Wendt, D.D.,
Author of 'The Teaching of Jesus.'   Demy 8vo.   Nett $2.50

'A searching and discriminative criticism.'—*Speaker.*
'An important contribution to the study of the problems of the Fourth Gospel.'—
Critical Review.

A Short History of the Westminster Assembly.   By the
Rev. W. Beveridge, M.A., of New Deer.   Crown 8vo.   Nett $1.00

*The Author has worked up this History from original documents, and has had it in preparation
for several years. In view of the present crisis of the Churches in Scotland, the book will be found
of special interest, as the Author, more particularly in the chapters on the Westminster 'Confession,' has had before him the decision of the House of Lords in the Free Church Appeal Case.
Mr. Beveridge is well known as an authority upon the subject of his book.*

'A volume full of valuable information and casting much light on the far-reaching
questions at present occupying the mind of the Scottish people.'—*Critical Review.*

Apostolic Order and Unity.   By Robert Bruce, M.A., D.D.,
Hon. Canon, Durham.   Crown 8vo.   Nett $1.00

'As Christian in tone as it is scholarly in its treatment of the subject.'—*Examiner.*

The Testament of Our Lord.   Translated into English from
the Syriac, with Introduction and Notes, by James Cooper, D.D.
Professor of Ecclesiastical History in Glasgow University ; and
the Right Rev. A. J. Maclean, D.D., Bishop of Moray and Ross.
8vo.   Nett $3.00

'Excellently conceived and well executed, and the information given is unique in its
way.'—*Living Church.*
'In making the work known, the Editor has done considerable service to the study
both of ecclesiastical history and of liturgy. It is a real service, which deserves the
gratitude of scholars.'—*Guardian.*
The *Testament* possesses the special interest of being the production of the very
period when the great transition in the Church's fortunes, from Imperial persecution to
Imperial favour, was leading to the inevitable transformation of her buildings and her
services to suit her altered circumstances. . . . The *Testament* reflects this state of
things as a mirror. It vibrates, moreover, with the pulsation of the great controversies
through which the Church was passing. The volume is thus far more than a mere
antiquarian curiosity. It had a message to its own time ; it has a message to all time,
and very distinctly to the time now present. The *Testament* is also a veritable mine at
once of devotional expression and liturgical lore.

The Pentateuch in the Light of To-day. Being a simple Introduction to the Pentateuch on the Lines of the Higher Criticism. By ALFRED HOLBORN, M.A. Second Edition. Crown 8vo.
Nett 75 cents

'Eminently serviceable for a reconstruction of traditional views upon the only ground now tenable for faith in a divine revelation to ancient Israel.'—*Outlook.*

The Words of Jesus. Considered in the Light of Post-Biblical Jewish Writings and the Aramaic Language. By Professor G. DALMAN, Leipzig. *Authorised English Translation* by Professor D. M. Kay, St. Andrews. Post 8vo.
Nett $2.50

'A very exhaustive study, and deserves attention as an example of searching method and cautious scholarship.'—*Living Church.*
'The most critical and scientific examination of the leading conceptions of the Gospels that has yet appeared.'—Prof. W. SANDAY, LL.D.
'He who does not know that Dalman is necessary, does not know much yet about the study of the New Testament in Greek.'—*Expository Times.*
'Absolutely indispensable to the understanding of the New Testament.'—*British Weekly.*

Selections from the Literature of Theism. Some Principal Types of Religious Thought. With Introductory and Explanatory Notes. By Prof. ALFRED CALDECOTT, M.A., D.D., King's College, London, and Prof. H. R. MACKINTOSH, M.A., D.Phil., Edinburgh. Post 8vo.
Nett $2.50

This volume has been prepared with the aim of bringing together within a small compass some of the leading positions in the philosophy of religion. It is agreed on all hands, in our day, that no one, except here and there an original genius, can expect to be in line with twentieth-century thought who dispenses himself from reference to the positions held by great minds. It is by training his mind in their high thoughts that he can expect to win power and insight for himself.

'Will meet a very wide felt want by bringing within the reach of ordinary book-buyers full summaries of the treatises of the great leaders of thought who have written upon Theism.'—*Bibliotheca Sacra.*
'Who would ever have expected so beautiful and delightful a book with such an unpretending and commonplace title? . . . Those are the passages which make Descartes, Spinoza, Martineau, Janet live; and those passages, interpreted as they are interpreted here, make the study of the doctrine of God, even in its philosophical side, alive and practical for all men.'—*Expository Times.*

St. Paul and the Roman Law, and other Studies on the Origin of the Form of Doctrine. By W. E. BALL, LL.D. Post 8vo.
Nett $1.50

'Reverent and acute. . . . We have said perhaps enough to show how varied and vital are the subjects of interest touched on in Dr. Ball's essays.'—*Churchman.*
'Dr. Ball has two rare gifts. He is a discoverer and a writer. . . . Every discovery is made known by the same unconscious skill—the touch of nature.'—*Expository Times.*

The Religious Controversies of Scotland. By Rev. HENRY F. HENDERSON, M.A., Dundee. Post 8vo.
Nett $1.75

CONTENTS:—Prof. Simson's *Affair*—The Marrow Men—Hume's *Essay on Miracles*—The Playhouse Battle—An Ayrshire *New Light*—The Apocrypha Controversy—Edward Irving—The *Row Heresy*—The Rise of Morisonianism—The *Scotch Sermons*—Robertson Smith and the Higher Criticism—The *Dods-Bruce Case.*

This volume forms the first of a Series entitled 'Religion in Literature and Life.'

'We can remember no book devoted to the topic which Mr. Henderson handles with such ease and power. It has been read by us with genuine enjoyment and appreciation.'—Principal PATRICK, D.D.

New Testament Theology; or, Historical Account of the Teaching of Jesus and of Primitive Christianity according to the New Testament Sources. By Professor WILLIBALD BEYSCHLAG, Halle. Authorised Translation. Two Vols. 8vo. Nett $6.00

'Dr. Beyschlag has achieved so large a measure of success as to have furnished one of the best guides to an understanding of the New Testament. . . . These pages teem with suggestions.'—*Methodist Recorder.*

The Teaching of Jesus. By Professor HANS HINRICH WENDT, D.D., Jena. Authorised Translation. Two Vols. 8vo. Nett $5.00

'An admirable translation of the greatest systematic study of the teachings of Jesus thus far produced in Germany.'—*Biblical World* (Chicago).

'No greater contribution to the study of biblical theology has been made in our time. A brilliant and satisfactory exposition of the teaching of Jesus.'—Prof. J. IVERACH, D.D., in the *Expositor.*

Dr. R. F. HORTON refers to Beyschlag's 'New Testament Theology' and Wendt's 'Teaching of Jesus' as 'two invaluable books.'

Old Testament Theology. The Religion of Revelation in its Pre-Christian Stage of Development. By Professor HERMANN SCHULTZ, D.D., Göttingen. Authorised English Translation by Professor J. A. PATERSON, D.D. Two Vols. 8vo. Second Edition.
Nett $6.00

'A standard work on this subject may be said to be indispensable to every theologian and minister. The book to get, beyond all doubt, is this one by Schultz, which Messrs. Clark have just given to us in English. It is one of the most interesting and readable books we have had in our hands for a long time.'—Professor A. B. BRUCE, D.D.

The Truth of the Christian Religion. By Prof. KAFTAN, Berlin. Authorised Translation. With Prefatory Note by Professor FLINT, D.D. Two Vols. 8vo. Nett $5.00

'Quite apart from the immediate question of obtaining a knowledge of the Ritschlian theology at first hand, these volumes are welcome. For Kaftan is no imitator, but a fertile and able writer. In the near future his view of theology, its essence and its accidents, will exercise a deep influence in our land.'—*Expository Times.*

History of the Jewish People in the Time of Our Lord. By Prof. EMIL SCHÜRER, D.D., Göttingen. Complete in Five Vols., with exhaustive Index. 8vo. Nett $8.00

'This monumental work by Schürer has made all other histories almost superfluous. In no other account of the period is there to be found such wealth of learning and such admirable arrangement of material.'—*Biblical World* (Chicago).

'Recognised as the standard authority on the subject.'—*Critical Review.*

'Every English commentary has for some years contained references to "Schürer" as the great authority upon such matters. . . . There is no guide to these intricate and difficult times which even approaches him.'—*Record.*

The Ethics of the Old Testament. By W. S. BRUCE, D.D. Crown 8vo. Nett $1.25

'An excellent work. . . . I have found it most interesting and instructive. I hope that the book may have the success which it well deserves.'—Prof. R. FLINT, D.D., LL.D.

The Formation of Christian Character: A Contribution to Individual Christian Ethics. By W. S. BRUCE, D.D. Crown 8vo. Nett $1.50

'A book which combines with a scholarly grasp of the subject a popular gift of interpretation.'—*Examiner.*

'Altogether, this is a spiritually instructive, suggestive, and refreshing book. Ministers of the gospel will find the volume extremely helpful in the presentation of gospel truth in its ethical issues.'—*Interior.*

Lexicon Syriacum. Auctore CAROLO BROCKELMANN. Præfatus est TH. NÖLDEKE. In handsome Roxburghe binding. Nett $10.50

'The appearance of a new Syriac Lexicon, designed to meet the wants of students, is an event of considerable importance for the progress of Semitic studies at home and abroad. The work will be welcomed on all hands as fulfilling what has long been the most conspicuous *lacuna* in Semitic bibliography. . . . The publishers have earned, and will certainly receive, the thanks of every Semitic student for thus coming forward to remove what had almost become a scandal to international scholarship, the lack of a student's dictionary of a language so important to the philologist, the historian, and the theologian.'—A. R. S. KENNEDY, D.D. (Professor of Oriental Languages in the University of Edinburgh) in the *Expository Times.*

A Concordance to the Greek Testament. Edited by W. F. MOULTON, D.D. (Editor of the English Edition of *Winer's Grammar*), and Prof. A. S. GEDEN, M.A. In crown 4to (pp. 1040). Nett $7.00

It is generally allowed that such a work is much needed in the interests of sacred scholarship. There exists no concordance whatever to the text of the Greek Testament as exhibited in modern critical editions. . . . The present work is a full and complete concordance to the text of the Greek Testament as it is set forth in the editions of WESTCOTT AND HORT, TISCHENDORF *(8th), and the English Revisers.*

'A Concordance which must displace all others, and which will remain for many a year the trusted companion of the student of the New Testament.'—*Critical Review.*

'I have no hesitation in saying that this work is one of the most important contributions to New Testament study that has been made during the present century. The need of such a work has long been felt by critical students. . . . The typographical execution of the work is beautiful. It will be a boon to all New Testament students, and must supersede all similar works.'—MARVIN R. VINCENT, D.D., Professor of Biblical Literature, Union Theological Seminary, N.Y.

Biblico - Theological Lexicon of New Testament Greek. By Prof. HERMANN CREMER, D.D., Greifswald. Authorised Translation. Demy 4to. Fourth Edition. Nett $8.00

This Lexicon deals with words whose meaning in the Classics is modified or changed in Scripture, words which have become the bases and watchwords of Christian theology, tracing their history in their transference from the Classics into the LXX., and from the LXX. into the New Testament, and the gradual deepening and elevation of their meaning till they reach the fulness of New Testament thought.

'Dr. Cremer's work is highly and deservedly esteemed in Germany. It gives with care and thoroughness a complete history, as far as it goes, of each word and phrase that it deals with. . . . Dr. Cremer's explanations are most lucidly set out.'—*Guardian.*

'It is hardly possible to exaggerate the value of this work to the student of the Greek Testament. . . . The translation is accurate and idiomatic, and the additions to the later edition are considerable and important.'—*Church Bells.*

LOTZE'S MICROCOSMUS.

Microcosmus: Concerning Man and His Relation to the World. By HERMANN LOTZE. Translated from the German. In one large Vol. 8vo (1450 pp.). Nett $5.00

'The English public have now before them the greatest philosophic work produced in Germany by the generation just past. The translation comes at an opportune time, for the circumstances of English thought, just at the present moment, are peculiarly those with which Lotze attempted to deal when he wrote his "Microcosmus" a quarter of a century ago. . . . Few philosophic books of the century are so attractive both in style and matter.'—*Athenæum.*

'These are indeed two masterly volumes, vigorous in intellectual power, and translated with rare ability. . . . This work will doubtless find a place on the shelves of all the foremost thinkers and students of modern times.'—*Evangelical Magazine.*

Pseudepigrapha: An Account of certain Apocryphal Sacred Writings of the Jews and Early Christians. By Rev. W. J. DEANE, M.A. Post 8vo. Nett $2.00

'It is the most complete book on the subject in the English language, and contains the most ample information on these writings. It is indispensable to every scholar who wishes to be acquainted with this class of literature, and should occupy a place in the library of every theologian.'—PATON J. GLOAG, D.D.

Delivery and Development of Christian Doctrine. By
Principal R. RAINY, D.D., New College, Edinburgh. 8vo.

Nett $3.00

'We gladly acknowledge the high excellence and the extensive learning which these lectures display. They are able to the last degree, and the author has, in an unusual measure, the power of acute and brilliant generalisation.'—*Literary Churchman.*

BY THE LATE PROF. A. B. DAVIDSON, D.D., LL.D., EDINBURGH.

*'Whatever subject Prof. Davidson touched, there are always two epithets which may be applied to his treatment of it: it is masterly and it is judicial. No one had a better power of penetrating to the heart of a subject, no one was more skilful in the discovery of characteristics of an age, the drift of an argument, the aim of a writer. . . . His mastery of a subject was almost complete.'—*CANON DRIVER.*

An Introductory Hebrew Grammar, with Progressive
Exercises in Reading and Writing. By the late Professor A. B. DAVIDSON, D.D., LL.D., New College, Edinburgh. Eighteenth Edition. 8vo.

Nett $2.50

'A text-book which has gone into its tenth [now eighteenth] edition needs no recommendation here. . . . Certain changes, in the introduction of new examples and the enlargement of some parts where brevity tended to obscurity, will add to the already great merits and widely acknowledged usefulness of the book.'—*Critical Review.*
'The best Hebrew Grammar is that of Professor A. B. Davidson.'—*British Weekly.*

Hebrew Syntax. Third Edition. In demy 8vo. Nett $2.50

'The whole is, it is needless to say, the work of a master; but it is the work of a master who does not shoot over the learners' heads, one who by long experience knows exactly where help is most needed, and how to give it in the simplest and clearest fashion.'—*Methodist Recorder.*

Old Testament Prophecy. Edited by Prof. J. A. PATERSON,
D.D. One large 8vo Volume.

Nett $3.50

'This must long remain the standard work on Old Testament prophecy.'—Professor MARCUS DODS.

The Called of God. With Biographical Introduction by A.
TAYLOR INNES, Esq., Advocate, and Portraits. Post 8vo.

Nett $2.00

'The biographical introduction is admirable. . . . The sermons have thoughts that startle with their depth, they have passages that thrill us with their suppressed emotion.'—*Aberdeen Free Press.*

Waiting upon God. Post 8vo. Nett $2.00

'All through the book we meet with flashes of true insight and almost startling examples of that deep experimental knowledge of the human heart at its worst and its best, which is so characteristic of Davidson's preaching. . . . A striking book.'—*Glasgow Herald.*

The Epistle to the Hebrews. (*Handbook Series.*) Crown
8vo.

75 cents

'For its size and price one of the very best theological handbooks with which I am acquainted—a close grappling with the thought of the Epistle by a singularly strong and candid mind.'—Professor SANDAY in the *Academy.*

The Exile and the Restoration. With Map and Plan. (*Bible
Class Primer Series.*)

Nett 20 cents

'A remarkable instance of Professor Davidson's gift of compressed lucid statement. . . . It may be safely said that nowhere within anything like the same narrow limits will one get so vivid a view of that period of Old Testament history.'—*Expository Times.*

The Christian Doctrine of Immortality. By Rev. S. D. F. SALMOND, D.D., Principal, and Professor of Systematic Theology, United Free Church College, Aberdeen. New and Cheaper Edition (the Fourth), Revised throughout and Re-set. Post 8vo. Nett $3.00

' It is doubtful whether any book so wide and comprehensive in its scope, so thoughtful and faithful in its statements, so suggestive and quickening in its influence, so valuable in the contribution it makes to our knowledge and our faith respecting the ultimate fact of Immortality.'—*Presbyterian and Reformed Review.*

' This is beyond all doubt the *one* book on the transcendent subject of which it treats. There is none like it — sound, frank, fearless, and yet modest in every page.'— *Methodist Times.*

Life after Death and the Future of the Kingdom of God. By Bishop L. N. DAHLE, Knight of St. Olaf. Authorised Translation from the Norse. 8vo. Nett $2.50

' A work of great ability. . . . He traverses the whole field with the utmost patience, thoroughness, learning, and candour, and, we venture to say, leaves no part of it without helpful illumination.'—Prof. J. ORR, D.D.

Forerunners of Dante: An Account of some of the more Important Visions of a Future Life from the Earliest Times. By MARCUS DODS, M.A., B.A. Crown 8vo. Nett $1.50

This work presents a series of typical visions of Heaven, Purgatory, and Hell, beginning with Babylonian and Egyptian examples and ending in the European literature of the age of Dante, and exhibiting the gradual development of the ideas of punishment and reward in a future state.

' The author has gathered the conceptions of the future life, shown in visions and legends from the earliest dawn of Babylonian and Egyptian literature and the classical period of Greece and Rome down to the invention of St. Patrick's Purgatory and the fiercely dramatic imaginings of Thurcill.'—*New York Churchman.*

Morality and Religion. By JAMES KIDD, D.D. 8vo. Nett $3.50

' We are not acquainted with any other book that has so clearly shown the vital unity between religion and morality. . . . A strong book by a strong man.'—*Methodist Times.*

' It is the work of a master of psychological analysis.'—*Record.*

The Hope of Israel: A Review of the Argument from Prophecy. By Rev. F. H. WOODS, B.D., Oxford. Crown 8vo. Nett $1.25

' It is obvious that the argument from Prophecy must require modification from time to time, as fresh light is continually thrown on exegesis by modern scholarship and criticism. The great advance which has been made in these last of late years has indeed so largely affected it, that in its old form it was already beginning to do more harm than good to the cause of Christian truth.'—*From the Preface.*

Truth and Reality, with special reference to Religion ; or, A Plea for the Special Unity of Life in all its Manifestations. By JOHN SMYTH, M.A., D.Phil. (Edin.). With Introductory Note by Professor R. FLINT, D.D. Crown 8vo. Nett $1.50

' Admirably adapted both as regards content and form—thought and style—to interest and profit not only all philosophical readers, but thoughtful and educated men in general.'—Professor FLINT in his *Introduction.*

The Sinlessness of Jesus. An Evidence for Christianity. By CARL ULLMANN, D.D. Crown 8vo. Nett $1.50

Dean FARRAR, in his *Life of Christ,* says : ' Ullmann has studied the sinlessness of Christ more profoundly, and written upon it more beautifully, than any other theologian.'

WORKS BY PROFESSOR F. GODET, D.D.

(Copyright, by arrangement with the Author.)

*For devotional warmth and practical application, Godet is perhaps unsurpassed by any modern commentator amongst foreign Protestants.'—*GUARDIAN.

Introduction to the New Testament. The Epistles of St. Paul. By Prof. F. GODET, D.D., Neuchâtel. 8vo (pp. 630).

(In course of publication. Not yet completed in the Original.)

Two Volumes of the English Translation are now ready, viz :—

  I. **THE EPISTLES OF ST. PAUL.** 8vo, Nett $3.50
  II. **THE GOSPEL COLLECTION, AND ST. MATTHEW'S GOSPEL.** 8vo. Nett $2.25

'Anything that comes from Dr. Godet is sure to receive a cordial welcome, and our familiarity with his eloquent and luminous commentaries prepares us to appreciate very highly a work in which the venerable Swiss thus gathers up the harvest of a lifetime.'—*Critical Review.*

'In every particular it is fully abreast of the times. For the purposes of the hard-working preacher there is no book on St. Paul's Epistles quite equal to this. For the student, it must always lie in a place that his hand can reach. It is delightful reading.' —*Methodist Times.*

Commentary on St. Luke's Gospel. 2 Vols. 8vo. Nett $4.50

'Marked by clearness and good sense, it will be found to possess value and interest as one of the most recent and copious works specially designed to illustrate this Gospel.'—*Guardian.*

Commentary on St. John's Gospel. 3 Vols. 8vo. Nett $6.75

'This Gospel forms one of the battlefields of modern inquiry, and is itself so rich in spiritual truth that it is impossible to examine it too closely ; and we welcome this treatise from the pen of Dr. Godet. We have no more competent exegete, and this new volume shows all the learning and vivacity for which the author is distinguished.'—*Freeman.*

Commentary on St. Paul's Epistle to the Romans. Two Vols. 8vo. Nett $4.50

'We prefer this commentary to any other we have seen on the subject.'—*British and Foreign Evangelical Review.*

Commentary on St. Paul's First Epistle to the Corinthians. Two Vols. 8vo. Nett $4.50

'We do not know any better commentary to put into the hands of theological students.'—*Guardian.*

'A perfect masterpiece of theological toil and thought. . . . Scholarly, evangelical, exhaustive, and able.'—*Evangelical Review.*

Defence of the Christian Faith. Crown 8vo. New and Cheaper Edition. Nett $1.25

'There is trenchant argument and resistless logic in these lectures ; but withal, there is cultured imagination and felicitous eloquence, which carry home the appeals to the heart as well as the head.'—*Sword and Trowel.*

Nature and the Bible: Lectures on the Mosaic History of Creation in its relation to Natural Science. By Dr. FR. H. REUSCH. Authorised Translation. Two Vols. 8vo. Nett $5.00

'Other champions much more competent and learned than myself might have been placed in the field ; I will only name one of the most recent, Dr. Reusch, author of "Nature and the Bible." '—W. E. GLADSTONE.

'We owe to Dr. Reusch, a Catholic theologian, one of the most valuable treatises on the relation of Religion and natural science that has appeared for many years.'—*Literary World.*

BY THE LATE PROFESSOR A. B. BRUCE, D.D.

The Kingdom of God; or, Christ's Teaching according to the Synoptical Gospels. By the late Professor A. B. BRUCE, D.D., Glasgow. Sixth Edition. Post 8vo. Nett **$2.00**

' As satisfactory a treatment of the central teachings of Jesus as exists.'—*Biblical World* (Chicago).

' To Dr. Bruce belongs the honour of giving to English-speaking Christians the first really scientific treatment of this transcendent theme. . . . His book is the best monograph on the subject in existence.'—Rev. JAMES STALKER, D.D., in the *British Weekly*.

The Epistle to the Hebrews: The First Apology for Christianity. An Exegetical Study. Second Edition. Post 8vo.
Nett **$2.00**

This book, the fruit of thirty years' study, is a companion volume to Professor Bruce's 'The Kingdom of God,' and 'St. Paul's Conception of Christianity.'

The Training of the Twelve; or, Exposition of Passages in the Gospels exhibiting the Twelve Disciples of Jesus under Discipline for the Apostleship. Fifth Edition. 8vo. Nett **$3.50**

' That minister who has not read "The Training of the Twelve" betrays an indifference to modern thought which is unpardonable.'—President HARPER in the *Biblical World*.

' A volume which can never lose its charm either for the preacher or for the ordinary Christian reader.'—*London Quarterly Review*.

The Humiliation of Christ, in its Physical, Ethical, and Official Aspects. Fourth Edition. 8vo. Nett **$3.50**

' These lectures are able and deep-reaching to a degree not often found in the religious literature of the day; withal, they are fresh and suggestive. . . . The learning and the deep and sweet spirituality of this discussion will commend it to many faithful students of the truth as it is in Jesus.'—*Congregationalist*.

BY PROFESSOR JAMES STALKER, D.D.

The Life of Jesus Christ. New Edition, in larger type, and handsomely bound, crown 8vo. Nett **$1.25**

' Even with all our modern works on the exhaustless theme, from Neander to Farrar and Geikie, there is none which occupies the ground of Dr. Stalker's. . . . We question whether any one popular work so impressively and adequately represents Jesus to the mind. . . . It may be despised because it is small, but its light must shine.'—*Christian*.

The Life of St. Paul. Uniform with the 'Life of Christ' in size and price. Nett **$1.25**

' Even to those who know by heart the details of the great apostle's life, this glowing sketch will be a revelation. Written with a fine sympathy for the more tender and personal aspects of his theme, Dr. Stalker has portrayed the outer and the inner life of Paul with a mingled power and beauty which is as rare as it is needed in evangelical writing.'—*Christian*.

*** *Small type Editions of both Volumes in the* 'BIBLE CLASS HANDBOOK *Series*,' *price* 45 *cents* (*nett*) *each.*—See page 35.

The Resurrection of the Dead. By the late Prof. W. MILLIGAN, D.D. Second Edition, crown 8vo. Nett **$1.50**

' In the treatment of such passages as these, Dr. Milligan's thoughtfulness, judgment, and scholarship reach their highest expression. We can but lament that this is the last volume for which we shall be indebted to him.'—*Record*.

The Incarnate Saviour: A Life of Jesus Christ. By W. ROBERTSON NICOLL, LL.D., Editor of 'The Expositor,' 'The British Weekly,' etc. *New and Cheaper Edition.* Crown 8vo. Nett **$1.00**

' It commands my warm sympathy and admiration. I rejoice in the circulation of such a book, which I trust will be the widest possible.'—Canon LIDDON.

Messianic Prophecy: Its Origin, Historical Growth, and Relation to New Testament Fulfilment. By Dr. EDWARD RIEHM. New Edition. With an Introduction by the late Prof. A. B. DAVIDSON, D.D.   Post 8vo.   Nett $2.25

'No work of the same compass could be named that contains so much that is instructive on the nature of prophecy in general, and particularly on the branch of it specially treated in the book.'—Professor A. B. DAVIDSON, D.D.

The Right of Systematic Theology. By Professor B. B. WARFIELD, D.D., Princeton University. With an Introduction by Professor J. ORR, D.D.   Crown 8vo.   Nett 60 cents

'A powerful blow directed against the attempt to abolish doctrine and creeds and reduce Christianity to mere sentiment. The protest made in this strong essay is most timely. We join Dr. Orr and other Scottish divines in earnestly commending it to the notice of theological readers.'—*Methodist Times.*

Pre-Organic Evolution and the Biblical Idea of God: An Exposition and a Criticism. By Principal L. CHAPMAN, LL.D.   Crown 8vo.   Nett $1.75

'A volume which will take an important position among Theistic, not to say Christian apologetics, and which, in the present growth of scepticism, we may well be thankful for.'—*Literary Churchman.*

Darwinianism: Workmen and Work. By J. HUTCHISON STIRLING, F.R.C.S., and LL.D. Edinburgh.   Post 8vo.   Nett $3.00

'Undoubtedly the most trenchant criticism of Darwinianism that has yet appeared. . . . The book is a work of art.'—Professor M'KENDRICK in the *Critical Review.*

Philosophy and Theology, The First Edinburgh University Gifford Lectures. By J. HUTCHISON STIRLING, LL.D.   Post 8vo.   Nett $3.00

'This volume will make for itself many friends. 'There is a bracing, stimulating masterfulness about the lectures, which on a careful perusal of them will be found to lead to many rich veins of thought.'—Professor STEWART in the *Critical Review.*

What *is* Thought? or, the Problem of Philosophy by Way of a General Conclusion so far. By JAS. H. STIRLING, LL.D.   Post 8vo.   Nett $3.00

'A noble contribution to the philosophy of our time. British philosophy is permanently enriched by Dr. Stirling's remarkable and penetrating piece of work.'—*Critical Review.*

History of the Christian Philosophy of Religion, from the Reformation to Kant. By BERNHARD PÜNJER. Translated by Prof. W. HASTIE, D.D. With a Preface by Prof. FLINT, D.D., LL.D.   8vo.   Nett $4.00

'The merits of Pünjer's history are not difficult to discover; on the contrary, they are of the kind which, as the French say, *sautent aux 'yeux*. The language is almost everywhere as plain and easy to apprehend as, considering the nature of the matter conveyed, it could be made. The style is simple, natural, and direct; the only sort of style appropriate to the subject. The amount of information imparted is most extensive, and strictly relevant. Nowhere else will a student get nearly so much knowledge as to what has been thought and written, within the area of Christendom, on the philosophy of religion. He must be an excessively learned man in that department who has nothing to learn from this book.'—*Extract from Preface by* Prof. FLINT.

Handbook of Church History : From the Reformation. By Prof. J. H. KURTZ, D.D. 8vo. Nett $2.50

' A work executed with great diligence and care, exhibiting an accurate collection of facts, and succinct though full account of the history and progress of the Church, both external and internal. . . . The work is distinguished for the moderation and charity of its expressions, and for a spirit which is truly Christian.'—*English Churchman.*

The First Epistle of Peter : With Introduction and Commentary. By Prof. R. JOHNSTONE, D.D., Edinburgh. 8vo. Nett $1.50

' Dr. Johnstone has done excellent service in publishing this work.'—*Record.*

' Full of thoughtfulness and spiritual power and suggestiveness, and likely to be a valuable book to all Christian teachers.'—*Literary World.*

BY THE LATE PATON J. GLOAG, D.D.

Introduction to the Synoptic Gospels. By the late PATON J. GLOAG, D.D., Edinburgh. 8vo. Nett $2.25

' A volume of sterling value ; learned, clear, candid, cautious, thoroughly well-considered ; it should be a welcome addition to the library of the biblical student.'—*London Quarterly Review.*

Introduction to the Catholic Epistles. 8vo. Nett $3.50

' Ought to be eagerly welcomed as a solid contribution to theological literature ; it is a work of masterly strength and uncommon merit.'—*Evangelical Magazine.*

Exegetical Studies. Crown 8vo. Nett $1.50

' Dr. Gloag handles his subjects very ably, displaying everywhere accurate and extensive scholarship, and a fine appreciation of the lines of thought in those passages with which he deals.'—*Baptist.*

The Messianic Prophecies. Crown 8vo. Nett $2.25

' We regard Dr. Gloag's work as a valuable contribution to theological literature. We have not space to give the extended notice which its intrinsic excellence demands, and must content ourselves with cordially recommending it to our readers.'—*Spectator.*

Evening Thoughts. Being Notes of a Threefold Pastorate. Crown 8vo. Nett $1.50

' Able, vigorous, and logical, marked by deep and robust thought, and stimulating in the highest degree.'—*Aberdeen Journal.*

Commentary on St. Paul's Epistle to the Ephesians. By Rev. J. MACPHERSON, M.A. 8vo. Nett $3.00

' It is an advance, and a great one, on anything we yet possess. . . . The author goes to the root, and neglects nothing that usually comes under the eye of a careful student. . . . Besides all this, the book is a living book. One is conscious of the heart of a man in it, as well as the brains.'—*Methodist Times.*

Christian Dogmatics. By Rev. J. MACPHERSON, M.A., Author of ' Commentary on St. Paul's Epistle to the Ephesians,' etc. Post 8vo. Nett $3.00

' Works on systematic theology are so few that we gladly welcome a well-informed and well-written compendium like the present one. . . . The work deserves a wide circulation among readers of theology.'—*Methodist Times.*

BY DR. C. VON ORELLI, BASEL.

The Twelve Minor Prophets. 8vo.   Nett $2.25

'A very valuable and trustworthy compendium of the latest results of critical research, written in a sober and devout spirit.'—*Christian World.*

The Prophecies of Isaiah. 8vo.   Nett $2.25

'The characteristics of this admirable commentary are brevity, separation of the more grammatical from the more expository notes, and general orthodoxy combined with first-rate scholarship.'—*Record.*

The Prophecies of Jeremiah. 8vo.   Nett $2.25

'Will be found a most trustworthy aid to the study of a book that presents many difficult problems.'—*John Bull.*

The Old Testament Prophecy of the Consummation of God's Kingdom. Traced in its Historical Development. 8vo.   Nett $2.25

'Cannot fail to be regarded as a standard work upon the subject of Old Testament prophecy.'—*Sword and Trowel.*

The Apostolic and Post-Apostolic Times. By Prof. G. V. LECHLER, D.D. Third Edition, thoroughly Revised and Re-written. Two Vols. crown 8vo.   Nett $5.00

'It contains a vast amount of historical information, and is replete with judicious remarks. . . . By bringing under the notice of English readers a work so favourably thought of in Germany, the translator has conferred a benefit on Theology.'—*Athenæum.*

THE LATE PROFESSOR FRANZ DELITZSCH, D.D., LEIPZIG.

'Probably no commentator of the age brought so many gifts to the interpretation of the Bible as did Franz Delitzsch. . . . Walking hand in hand with such a guide through the garden of the Lord, one cannot only gather its ripened fruit, but also breathe the fragrance of its flowers and gaze upon their loveliness.—Professor J. F. M'CURDY, Toronto.

A New Commentary on Genesis. By the late Prof. FRANZ DELITZSCH, D.D., Leipzig. Specially Revised by the Author for the English Translation. Two Vols. 8vo.   Nett $4.50

'We congratulate Professor Delitzsch on this new edition. By it, not less than by his other commentaries, he has earned the gratitude of every lover of biblical science, and we shall be surprised if, in the future, many do not acknowledge that they have found in it a welcome help and guide.'—Professor S. R. DRIVER in the *Academy.*

The Prophecies of Isaiah. Translated from the Fourth and Last Edition. *The only Authorised Translation.* With Introduction by Prof. S. R. DRIVER, D.D. Two Vols. 8vo.   Nett $4.50

'Delitzsch's last gift to the Christian Church. . . . In our opinion, those who would enter into the meaning of that Spirit as He spake long ago by Isaiah, words of comfort and hope which have not lost their significance to-day, cannot find a better guide ; one more marked by learning, reverence, and insight, than Franz Delitzsch.'—*Expository Times.*

A System of Biblical Psychology. 8vo.   Nett $2.25

'Still the best book on the whole of the subject.'—Principal CAVE, D.D.

*** *For other works by Professor Delitzsch, see 'The Foreign Theological Library,' p. 39.*

Franz Delitzsch : A Memorial Tribute. By Prof. S. I. CURTISS, D.D., Chicago. With a Portrait. Crown 8vo.   Nett $1.00

'A highly interesting little monograph on the personality of the great theologian, and on his work.'—*Spectator.*

BY THE LATE PROFESSOR W. HASTIE, D.D.

The Theology of the Reformed Church in its Fundamental Principles. By the late Professor W. HASTIE, D.D., Glasgow. Crown 8vo. Nett $1.50

'The work so long looked for is now published, and it is to be hoped that it will be widely and kindly received. No intelligent reader of it can fail to find in its pages much information, eloquently stated, regarding both the history and the characteristics of the reformed Theology.'—From Prefatory Note by Prof. R. FLINT, D.D.

'The logical cohesion of the Calvinistic system finds here an excellent expression by an advocate no less skilful than convinced.'—New York Churchman.

Outlines of Pastoral Theology for Young Ministers and Students. Crown 8vo. Nett 75 cents

'We have seldom read a book of loftier ideal or more practical value to parish priests than this volume.'—New York Churchman.

'How Professor Hastie discovered this book, and how he was drawn to it, how it had to be laid aside, and how it would not lie,—all this is told with thrilling simplicity in the Introduction. We do greatly need a small competent sympathetic guide to the work of the ministry. This is the book we need.'—Expository Times.

St. Paul's Conception of Christ; or, The Doctrine of the Second Adam. By Rev. DAVID SOMERVILLE, D.D., Edinburgh. 8vo. Nett $3.00

'The book gives evidence throughout of wide familiarity with recent literature, both exegetical and dogmatic, and manifests in many features a mastery of Pauline thought that makes it very welcome to students of the great apostle.'—American Journal of Theology.

Theologia Pectoris: Outlines of Religious Faith and Doctrine, founded on Intuition and Experience. By the Rev. J. M. HODGSON, M.A., D.Sc., D.D., Principal of the Theological Hall of the Congregational Churches of Scotland. In crown 8vo. Nett $1.25

A System of Biblical Theology. By the late W. LINDSAY ALEXANDER, D.D., LL.D. Two Vols. 8vo. Nett $6.00

'Oh that Scotland and Congregationalism had many worthies like Dr. Lindsay Alexander! . . . The ripe man, full of rich experience and heavenly knowledge, will prize each leaf, and give himself a glorious drilling as he masters chapter by chapter.'—Mr. SPURGEON in the Sword and Trowel.

The Ancient Faith in Modern Light.

A series of Essays by eminent Congregational and Baptist ministers on some theological questions much discussed in modern days. The subjects include such topics as 'Theism,' 'The Bible,' 'Sin,' 'The Incarnation,' 'The Atonement,' with practical questions such as 'The Church in Modern Society,' 'The Pulpit in relation to Literature,' etc. The Contributors include Dr. GUINNESS ROGERS, Dr. JOSEPH PARKER, Principals VAUGHAN PRYCE, CAVE, and TYMMS, Dr. NEWTH, Rev. W. BROCK, E. MEDLEY, and Dr. SAMUEL G. GREEN, who has edited the work. The object of the book is to vindicate the belief of the Churches in those important topics, and the harmony of that belief with a true philosophy, and its adaptation to the thought of the age. The Volume may therefore be regarded in some sense as a manifesto of modern liberal belief. Nett $3.50

From Apostle to Priest. A Study of Early Church Organisation. By JAMES W. FALCONER, M.A., B.D. In crown 8vo. Nett $1.50

'The story is told with the greatest clearness and convincing force. To any one who wishes a plain accurate account of the growth of the sacerdotal theory of the ministry we confidently recommend this work.'—London Quarterly Review.

How to Read the Prophets: Being the Prophecies arranged
Chronologically in their Historical Setting, with Explanations,
Maps, and Glossary. By BUCHANAN BLAKE, B.D.

PART I. **THE PRE-EXILIAN MINOR PROPHETS (with JOEL).** Second Edition.—
PART II. **ISAIAH** (Chaps. i.–xxxix.). Second Edition.—PART III. **JEREMIAH.**—
PART IV. **EZEKIEL.**—PART V. **ISAIAH** (Chaps. xl.–lxvi.) and **THE POST-EXILIAN
PROPHETS.** (Complete in 5 Vols. crown 8vo.)   Each, Nett $1.00

*'It has often been found a difficulty to profit fully from the reading, especially of the smaller
prophecies of the Old Testament. To make these prophecies intelligible to the plainest reader, it
seems desirable that a chronological arrangement of the prophetic books should be attempted.
Alongside of the several prophecies should be placed those portions of the Old Testament historical
books which deal with the same period. The aim of these manuals is consequently in this direction :
to bring within the reach of the many a clear and succinct presentation of these prophets in their
historical environment.'*—From the AUTHOR'S INTRODUCTION.

'Mr. Blake seems to have hit upon the right thing, and he has proved himself competent to do it rightly. While these books are the very best introductions to the
study of the prophets, even the accomplished scholar will find them indispensable.'—
Expository Times.

Joseph and Moses the Founders of Israel: Being their
Lives as read in the Light of the Oldest Prophetic Writings of the
Bible. Crown 8vo.   Nett 1.25

'Mr. Blake hit upon a fresh idea when he wrote his books on "How to Read the
Prophets." Nothing has made the prophets so accessible to the average man. He
has hit upon a fresh idea again. . . . Have we come to the point as preachers when we
desire to make a new start with the Old Testament? This book will enable us to make
it.'—*Expository Times.*

'This instructive and always vivid exposition of the narrative.'—*Princeton Theological
Review.*

The Voice from the Cross: A Series of Sermons on our
Lord's Passion by Eminent Living Preachers of Germany, includ-
ing Drs. Ahlfeld, Baur, Bayer, Couard, Faber, Frommel, Gerok,
Hähnelt, Hansen, Kögel, Luthardt, Mühe, Müllensiefen, Nebe,
Quandt, Schrader, Schröter, Stöcker, and Teichmüller. With
Biographical Sketches and Portrait of Dr. Kögel. Crown 8vo.
                                                        Nett $1.50

'Is certain to be welcomed with devout gratitude by every Evangelical Christian.'—
Christian Leader.

BY PRINCIPAL A. CAVE, D.D.

An Introduction to Theology: Its Principles, Its Branches,
Its Results, and Its Literature. By ALFRED CAVE, D.D., Principal
of Hackney College, London. New Edition just published, Revised
and largely Re-written. The Bibliography brought up to date.
8vo.   Nett $3.50

'I have just seen your excellent "Introduction to Theology," and feel prompted to
thank you for this excellent help to students. I have been lecturing on this subject for
forty years, and long wished for some such substitute for Hagenbach (too German to be
translated or even reproduced) which I could recommend to my students. . . . It is
the best original work on the subject in the English language.'—PHILIP SCHAFF, D.D.,
LL.D.

The Scriptural Doctrine of Sacrifice and Atonement.
New Edition, Revised throughout. 8vo.   Nett $3.00

'Let readers judge—is this not now the best study of the Atonement in the English
language?'—*Expository Times.*

The Prophecies of Jesus Christ relating to His Death, Resurrection, and Second Coming, and their Fulfilment. By Dr. P. SCHWARTZKOPFF. Crown 8vo. Nett $1.50

'A book blossoming on every page with suggestions, and worthy of the most serious study of the theologians.'—Prof. MARCUS DODS in the *Critical Review*.

BY PROFESSOR I. A. DORNER, D.D., BERLIN.

History of the Development of the Doctrine of the Person of Christ. By Prof. I. A. DORNER, Berlin. Five Vols. 8vo. Nett $11.25

'The stupendous work upon *The Person of Christ* has now become in Great Britain and America, what it had been in Germany from its publication, a classic in Christology.' —Principal CAVE, D.D.

A System of Christian Doctrine. Four Vols. 8vo. Nett $9.00

'Had it been the work of an entire lifetime, it would have been a monument of marvellous industry and rare scholarship. It is a tribute alike to the genius, the learning, and the untiring perseverance of its author.'—*Baptist Magazine*.

System of Christian Ethics. 8vo. Nett $3.00

'This noble book is the crown of the Systematic Theology of the author. . . . It is a masterpiece. It is the fruit of a lifetime of profound investigation in the philosophical, biblical, and historical sources of theology.'—Prof. C. A. BRIGGS, D.D.

BY PROFESSOR BERNHARD WEISS, D.D., BERLIN.

The Life of Christ. Three Vols. 8vo. Nett $6.75

'The authority of John's Gospel is vindicated with great fulness and success. Altogether the book seems destined to hold a very distinguished, if not absolutely unique, place in the criticism of the New Testament. Its fearless search after truth, its independence of spirit, its extent of research, its thoughtful and discriminating tone must secure for it a very high reputation.'—*Congregationalist*.

Biblical Theology of the New Testament. Two Vols. 8vo. Nett $4.50

'This is a field which Weiss has made his own. His work far excels the numerous works of his predecessors in thoroughness and completeness.'—*Methodist Recorder*.

Apologetics; or, The Scientific Vindication of Christianity. By Prof. J. H. A. EBRARD, D.D., Erlangen. Three Vols. 8vo. Nett $6.75

'The author of this work has a reputation which renders it unnecessary to speak in words of general commendation of his "Apologetics." . . . Dr. Ebrard takes nothing for granted. He begins at the beginning, laying his foundations deep and strong, and building upon them patiently and laboriously, leaving no gaps, no loose work, but adjusting each stone in its place and use.'—*Church Bells*.

The Miracles of our Lord, in relation to Modern Criticism. By Professor F. L. STEINMEYER. 8vo. Nett $2.25

'This work vindicates in a vigorous and scholarly style the sound view of miracles against the sceptical assaults of the time.'—*Princeton Review*.

History of the Passion and Resurrection of our Lord, considered in the light of Modern Criticism. By Professor F. L. STEINMEYER. 8vo. Nett $2.25

'Our readers will find this work a most valuable and suggestive help for their thoughts and teaching during Passion-tide and Easter.'—*English Churchman*.

BISHOP HEFELE'S COUNCILS OF THE CHURCH.

A History of the Councils of the Church. From the Original Documents. By the Right Rev. C. J. Hefele, D.D., Bishop of Rottenburg. Now complete in Five Vols. 8vo. Vol. I., to A.D. 325. Vol. II., A.D. 326 to 429. Vol. III., A.D. 431 to 451. Vol. IV., A.D. 451 to 680. Vol. V., completing the series, A.D. 626 to close of Second Council of Nicæa, 787. With Appendix and Indices. 8vo. Per Vol. Nett **$3.50**

'To all who have the slightest pretension to the name of scientific theologians it must afford the greatest satisfaction to receive a new volume of Bishop Hefele's standard work on the Councils. It is quite unnecessary to commend this great and learned book. No one would think of studying the subject of the Councils without consulting it.'— *Church Bells.*

Declarations and Letters on the Vatican Decrees, 1869-1887. By Ignaz von Döllinger. Authorised Translation. Crown 8vo. Nett **$1.00**

Dr. Alfred Plummer says: 'This intensely interesting collection of Declarations and Letters gives us in a short compass the main historical facts which Dr. Döllinger considered to be absolutely fatal to the truth of the dogma respecting the infallibility of the Pope, and the reason which for nineteen years prevented him from "submitting" even to the Pope with the whole of the Roman episcopate at his back. . . . Indispensable to every one who would have an intelligent grasp of the Infallibility Question.'

Hippolytus and Callistus; or, The Church of Rome in the First Half of the Third Century. By Ign. von Döllinger. Translated, with Introduction, Notes, and Appendices, by A. Plummer, D.D., Durham. 8vo. Nett **$2.00**

'We are impressed with profound respect for the learning and ingenuity displayed in this work. The book deserves perusal by all students of ecclesiastical history. It clears up many points hitherto obscure, and reveals features in the Roman Church at the beginning of the third century which are highly instructive.'—*Athenæum.*

The Early Church: A History of Christianity in the First Six Centuries. By the late Prof. David Duff, D.D., LL.D., Edinburgh. 8vo. Nett **$3.50**

'A more uniformly chastened and dignified style could not be desired. . . . There is no history of this time at once so full and so concise, no safer guide or more agreeable companion.'—*Expository Times.*

BY J. J. VAN OOSTERZEE, D.D.

The Year of Salvation: Words of Life for Every Day. A Book of Household Devotion. Two Vols. large crown 8vo.
Per Vol. Nett **$1.75**

'This charming and practical book of household devotion will be welcomed on account of its rare intrinsic value, as one of the most practical devotional books ever published.'—*Standard.*

Moses: A Biblical Study. Crown 8vo. Nett **$1.75**

'Our author has seized, as with the instinct of a master, the great salient points in the life and work of Moses, and portrayed the various elements of his character with vividness and skill.'—*Baptist Magazine.*

The Bible Doctrine of Man; or, The Anthropology and Psychology of Scripture. By Professor J. LAIDLAW, D.D., Edinburgh. New Edition, Revised and Re-arranged. Post 8vo. Nett $2.25

'The standard work in English on the Anthropology and Psychology of the Bible. . . . A volume worthy of its subject, and likely to hold the first place in it for many days to come.'—*Expository Times.*

Kant, Lotze, and Ritschl. A Critical Examination. By LEONHARD STÄHLIN, Bayreuth. Translated by Principal SIMON, D.D. 8vo. Nett $3.00

'This learned work goes to the very root of the philosophical and metaphysical speculations of recent years.'—*Ecclesiastical Gazette.*

BY THE REV. J. B. HEARD, M.A.

Alexandrian and Carthaginian Theology Contrasted. (Hulsean Lectures.) Crown 8vo. Nett $1.75

'We can heartily recommend these lectures as pursuing a most interesting branch of inquiry in a thoroughly able, scholarly, and instructive way.'—*Scotsman.*

Old and New Theology: A Constructive Critique. Crown 8vo. Nett $1.75

'Progressive theologians, who desire to find "the old in the new, and the new in the old," will be deeply grateful to Mr. Heard for this courageous and able work.'—*Christian World.*

The Tripartite Nature of Man: Spirit, Soul, and Body. Fifth Edition. Crown 8vo. Nett $1.75

'An elaborate, ingenious, and very able book.'—*London Quarterly Review.*

WORKS BY ERNEST NAVILLE.

The Christ. By ERNEST NAVILLE, Corresponding Member of the Institute of France. Crown 8vo. Nett $1.25

'M. Naville is well known as an earnest, faithful, and eloquent defender of the Christian faith, master of a rich French style, and endowed with exquisite tact in adapting his apology to the thoughts and needs of his readers.'—*London Quarterly Review.*

Modern Physics: Studies Historical and Philosophical. Crown 8vo. Nett $1.25

'This work meets, with rare skill, some of the more subtle speculations of prominent writers in our midst.'—*Record.*

The Problem of Evil. Crown 8vo. Nett $1.25

'We give this book our warmest commendation. . . . The brilliant sparkle of the French original is as nearly preserved as could be expected in any version.'—*Literary Churchman.*

Kant's Principles of Politics, including His Essay on Perpetual Peace. A Contribution to Political Science. Edited and Translated by Professor HASTIE, D.D. Crown 8vo. Nett $1.00

Kant's Metaphysic of Ethics. Edited by Professor H. CALDERWOOD, LL.D. Crown 8vo. Fourth Edition. Nett $1.75

'This translation has been accepted by scholars as a real success.'--*Contemporary Review.*

BY PRINCIPAL D. W. SIMON, D.D.

Reconciliation by Incarnation: The Reconciliation of God and Man by the Incarnation of the Divine Word. By Principal D. W. SIMON, D.D., The United College, Bradford. 8vo.

Nett $2.25

'A treatise of great value, for its broad philosophical grasp, its subtle spiritual insight, and its apt illustrations. It is a fresh, timely, and independent study of a subject which must ever be to the fore.'—*Baptist Magazine.*

The Bible an Outgrowth of Theocratic Life. Crown 8vo. Nett $1.50

' This book will well repay perusal. It contains a great deal of learning as well as ingenuity, and the style is clear.'—*Guardian.*

BY THE REV. JOHN HUTCHISON, D.D.

Our Lord's Signs in St. John's Gospel: Discussions, chiefly Exegetical and Doctrinal, on the Eight Miracles in the Fourth Gospel. 8vo. Nett $2.25

' A learned, thoughtful, and delicate study of the Miracles of the Fourth Gospel.'— *Bookman.*

Lectures on Paul's Epistle to the Philippians. 8vo.

Nett $2.25

' This book has one great merit which separates it from the mass of commentaries and expository lectures—it is not only instructive, but it is also delightfully interesting. . . . The author's moral and spiritual tone is lofty, and these sermons are characterised by a sweet and sunny grace, which cannot but charm and make better those who read them.'—*Literary World.*

Lectures on Paul's Epistles to the Thessalonians. 8vo. Nett $3.00

' The text is at once treated with scholarly ability, and turned to popular and practical account. Such is the character of Dr. Hutchison's work—his exegesis of crucial passages strikes us at once as eminently clear.'—*Baptist.*

Pastoral Theology of the New Testament. By Professor J. T. BECK, D.D., Tübingen. Authorised Translation. Crown 8vo. Nett $1.75

' Thorough knowledge of the Scripture, rigid fidelity to its principles, robust common sense, perfect lucidity of statement and orderliness of arrangement, combined with profound reverence for Christ and fervent love for men, make this by a long way the best exposition of *The Teaching of the New Testament* on all questions relating to the pastoral office and work which we yet possess. . . . Whatever other books are used in our colleges, and studied by our ministers, we believe that Dr. Beck's "Pastoral Theology" will soon be universally regarded as indispensable.'—*Baptist Magazine.*

Outlines of Biblical Psychology. By Professor J. T. BECK, D.D. Crown 8vo. Nett $1.25

' A useful, handy volume, which compresses into small space the results of scholarly and elaborate investigations.'—*Baptist Magazine.*

The Jewish and the Christian Messiah: A Study in the Earliest History of Christianity. By Professor V. H. STANTON, D.D., Cambridge. 8vo. Nett. $3.00

' Mr. Stanton's book answers a real want, and will be indispensable to students of the origin of Christianity.'—*Guardian.*

Biblical Essays; or, Exegetical Studies on the Books of Job and Jonah, Ezekiel's Prophecy of Gog and Magog, St. Peter's 'Spirits in Prison,' and the Key to the Apocalypse. By C. H. H. WRIGHT, D.D. Crown 8vo. Nett $1.50

'Solid scholarship, careful and sober criticism, and a style which is pure and lucid.' —*Church Bells.*

BY PROFESSOR C. E. LUTHARDT, D.D., LEIPZIG.

A History of Christian Ethics before the Reformation. Authorised Translation by Professor W. HASTIE, D.D. 8vo. Nett $2.25

'Charmingly written and adequately covers the ground. . . . The ablest and most thorough historical exposition of the subject of Christian Ethics that has been made accessible to English-speaking people.'—*Presbyterian and Reformed Review.*

The Truths of Christianity. Three Vols. Crown 8vo. Each, Nett $1.75

1. THE FUNDAMENTAL TRUTHS OF CHRISTIANITY. Seventh Edition.
2. THE SAVING TRUTHS OF CHRISTIANITY. Fifth Edition.
3. THE MORAL TRUTHS OF CHRISTIANITY. Fourth Edition.

'We do not know any volumes so suitable in these times for young men entering on life, or, let us say, even for the library of a pastor called to deal with such, than the three volumes of this series. We commend the whole of them with the utmost cordial satisfaction. They are altogether quite a specialty in our literature.'—*Weekly Review.*

Commentary on St. John's Gospel. Three Vols. 8vo. Nett $6.75

'Full to overflowing with a ripe theology and a critical science worthy of their great theme.'—*Irish Ecclesiastical Gazette.*

St. John the Author of the Fourth Gospel. Translated, and the Literature enlarged, by Dr. C. R. GREGORY, Leipzig. 8vo. Nett $2.25

'A work of thoroughness and value.'—*Guardian.*

The Church: Its Origin, Its History, and Its Present Position. By Professors LUTHARDT, KAHNIS, and BRÜCKNER. Crown 8vo. Nett $1.50

'A comprehensive review of this sort, done by able hands, is both instructive and suggestive.'—*Record.*

The Kingdom of God, Biblically and Historically considered. By Professor J. S. CANDLISH, D.D., Glasgow. 8vo. Nett $3.00

'Dr. Candlish treats his subject with an admirable combination of scholarly comprehensiveness, historical candour, and regard to the practical demands of mankind.'—*Christian World.*

'As to the ability of this volume there can be no question: it is worthy of the reputation and position of its author.'—*Evangelical Magazine.*

Central Truths and Side Issues. By R. G. BALFOUR, D.D., Edinburgh. Crown 8vo. Nett $1.25

'The book is well worth buying and keeping. The chapter on the Incarnation and Humiliation of the Son of God is admirable in every way—reasonable, liberal, and full of acute and forcible argument.'—*Review of the Churches.*

Ephesians, Philippians, Colossians. By the late Professor J. EADIE, D.D. Three Vols. 8vo. Per Vol. Nett $3.00

The World of Faith and the Everyday World. As displayed in the Footsteps of Abraham. By Pastor OTTO FUNCKE, Post 8vo. Nett $2.00

' A remarkable volume. . . . The plainness and freedom of his speech, the homeliness and force of his illustrations, the general directness and vigour of his method, are such as one does not often meet with. . . . To describe the author in short, we should say that he was a German Spurgeon.'—*Spectator*.

The Footsteps of Christ. Translated from the German A. of CASPERS. Crown 8vo. Nett $2.50

' There is much deeply experimental truth and precious spiritual love in Caspers' book. . . . I own myself much profited by his devout utterances.'—Rev. C. H. SPURGEON.

Gotthold's Emblems; or, Invisible Things understood by Things that are Made. By CHRISTIAN SCRIVER. Crown 8vo. Nett $1.50

' A peculiarly fascinating volume. It is rich in happy and beautiful thoughts, which grow on the root of genuine piety.'—*Witness*.

Sermons for the Christian Year: Advent-Trinity. By Professor ROTHE, Heidelberg. Crown 8vo. Nett $1.25

' The volume is rich in noble thoughts and wholesome lessons.'—*Watchman*.

BY REV. NEWMAN HALL, D.D.

Gethsemane; or, Leaves of Healing from the Garden of Grief. Second Edition. Crown 8vo. Nett $1.25

' A series of meditations, designed for the consolation of the afflicted. Written in the devout spirit and direct style to which we are accustomed in their author, they are admirably adapted to the object they have in view.'—*Critical Review*.

Divine Brotherhood in 'The Man Christ Jesus.' Third Edition. Crown 8vo. Nett $1.25

' This book will receive a cordial welcome from those—and their name is legion—who esteem and admire the venerable author. It is characterised by all his well-known excellences as a writer. It is altogether admirable.'—*Scotsman*.

The Lord's Prayer: A Practical Meditation. 8vo. Nett $1.50

Dr. THEODORE CUYLER writes : ' It is the very book to assist ministers of the gospel in the study of the Model Prayer ; it is equally stimulating and quickening to private Christians in their quiet hours of meditation and devotion.'

The Spirit of Power as set forth in the Book of the Acts of the Apostles. By T. ADAMSON, D.D. Second Edition. Fcap. 8vo. Nett 40 cents

Principal MOULE writes : ' It will repay not only reading, but reading again and again. . . . A book of rare and solid value.'

The Gospel of a Risen Saviour. By R. M'CHEYNE EDGAR, D.D., ex-Moderator of the General Assembly, Irish Presbyterian Church. Post 8vo. Nett $2.25

Principal FAIRBAIRN writes :—' Let me thank you for a most instructive and stimulating book. I am struck with its careful workmanship and the way in which it has grouped its material round its central idea. I am sure every evangelical theologian must feel that you have made a most helpful contribution to a great subject.'

An Explanatory Commentary on Esther. With Four
Appendices : the Second Targum translated from the Aramaic with
Notes, Mithra, the Winged Bulls of Persepolis, and Zoroaster. By
Professor P. CASSEL, D.D., Berlin. Authorised Translation. 8vo.
Nett $2.25

' No one whose fortune it is to secure this commentary will rise from its study without
a new and lively realisation of the life, trials, and triumphs of Esther and Mordecai.'—
Ecclesiastical Gazette.

Handbook of Biblical Archæology. By Prof. C. F. KEIL,
D.D. Two Vols. Authorised Translation. 8vo.   Nett $4.50

' This work is the standard scientific treatise on Biblical Archæology. It is a very
mine of learning.'—*John Bull.*

**Manual of Historico-Critical Introduction to the
Canonical Scriptures of the Old Testament.** By
Professor C. F. KEIL, D.D. Two Vols. 8vo.   Nett $4.50

What Think Ye of the Gospels? A Handbook of Gospel
Study. By Rev. J. J. HALCOMBE, M.A. 8vo.   Nett $1.25

' The author has given the matter much earnest study, and his theory, which can
only be thoroughly understood by studying his work, appears to have much in it worthy
of commendation.'—*Christian Commonwealth.*

BY PROFESSOR H. EWALD.

Revelation: Its Nature and Record. By Professor H. EWALD, D.D.
8vo.   Nett $2.25

' Ewald is one of the most suggestive and helpful writers of this century. This is
certainly a noble book, and will be appreciated not less than his other and larger works.
. . . There is a rich poetic glow in his writing which gives to it a singular charm.'—
Baptist Magazine.

Old and New Testament Theology. 8vo.   Nett $2.25

' Suggestive on every page, and therefore essential to every student of theology.'—
Record.

**Syntax of the Hebrew Language of the Old Testa-
ment.** 8vo.   Nett $2.25

' The work stands unique as regards a patient investigation of facts, written with a
profound analysis of the laws of thought, of which language is the reflection.'—*British
Quarterly Review.*

The Church in the Mirror of History: Studies on the
Progress of Christianity. By KARL SELL, D.D., Ph.D., Darmstadt,
Editor of ' Life and Letters of H.R.H. Princess Alice.' Translated
by ELIZABETH STIRLING. Crown 8vo.   Nett $1.00

' Eminently thoughtful and instructive lectures.'—*Glasgow Herald.*

Hymns and Thoughts on Religion. By NOVALIS. With
a Biographical Sketch and Portrait. Translated and Edited by
Professor HASTIE, D.D. Crown 8vo.   Nett $1.25

' As a poet, Novalis is no less idealistic than as a philosopher. His poems are
breathings of a high, devout soul.'—CARLYLE.

BY THE LATE REV. JAMES MACGREGOR, D.D.

(SOMETIME PROFESSOR OF SYSTEMATIC THEOLOGY, NEW COLLEGE, EDINBURGH.)

Studies in the History of New Testament Apologetics. 8vo. Nett $2.25

'Dr. Macgregor is a man of vast knowledge and exceptional cleverness; deft in the use of his weapons and always wide awake. His present volume abounds in brilliant passages, clever hits, and decisive argument. . . . The book is lively reading, and carries conviction.'—*British Weekly*.

The Apology of the Christian Religion, Historically regarded with reference to Supernatural Revelation and Redemption. 8vo. Nett $3.00

'Fresh and original, sustained and powerful, it is an apology of the noblest kind. . . . His book does indeed reach the magnificent claim which its title makes for it.'—*Expository Times*.

The Revelation and the Record: Essays on Matters of Previous Question in the Proof of Christianity. 8vo. Nett $2.25

'The book gives us the thoughts of a strong theologian, who has studied many questions deeply, and is able to hold his own with most opponents.'—*Critical Review*.

Those Three Volumes form Dr. Macgregor's 'Apologetic Series.' Independent works, they yet combine in representation of the view that proof of Christianity (the *proof*) is constituted by the whole historical appearance of this religion among mankind.

The Life and Writings of Alexander Vinet. By LAURA M. LANE. With Introduction by Dean FARRAR. Post 8vo. Nett $2.00

'I may say without hesitation that readers will here find a deeply interesting account of a sincere and brilliant thinker. . . . The publication of this book will be a pure gain, if it calls the attention of fresh students to the writings of a theologian so independent as Vinet was, yet so supreme in his allegiance to the majesty of truth.'—Dean FARRAR.

The Work of the Holy Spirit in Man. By Pastor G. TOPHEL, Geneva. Crown 8vo. Nett $1.00

'These pages are replete with clear, mellow, tender, beautiful, elevating thoughts, eminently instructive to inquiring minds, and such as the devout must delight contemplatively and prayerfully to linger upon.'—*Baptist Magazine*.

Mediæval Missions. By Professor T. SMITH, D.D., Edinburgh. Crown 8vo. Nett $1.25

'This is a work which will well repay careful study.'—*Watchman*.

The Kingdom of God: A Plan of Study. By F. HERBERT STEAD, M.A. (*Bible-Class Primers.*) Three parts in One Vol. Nett 50 cents

'It is a plan well worth a trial from every Bible-class teacher.'—*Expository Times*.

A Chronological and Geographical Introduction to the Life of Christ. By C. E. CASPARI. 8vo. $2.25

'The work is handy, and well suited for the use of the student.'—*Guardian*.

The Christian Doctrine of Sin. By Dr. JULIUS MÜLLER. Two Vols. 8vo. Nett $4.50

The Form of the Christian Temple: Being a Treatise on the Constitution of the New Testament Church. By T. WITHEROW, D.D., LL.D. 8vo. Nett $1.75

'A model of clear writing, and of satisfactory arrangement.'—*Record*.

Modern Pantheism. Essay on Religious Philosophy. Translated from the French of EMILE SAISSET. Two Vols. 8vo. Nett $4.00

Christmas Eve: A Dialogue on the Celebration of Christmas. By SCHLEIERMACHER. Translated by Professor HASTIE, D.D. Crown 8vo. Nett **75** cents

'A genuine Christmas book, an exquisite prose-poem.'—*Baptist Magazine.*

Studies in the Christian Evidences: Being Apologetics for the Times. By ALEX. MAIR, D.D. Third Edition. Revised and Enlarged. Crown 8vo. Nett **$1.75**

N.B.—For this book the American Tract Society awarded to the Author the George Wood Gold Medal and Premium, as '*the publication of that year best fitted to promote the glory of Christ as the Son of God and the Saviour of sinners.*'

The Lord's Supper: Its Origin, Nature, and Use. By Rev. J. P. LILLEY, M.A. Crown 8vo. Nett **$1.50**

'Mr. Lilley supplies us with an excellent and much-needed book. . . . Altogether the volume can be cordially recommended to all who seek clear and reasonable views on the Sacrament.'—Professor MARCUS DODS, D.D., in the *Expositor.*

Words to Young Christians: Addresses to Young Communicants. By G. E. TROUP, M.A. On antique laid paper. Handsomely bound. Crown 8vo. Nett **$1.25**

'These addresses have a most fascinating charm. Full of literary grace, spiritual insight, and moral elevation.'—*Review of the Churches.*

Homiletic: Lectures on Preaching. By Professor T. CHRISTLIEB, Bonn University, Author of 'Modern Doubt and Christian Belief.' Post 8vo. Nett **$2.25**

'A new manual of Homiletic was greatly needed. . . . Surely he is a foolish man, and a pithless preacher, who would despise the knowledge which such a master in the art of preaching could impart to him.'—*Expository Times.*

Scenes from the Life of Jesus. By Pastor E. LEHMANN. Crown 8vo. Nett **$1.00**

'There is in these lectures a tender sympathy, and a spiritual devoutness and simplicity, which gives to them a real charm.'—*Literary World.*

The World of Prayer; or, Prayer in relation to Personal Religion. By Bishop MONRAD. Crown 8vo. Nett **$1.25**

'One of the richest devotional books that we have read.'—*Prim. Meth. Magazine.*

So Great Salvation. By Rev. G. H. C. MACGREGOR, M.A., London. With Introduction by Principal MOULE. Neatly bound in cloth. Nett **40** cents

'The truth rings from the very first page, and its note is very clear and convincing.'—*Expository Times.*

The Doctrine of Divine Love; or, Outlines of the Moral Theology of the Evangelical Church. By ERNEST SARTORIUS, D.D., Senior Court Preacher at Königsberg. 8vo. Nett **$2.25**

'An exhaustive treatise, handled with the inevitable copiousness of a favourite subject.'—*Saturday Review.*

Principles of New Testament Quotation. By J. Scott, D.D. Crown 8vo. Second Edition. Nett $1.25

'In terse and well-ordered style the author deals with a subject too little studied and less understood.'—*Record.*

The Free Church of Scotland: Her Origin, Founders, and Testimony. By Peter Bayne, LL.D. New and Cheaper Edition. Nett $1.25

'Among the books called forth by the great northern Jubilee, this is by far and away the first. . . . We have seldom read a book with such a glow, with such a lofty, moral, and spiritual fervour.'—*Review of the Churches.*

The Scripture Doctrine of the Church Historically and Exegetically Considered. By D. D. Bannerman, D.D. 8vo. Nett $2.50

'Dr. Bannerman has executed his task with commendable impartiality and thoroughness. His learning is ample, his materials have been carefully sifted and clearly arranged, his reasoning is apt, lucid, and forcible, while he has none of the bitterness which so frequently mars controversial works of this class.'—*Baptist Magazine.*

The Text of Jeremiah; or, A Critical Investigation of the Greek and Hebrew, with the Variations in the LXX. retranslated into the Original and explained. By Prof. G. C. Workman, M.A. With Introduction by Prof. F. Delitzsch, D.D. Post 8vo. Nett $1.50

'The most painstaking and elaborate illustration of the application of his principles to this end that has yet been given to the world. . . . Scholars will hail it with gratitude, and peruse it with interest.'—*Guardian.*

The Doctrine of the Apocalypse. By Pastor H. Gebhardt. 8vo. Nett $2.25

The Doctrine of the Holy Spirit. By the late Prof. Geo. Smeaton, D.D., Edinburgh. 8vo. Second Edition. $3.00

'A valuable monograph. . . . The masterly exposition of doctrine given in these lectures has been augmented in value by the wise references to current needs and common misconceptions.'—*Brit. and For. Evangelical Review.*

System of the Christian Certainty. By Prof. F. H. R. Frank, Erlangen. 8vo. Nett $2.25

'No weightier or more valuable theological work has come to us from Germany since the publication of Dr. Dorner's "Christian Doctrine."'—*Literary World.*

Elements of Logic as a Science of Propositions. By E. E. C. Jones, Lecturer in Moral Sciences, Girton College, Cambridge; Joint-Translator and Editor of Lotze's *Microcosmus.* 8vo. Nett $2.00

'We must congratulate Girton College upon the forward movement of which the publication of this work is one of the first steps.'—*Cambridge Review.*

Encyclopædia of Theology. By Professor J. F. Räbiger, D.D. Two Vols. 8vo. Nett $4.50

'Räbiger's Encyclopædia is a book deserving the attentive perusal of every divine. . . . It is at once instructive and suggestive.'—*Athenæum.*

Historical Theology: A Review of the Principal Doctrinal Discussions in the Christian Church since the Apostolic Age. By the late Principal Wm. Cunningham, D.D., Edinburgh. Two Vols. 8vo. Second Edition. Nett $3.50

The Servant of Jehovah. A Commentary upon Isaiah lii. 13–liii. 12. With Dissertations upon the Authorship of Isaiah xl.–lxvi., etc. By W. URWICK, M.A., Tutor in Hebrew, New College, London. 8vo. Nett $1.25

'A work of great and permanent value.'—*Weekly Review.*

Is Christ Infallible and the Bible True? (Giving the Teaching of Jesus on Holy Scripture, and other burning Questions in Theology and Religious Life.) By Rev. HUGH M'INTOSH, M.A., London. Post 8vo. Nett $3.00

'Such a title is calculated to arrest attention and awaken interest. Nor will any one who reads the book find his attention allowed to flag or his interest to wane, for the points discussed are in themselves most attractive and important, whilst the method of treatment is both vigorous and vivid.'—*Presbyterian.*

BISHOP MARTENSEN'S WORKS.

'The greatest Scandinavian, perhaps the greatest Lutheran, divine of our century.'—EXPOSITOR.

Christian Ethics. Three Vols. 8vo. Each nett $2.25

Volume I. GENERAL ETHICS.—II. INDIVIDUAL ETHICS.—III. SOCIAL ETHICS.

'Dr. Martensen's work on Christian Dogmatics reveals the strength of thought as well as the fine literary grace of its author. . . . His chief ethical writings comprise a system of Christian Ethics, general and special, in three volumes. Each of these volumes has great and singular excellence, and it might be generally felt that in them the author has surpassed his own work on "Christian Dogmatics."'—Principal CAIRNS.

Christian Dogmatics. One Vol. 8vo. Nett $2.25

'The famous "Dogmatics," the eloquent and varied pages of which contain intellectual food for the laity no less than for the clergy. . . . His "Christian Dogmatics" has exercised as wide an influence on Protestant thought as any volume of our century.'—*Expositor.*

Inspiration, and other Lectures. By the late President T. GEORGE ROOKE, B.A., Rawdon College. Edited by TWO OF HIS STUDENTS. One Vol. 8vo. Nett $2.25

'Intrinsically good. . . . The chapters on pastoral work glow with a whole-hearted devotion. The counsels given are excellent.'—*London Quarterly Review.*

The First Epistle of St. John: A Contribution to Biblical Theology. By Professor ERICH HAUPT. 8vo. Nett $2.25

The Atonement and Intercession of Christ. By the late Principal DAVID C. DAVIES, M.A., Trevecca. Edited by D. E. JENKINS, Portmadoc. Crown 8vo. Nett $1.25

'Can hardly fail to be helpful to all who wish to understand what the Bible teaches concerning the most profound and important of all subjects—that of the atonement.'—*American Journal of Theology.*
'It is an able defence and exposition of orthodox doctrine—substitution and propitiation. . . . Full of suggestion and edification.'—*Methodist Times.*

Our Father's Kingdom: Lectures on the Lord's Prayer. By C. B. ROSS, B.D., Lachine, Canada. Crown 8vo. Nett 75 cents

'This is the book to get for clear and simple presentation of the best modern expository work on this all-important section of the Gospels.'—*Expository Times.*

Handbooks for Bible Classes and Private Students.

Edited by Prof. MARCUS DODS, D.D., and ALEX. WHYTE, D.D.

' I name especially the admirable Handbooks for Bible Classes issued by T. & T. Clark of Edinburgh. They are very cheap, and among them are some books unsurpassed in their kind.' Dr. W. ROBERTSON NICOLL in the *British Weekly*.

' Sound, intelligible, and sometimes brilliantly written handbooks, packed with wisdom and knowledge.'—*Methodist Recorder*.

' These volumes are models of the *multum in parvo* style.'—*Literary World*.

The Prices detailed below are Nett.

COMMENTARIES—

Professor MARCUS DODS, D.D.   Genesis. $.60
JAS. MACGREGOR, D.D.   Exodus. 2 Vols. Ea. .60
Principal DOUGLAS, D.D.   Joshua.   .45
Judges.   .45
Prof. J. G. MURPHY, LL.D.   Chronicles.   .45
Rev. JAMES AITKEN, M.A.   Job.   .45
Professor MARCUS DODS, D.D.   Haggai, Zechariah, Malachi.   .60
Principal DOUGLAS, D.D.   Obadiah to Zephaniah.   .45

Principal T. M. LINDSAY, D.D.   Mark. $.75
Prin. T. M. LINDSAY, D.D.   St. Luke.   2 Vols.—Vol. I., $.60.   Vol. II.,   .45
GEO. REITH, D.D.   St. John.   2 Vols. Each .60
Prin. T. M. LINDSAY, D.D.   Acts. 2 Vols. Ea. .45
Principal BROWN, D.D.   Romans.   .60
JAMES MACGREGOR, D.D.   Galatians.   .45
Professor J. S. CANDLISH, D.D.   Ephesians.   .45
Professor A. B. DAVIDSON, D.D.   Hebrews.   .75
J. P. LILLEY, D.D.   The Pastoral Epistles.   .75

GENERAL SUBJECTS—

Prof. JAMES STALKER, D.D.
The Life of Christ. $.45
The Life of St. Paul.   .45
(*Large-type Editions, price* $1.50 *each, see p.* 17.)
ALEXANDER WHYTE, D.D.
The Shorter Catechism.   .75
Professor J. S. CANDLISH, D.D.
The Christian Sacraments.   .45
The Christian Doctrine of God.   .45
The Work of the Holy Spirit.   .45
The Biblical Doctrine of Sin.   .45
NORMAN L. WALKER, D.D.
Scottish Church History.   .45
Rev. W. D. THOMSON, M.A.
The Christian Miracles and the Conclusions of Science.   .60
GEORGE SMITH, LL.D., F.R.G.S., C.I.E.
History of Christian Missions.   .75
ARCHIBALD HENDERSON, D.D.
Palestine : Its Historical Geography.   .75
Prin. T. M. LINDSAY, D.D.   The Reformation. .60
Professor BINNIE, D.D.   The Church.   .45
Professor T. B. KILPATRICK, D.D.
Butler's Three Sermons on Human Nature.   .45
Rev. W. SCRYMGEOUR, M.A.
Lessons on the Life of Christ.   .75

Rev. JOHN MACPHERSON, M.A.
The Sum of Saving Knowledge. $.45
The Confession of Faith.   .60
Presbyterianism.   .45
President HAMILTON, D.D.
History of the Irish Presbyterian Church.   .60
A. TAYLOR INNES, M.A., Advocate.
Church and State.   .75
Rev. J. FEATHER.
The Last of the Prophets—John the Baptist.   .60
Rev. W. FAIRWEATHER, M.A.
From the Exile to the Advent.   .60
Professor J. LAIDLAW, D.D.
Foundation Truths of Scripture as to Sin and Salvation.   .45
Rev. L. A. MUIRHEAD, B.D.
The Times of Christ.   .60
J. P. LILLEY, D.D.
The Principles of Protestantism.   .75
Rev. J. STRACHAN.
Hebrew Ideals from the Story of the Patriarchs. 2 Vols. $.60 each ; or bound together, $1
DAVID M. ROSS, D.D.
The Teaching of Jesus.   .60

Edited by Principal SALMOND, D.D.   Each Nett 20 cents.

BIBLE CLASS PRIMERS.

' An admirable series of *Bible Class Primers*. . . . Each new number is a distinct addition to the cause of intelligent Christianity.'—*Biblical World* (Chicago).

' A most useful series. With such helps as these, to be an inefficient teacher is to be blameworthy.'—Rev. C. H. SPURGEON.

The Covenanters, by J. BEVERIDGE, B.D.—Eli, Samuel, and Saul, by C. A. SALMOND, D.D.—Ezekiel, by HARVIE JELLIE, B.D.—Jeremiah, by J. ROBSON, D.D.—History of Egypt, by Prof. R. G. MURISON, B.D.—The Minor Prophets, by J. ADAMS, B.D.—History of Babylonia and Assyria, by Prof. ROSS G. MURISON, M.A.—The Mosaic Tabernacle, by J. ADAMS, B.D.—The History of the English Bible, by BURNETT THOMSON.—The Exile and the Restoration, by Prof. A. B. DAVIDSON, LL.D.—Geography of Palestine, by S. R. MACPHAIL, D.D.—Our Lord's Illustrations, by R. RESKER.—Elijah and Elisha, by R. G. MACINTYRE, B.D.—The Miracles of our Lord, by Prof. J. LAIDLAW, D.D.—Christian Conduct; Christian Character: A Study in New Testament Morality, by T. B. KILPATRICK, D.D.—The Free Church of Scotland, by C. G. M'CRIE, D.D.—The Truth of Christianity, by Prof. J. IVERACH. D.D.—The Making of Israel, by C. A. SCOTT, B.D.—The Sabbath, by the EDITOR—Our Christian Passover, by C. A. SALMOND, D.D.—The Kingdom of God, *Three Parts (or bound in one vol., 45 cents)*, by F. HERBERT STEAD, M.A.—The Parables of our Lord, by the EDITOR—Life of St. John, by PATON J. GLOAG, D.D.—The Story of Jerusalem, by H. CALLAN, M.A.—Life of Abraham, by C. A. SCOTT, B.D.—Historical Connection between the Old and New Testaments, by Prof. J. SKINNER, D.D.—Life of Christ, by the EDITOR—The Shorter Catechism, *Three Parts (or bound in one vol., 45 cents)*, by the EDITOR—The Period of the Judges, by Prof. J. PATERSON, D.D.—Outlines of Protestant Missions, by J. ROBSON, D.D.—The Apostle Peter, by the EDITOR—Outlines of Early Church History, by H. W. SMITH, D.D.—David, by P. THOMSON, M.A.—Moses, by Princ. J. IVERACH, D.D.—Paul, by P. J. GLOAG, D.D.—Solomon, by R. WINTERBOTHAM, LL.D.—Reformation, by Prof. WITHEROW—Kings of Israel, by W. WALKER, M.A.—Kings of Judah, by Prof. GIVEN.—Joshua and the Conquest, by Prof. CROSKERY.

Extra Vols.—Bible Words and Phrases, by C. MICHIE, M.A.   40 cents.—The Seven Churches of Asia, by DEBORAH ALCOCK.   40 cents.

THE ANTE-NICENE CHRISTIAN LIBRARY.

The Ante-Nicene Christian Library. A Collection of all the Works of the Fathers of the Christian Church prior to the Council of Nicæa. Edited by the Rev. Professor ROBERTS, D.D., and Principal JAMES DONALDSON, LL.D., St. Andrews. In Twenty-four handsome 8vo Vols. Per Vol. Nett $2.25

This Series has been received with marked approval by all sections of the Christian Church in this country and in the United States, as supplying what has long been felt to be a want, and also on account of the impartiality, learning, and care with which Editors and Translators have executed a very difficult task.

The following Works are included in the Series :—

Apostolic Fathers, comprising Clement's Epistle to the Corinthians ; Polycarp to the Ephesians ; Martyrdom of Polycarp ; Epistles of Barnabas ; Epistles of Ignatius (longer and shorter, and also the Syriac Version) ; Martyrdom of Ignatius : Epistle to Diognetus ; Pastor of Hermas ; Papias ; Spurious Epistles of Ignatius. One Volume. **Justin Martyr ; Athenagoras.** One Volume. **Tatian ; Theophilus ; The Clementine Recognitions.** One Volume. **Clement of Alexandria,** comprising Exhortation to Heathen ; The Instructor ; and the Miscellanies. Two Volumes. **Hippolytus,** Volume First ; Refutation of all Heresies, and Fragments from his Commentaries. **Irenæus,** Volume First. **Irenæus** (completion) and **Hippolytus** (completion) ; Fragments of Third Century. One Volume. **Tertullian against Marcion.** One Volume. **Cyprian :** The Epistles and Treatises ; **Novatian : Minucius Felix.** Two Volumes. **Origen :** De Principiis ; Letters ; Treatise against Celsus ; and Life of Origen. Two Volumes. **Tertullian :** To the Martyrs ; Apology ; to the Nations, etc. Three Volumes. **Methodius : Alexander of Lycopolis ; Peter of Alexandria Anatolius ; Clement on Virginity ;** and Fragments. One Volume. **Apocryphal Gospels, Acts, and Revelations ;** comprising all the very curious Apocryphal Writings of the first three Centuries. One Volume. **Clementine Homilies : Apostolical Constitutions.** One Volume. **Arnobius.** One Volume. **Gregory Thaumaturgus ; Dionysius ; Archelaus ; Syrian Fragments.** One Volume. **Lactantius ;** together with the Testaments of the Twelve Patriarchs, and Fragments of the Second and Third Centuries. Two Volumes. **Early Liturgies and Remaining Fragments.** One Volume.

ST. AUGUSTINE'S WORKS.

The Works of Aurelius Augustine, Bishop of Hippo. Edited by MARCUS DODS, D.D. In Fifteen Vols. 8vo.

Per Vol. Nett $2.25

The 'City of God.' Two Volumes.

Writings in connection with the Donatist Controversy. One Volume.

The Anti-Pelagian Works. Three Volumes.

Treatises against Faustus the Manichæan. One Volume.

On the Trinity. One Volume.

Commentary on John. Two Volumes.

The Harmony of the Evangelists, and the Sermon on the Mount. One Volume.

'Letters.' Two Volumes.

On Christian Doctrine, Enchiridion, on Catechising, and on Faith and the Creed. One Volume.

'Confessions.' With Copious Notes by Rev. J. G. PILKINGTON.

' For the reproduction of the "City of God" in an admirable English garb we are greatly indebted to the well-directed enterprise and energy of Messrs. Clark, and to the accuracy and scholarship of those who have undertaken the laborious task of translation.'—*Christian Observer*.

N.B.—A Selection of Twelve Volumes from either or both of those Series may be had for $24 nett,

'The ablest grammatical exegete of the age.'—PHILIP SCHAFF, D.D.

MEYER'S COMMENTARY ON THE NEW TESTAMENT.

'Meyer has been long and well known to scholars as one of the very ablest of the German expositors of the New Testament. We are not sure whether we ought not to say that he is unrivalled as an interpreter of the grammatical and historical meaning of the sacred writers. The Publishers have now rendered another seasonable and important service to English students in producing this translation.'—GUARDIAN.

Critical and Exegetical Commentary on the New Testament. By Dr. H. A. W. MEYER. Authorised Translation edited by Professor W. P. DICKSON, D.D. In Twenty handsome 8vo Vols. Per Vol. Nett $2.25

ST. MATTHEW'S GOSPEL, Two Vols.; MARK AND LUKE, Two Vols.; ST. JOHN'S GOSPEL, Two Vols.; ACTS OF THE APOSTLES, Two Vols.; ROMANS, Two Vols.; CORINTHIANS, Two Vols.; GALATIANS, One Vol.; EPHESIANS AND PHILEMON, One Vol.; PHILIPPIANS AND COLOSSIANS, One Vol.; THESSALONIANS, One Vol.; TIMOTHY AND TITUS, One Vol.; HEBREWS, One Vol.; JAMES AND JOHN, One Vol.; PETER AND JUDE, One Vol.

BENGEL'S GNOMON.

'Stands out among the exegetical literature not only of the eighteenth century, but of all centuries, for its masterly terseness and precision, and for its combination of spiritual insight with the best scholarship of his time.'—Professor W. SANDAY, D.D., Oxford.

Gnomon of the New Testament. By JOHN ALBERT BENGEL. Translated into English. With Original Notes, Explanatory and Illustrative. Edited by Rev. A. R. FAUSSET, M.A. The Original Translation, Five large Vols. 8vo. Nett $9.00

STIER'S WORDS OF THE LORD JESUS.

The Words of the Lord Jesus. By Dr. RUDOLPH STIER. Eight Vols. 8vo. Nett $18.00

The Words of the Risen Saviour. 8vo. Nett $2.25

The Words of the Apostles. 8vo. Nett $2.25

'The whole work is a treasury of thoughtful exposition. Its measure of practical and spiritual application, with exegetical criticism, commends it to the use of those whose duty it is to preach as well as to understand the Gospel of Christ.'—*Guardian*.

BY F. W. KRUMMACHER, D.D.

The Suffering Saviour; or, Meditations on the Last Days of the Sufferings of Christ. Cr. 8vo. Eighth Edition. Nett $1.75

David, the King of Israel. A Portrait drawn from Bible History and the Book of Psalms. Cr. 8vo. Second Edition. Nett $1.75

LANGE'S LIFE OF CHRIST.

The Life of the Lord Jesus Christ: A Complete Critical Examination of the Origin, Contents, and Connection of the Gospels. By Prof. J. P. LANGE, D.D., of Bonn. Edited, with additional Notes, by MARCUS DODS, D.D. Four Vols. 8vo. Nett $9.00

'Stands in the front rank of lives of Christ; it first presents the life of Christ as given in the four Gospels together, and then as given by each Gospel separately from its peculiar standpoint.'—Principal A. CAVE, D.D.

SPECIAL OFFER.

TEN VOLUMES for TWENTY DOLLARS.

The Foreign Theological Library.

THIS Series comprises Authorised Translations of the principal Works of the leading Continental Theologians. It is believed that the publication of this 'Library' has had considerable influence upon the progress of theological science in Great Britain and America.

The BISHOP OF GLOUCESTER AND BRISTOL, with regard to Sacred Study, says : 'It may be of some little service to the reader if I mention the long and valuable series of Commentaries on, I believe, every book of the Old Testament, that will be found translated from the German in the comprehensive Foreign Theological Library of Messrs. Clark of Edinburgh. The same Library may be mentioned in reference to the New Testament.'

President W. R. HARPER, of Chicago University, writes : 'THE FOREIGN THEOLOGICAL LIBRARY has exercised a great influence upon the biblical studies in this country and in England. It has introduced to students of the Scriptures some of the best work of German theologians and critics. The forty-five years of publication, at the rate of four volumes yearly, is an achievement to look back upon with pride, and the belief of the Messrs. Clark, that "through the care with which books have been selected, the series has exercised a healthful influence upon the progress of theological science," is amply justified. It is gratifying to learn that they do not propose entirely to give up this special work of publishing such translations, but will discontinue the serial publication, issuing books irregularly, as occasion offers.'

The Series being now completed, Messrs. Clark are desirous of bringing it within the reach of every biblical student, and they have therefore decided to offer any TEN VOLUMES for TWENTY DOLLARS, or a larger number at the same ratio. The published price of each Volume (with one or two exceptions) is $2.25 nett.

A complete list of the Series (173 Vols. in all) will be found on the opposite page, but Messrs. Clark invite special attention to the Standard Works mentioned below :—

History of the Jewish People in the Time of Jesus Christ. By Prof. E. SCHÜRER, D.D., University of Göttingen. Complete in 5 Vols. 8vo. INDEX VOL. 75 cents nett (100 pp. 8vo).

'Recognised as the standard authority on the subject.'—*Critical Review.*
'Every English commentary has for some years contained references to "Schürer" as the great authority upon such matters. . . . There is no guide to these intricate and difficult times which even approaches him.'—*Record.*

Christian Dogmatics, 1 Vol.—Christian Ethics, 3 Vols. (GENERAL, INDIVIDUAL, SOCIAL). By H. MARTENSEN, D.D., Bishop of Seeland.

'The greatest Scandinavian, perhaps the greatest Lutheran, divine of our century. The famous "Dogmatics," the eloquent and varied pages of which contain intellectual food for the laity no less than for the clergy. . . His "Christian Dogmatics" has exercised as wide an influence on Protestant thought as any volume of our century.'—*Expositor.*

Handbook of Biblical Archæology. By Prof. C. F. KIEL. 2 Vols.

'No mere dreary mass of details, but a very luminous, philosophical, and suggestive treatise. Many chapters are not simply invaluable to the student, but have also very direct homiletic usefulness.'—*Literary World.*

The Words of the Lord Jesus, 8 Vols. 8vo (or the 8 Vols. bound in 4). —The Words of the Risen Saviour.—The Words of the Apostles. By Dr. RUDOLPH STIER.

'The whole work is a treasury of thoughtful exposition.'—*Guardian.*

Professor Godet's Commentaries on St. Luke, 2 Vols.; St. John, 3 Vols. ; and 1st Corinthians, 2 Vols.

'For devotional warmth and practical application, Godet is perhaps unsurpassed by any modern commentator among foreign Protestants.'—*Guardian.*

Professor Dorner's 'System of Christian Doctrine,' 4 Vols.; and 'Doctrine of the Person of Christ,' 5 Vols.

Professor Weiss's 'Life of Christ,' 3 Vols.; and 'Biblical Theology,' 2 Vols.

Clark's Foreign Theological Library.

Octavo, cloth, price $2.25 per Volume, nett. Any Ten Volumes for $20.00 nett.

Baumgarten—The History of the Church in the Apostolic Age. Three vols.
Bleek—Introduction to the New Testament. Two vols.
Cassel's Commentary on Esther. One vol.
Delitzsch—New Commentary on Genesis. Two vols.
—— Commentary on the Psalms. Three vols.
—— Commentary on the Proverbs of Solomon. Two vols.
—— Commentary on Song of Solomon and Ecclesiastes. One vol.
—— Commentary on the Prophecies of Isaiah. Two vols. (Only Translation of the *Fourth* and *last* Edition.)
—— Commentary on Epistle to the Hebrews. Two vols.
—— A System of Biblical Psychology. One vol.
Dorner—A System of Christian Doctrine. Four vols.
—— History of the Development of the Doctrine of the Person of Christ. Five vols.
Ebrard—Commentary on the Epistles of St. John. One vol.
—— The Gospel History. One vol.
—— Apologetics. Three vols.
Ewald—Revelation: Its Nature and Record. One vol.
—— Old and New Testament Theology. One vol.
Frank's System of Christian Certainty. One vol.
Gebhardt—Doctrine of the Apocalypse. One vol.
Gerlach—The Pentateuch. One vol.
Godet—Commentary on St. Luke's Gospel. Two vols.
—— Commentary on St. John's Gospel. Three vols.
—— Commentary on the Epistle to the Romans. Two vols.
—— Commentary on First Corinthians. Two vols.
Goebel—On the Parables. One vol.
Hagenbach—History of the Reformation. Two vols.
—— History of Christian Doctrines. Three vols.
Harless—A System of Christian Ethics. One vol.
Haupt—Commentary on the First Epistle of St. John. One vol.
Hävernick—General Introduction to the Old Testament. One vol.
Hengstenberg—Christology of the Old Testament. Four vols.
—— Commentary on the Psalms. Three vols.
—— On the Book of Ecclesiastes. Etc. etc. One vol.
—— Commentary on the Gospel of St. John. Two vols.
—— Commentary on Ezekiel. One vol.
—— On the Genuineness of Daniel. One vol.
—— The Kingdom of God under the Old Covenant. Two vols.
Keil—Introduction to the Old Testament. Two vols.
—— Commentary on the Pentateuch. Three vols.
—— Commentary on Joshua, Judges, and Ruth. One vol.
—— Commentary on the Books of Samuel. One vol.
—— Commentary on the Books of Kings. One vol.
—— Commentary on the Books of Chronicles. One vol.
—— Commentary on Ezra, Nehemiah, and Esther. One vol.
—— Commentary on Jeremiah and Lamentations. Two vols.
—— Commentary on Ezekiel. Two vols.
—— Commentary on the Book of Daniel. One vol.
—— Commentary on the Minor Prophets. Two vols.
—— Biblical Archæology. Two vols.
Kurtz—History of the Old Covenant; or, Old Testament Dispensation. Three vols.
Luthardt—Commentary on the Gospel of St. John. Three vols.
—— History of Christian Ethics. One vol.
Martensen—Christian Dogmatics. One vol.
—— Christian Ethics. General—Social—Individual. Three vols.
Müller—The Christian Doctrine of Sin. Two vols.
Oehler—Biblical Theology of the Old Testament. Two vols.
Orelli—Prophecy regarding Consummation of God's Kingdom. One vol.
—— Commentary on Isaiah. One vol.
—— Commentary on Jeremiah. One vol.
—— The Twelve Minor Prophets. One vol.
Philippi—Commentary on Epistle to Romans. Two vols.
Räbiger—Encyclopædia of Theology. Two vols.
Sartorius—The Doctrine of Divine Love. One vol.
Schürer—The Jewish People in the Time of Christ. Five vols. and Index.
Steinmeyer—History of the Passion and Resurrection of our Lord. One vol.
Stier—The Words of the Lord Jesus. Eight vols.
—— The Words of the Risen Saviour, and Commentary on Epistle of St. James. One vol.
—— The Words of the Apostles Expounded. One vol.
Weiss—Biblical Theology of the New Testament. Two vols.
—— The Life of Christ. Three vols.

INDEX